"My friend Ralph O. M
we were both atheists who b
dence. In this powerful and
of history and science that

tianity is true. If you're a Christian, his story will breathe new life into your faith. If you're a skeptic or seeker, be prepared to be challenged and encouraged as Ralph takes you on a fascinating and exciting search for God."

—**Lee Strobel,** journalist and author of the bestselling books
The Case for Christ and *The Case for Faith*

———•———

"Ralph Muncaster's book is an indispensable tool for dealing with skeptics."

—**Rick Warren,** author of *The Purpose-Driven Church* and founder of Saddleback Church, Lake Forest, California

———•———

"It is often said that 'nobody erects statues to skeptics and critics,' but in this powerful book Ralph Muncaster has built a most impressive memorial to his own pilgrimage from atheism to Christianity.

"Already tested and proved by the eighteen *Examine the Evidence* booklets that he has published as the foundation blocks for this comprehensive volume, the present work deals realistically and convincingly with the barriers to faith that are raised against the whole truth of God as revealed in His Word and in Jesus Christ.

"Compelling and convicting arguments from start to finish, *A Skeptic's Search for God* is destined to bring many people to Christ in these difficult and challenging times in which we live."

—**D. James Kennedy,** author of *Why I Believe* and *What If Jesus Had Never Been?;* Senior Minister, Coral Ridge Presbyterian Church, Fort Lauderdale, Florida

A SKEPTIC'S
SEARCH
for GOD

Ralph O. Muncaster

HARVEST HOUSE™ PUBLISHERS

EUGENE, OREGON

Cover by Terry Dugan Design, Minneapolis, Minnesota

A SKEPTIC'S SEARCH FOR GOD
Copyright © 2002 by Ralph O. Muncaster
Published by Harvest House Publishers
Eugene, Oregon 97402

Library of Congress Cataloging-in-Publication Data
Muncaster, Ralph O.
   A skeptic's search for God / Ralph O. Muncaster.
       p. cm.
   Includes bibliographical references.
   ISBN 0-7369-0452-2
   1. God—Proof. I. Title.

BT103 .M86 2002
239—dc21   2001039811

Printed in the United States of America.

02 03 04 05 06 07 08 09 10 11 / DP-MS / 10 9 8 7 6 5 4 3 2 1

I dedicate this book to my parents, Bill and Frances Muncaster.

Even though I didn't learn much about God at home, my parents did teach me a great deal about life and morality, and I love them dearly for that. I'm also grateful for the years of church and Sunday school I had to attend. Because of this, when I started researching religion, I had a significant amount of information to start with. So indirectly it led to telling many thousands of skeptics about God.

Most important, I now have respect for how difficult it is to be a parent. (Too bad there aren't classes and degrees for parenting.) I've failed so many times, and am humbled by the awesome task of raising children—especially to teach them to really, truly know God. (My three sons are probably sick of hearing me talk about evidence for God!) The only thing we as parents can do, is to try to do our best.

God bless you, Mom and Dad—thanks, and I love you!

Contents

Part I

How I Became an
Atheist in Church

1

The Child Skeptic

Life can be so bizarre. Who would imagine that three boys, raised with 4368 hours of Sunday school and church teaching between them, would turn into two hard-core atheists and an agnostic only a few years later? What fed the move into atheism? Who would think that the most ardent atheist and Bible-basher (me) would later agree to a challenge to prove that the Bible really was *a fairy tale? Even more surprising, who would ever think that my quest would result in a life-changing discovery?*

———————•———————

"You're wrong!" I shouted as loudly as a six-year-old could, my voice cracking between sobs, tears streaming down my face. I had just received the results of my very first test in the first grade, with a large, red "minus 1" at the top. I couldn't bear the "defeat." I glared at my first-grade teacher, Mrs. Latham, in disbelief, and fighting back the quivering in my lips, I raised my hand to explain why I was right.

The question that I disagreed with was this:

"Do you cross the street when the light is a) red or b) green?" I answered "red"—and was certain of it.

To those of us living in the twenty-first century in big cities, it may seem obvious that green means "go." But as a six-year-old boy in the tiny town of Woodstown in south New Jersey—a town with a single stoplight and only 2000 people—I was right. In our town we didn't have lights to indicate when people should cross the street. So a prudent pedestrian would look at the stoplight of the street he was crossing relative to the automobile traffic. When it was *red* he would cross (the light stopped the traffic), not when it was green. The test had been designed by "big-city folk" who waited for green pedestrian-crossing lights. I was really upset. (And the teacher never gave me credit for my answer.)

When I was six, people just said I had an "inquisitive mind." Later they would say I had a "skeptical mind." I would prove to be a difficult challenge for many teachers and other people in the years to come. But I never forgot that single question. It was the first test question I ever got "wrong," but I knew I was really right relative to my world in Woodstown. I never forgot that "big people" can be wrong, or can misunderstand things, or can place things in the wrong perspective. This question, along with the reluctance of the teacher to see the question from the "world" I lived in, caused me to stop and analyze things throughout my life—to be skeptical. And never again did I accept a "grown-up" belief without some basis in evidence. I needed facts. Lots of facts. I needed a frame of reference—for example, Woodstown versus New York City.

Even at age five and six, I was very interested in God, and by age eight had become interested in such concepts as infinity and space. I frequently asked others to explain to me these paradoxes:

- Time—It had to have a beginning, yet this also seemed impossible. How could there not have been some kind of "time" before it?

- Space—It had to have a finite boundary, yet this also seemed impossible. How could there not be something that existed beyond it?

These were very difficult questions that no adult I knew could explain to a young child. The people I talked to didn't seem to understand it themselves. From age six through high school, I was very puzzled by these issues. I thought that, if God existed at all, he must be somehow "mixed up" with time and space.

The minister droned on and on. "The Father, the Son, and the Holy Ghost…The Father, the Son, and the Holy Ghost." Didn't he ever have anything else to say to an eight-year-old boy swallowed up among a bunch of grown-ups? Boring.

To me, he seemed like a giant of a man who never said anything that made much sense. Tall. Lanky. I thought he didn't eat enough. Maybe if he had a good meal or two, he'd gain some weight, be happier, and be more interesting.

"Oh well," I sighed as he went on and on. I glanced at my mother, sitting in the choir beside the altar, proud and seeming interested in what the minister had to say. She wore one of those fancy choir gowns. They seemed weird…why did choir people need to dress that way? I had to figure a way to kill some time. I didn't wear a watch and there were no clocks, I just knew that this part of the routine lasted forever before the choir would get up and sing again and they would pass the fancy silver plates to collect a bunch of money. I wondered whether, if I put bubble gum on my fingers, I might be able to actually take some money out as it went by. I never tried it, though.

Sometimes I counted things to kill time—like panes in the windows around the church. Or I counted people, or maybe the number of people wearing red. Othertimes I would fantasize about inventions I would create, or some adventure I would have with my friends in the woods where I lived, outside of Woodstown. Today, as always, I was bored.

Then I noticed that Mrs. Bee in front of me had a tuft of hair sticking out on the right side of her head, held by a red clasp. I wondered, could she feel it if I touched it?

I peered to my left, where I saw my older brother Tom (age 11), Rick (who had just started coming to church at age 5), and my father sitting. My father was trying to "control" Rick. Yep, it was a good situation to try something new. My father seemed totally involved in the sermon.

My church bulletin was always rolled up into a tube shape, so I decided to see if Mrs. Bee could feel it if I touched her hair. Carefully glancing at my father, I sneaked a touch of her hair with my rolled-up bulletin.

Cool! She raised her hand as if to get rid of a bug in the warm August air. This could be a new game to kill some time.

The minister was continuing his droning. Something about going to hell if we didn't repent. He didn't say why. I looked down to the front row on the right. Mr. Brennan was asleep as usual. In fact, he started snoring—until his wife gave him the elbow. I looked at Tom, and we both started snickering.

The bug thing worked, so I decided to do it again on Mrs. Bee's other side. Again, she brought her hand up to get rid of the bug. I looked at Tom, whose eyes were wide as saucers. He was probably thinking, *What are you doing, idiot? You're gonna get busted by Dad.*

I grabbed his rolled-up bulletin in my other hand and attacked Mrs. Bee from both sides. This time she waved her hands and spun around, and I felt a familiar slap as my father hit my arms. I saw his eyes. They were stern—the eyes of someone raised on a farm. The eyes of someone who insisted upon discipline and respect in church. Now I dreaded the drive home and the aftermath. I knew that being disrespectful in church was a major felony and that I would be in big trouble when I got home. *Oh well,* I thought. *Another week of Sunday school and church out of the way.*

To me, what was this "church"? How could I believe what was taught? All of it was in direct contradiction to what I learned in school. Little did I know how many questions this would raise in the future.

Planting Seeds of Agnosticism

Even as an eight-year-old, I liked to think a lot. By then I was done believing in Santa and the Easter Bunny, but I still would pretend I did—hoping to increase the number of presents I received. I also started having doubts about God, the Bible, and Jesus, despite having been made to go to both church and Sunday school ever since I was about five.

———•———

We started giggling at the same time, my friend Robert and me. The Sunday school teacher had just told us about Adam and

Eve, the first humans, and how they had lived to be more than 900 years old.

"What do you think is so funny?" Lynn, the teacher, asked as she looked at me.

"Nothing," I flatly stated. Robert started giggling again.

"How about you, Robert? What do you think is so funny?"

"Oh, I don't know," he said.

Then we both erupted in outright laughter, which started the entire class laughing. Now our teacher seemed to get upset. "If you can't take this seriously, I really don't know why you're here!" she exclaimed.

"Miss Lynn" (that was the name she told us to use), "do you have any 900-year-old relatives?" I asked.

"No, of course not," she replied.

"Do you know of anyone who lived 900 years?" I asked.

"Yes, Adam and many early biblical people," she replied.

"How about today? Do you know anyone living that long today?" I asked.

"Well, no," she said.

"Then why are you telling us Adam and others lived over 900 years?" At age eight, I wasn't frustrated over such things yet. It just seemed funny—here was yet one more time adults were trying to fool us with a bunch of ridiculous ideas.

Robert chimed in. "I bet I know the oldest person in the world."

"And who might that be?" Miss Lynn said sarcastically.

"Santa Claus!" Robert said. "I see him every year, and he never gets any older!"

Now Miss Lynn was in a dilemma, and I knew it, because not all the kids in class knew Santa Claus was a fake. "Well, let's stay focused on our topic for today. Adam lived 930 years, and the oldest living person on earth was Methuselah, who lived to be 969 years old."

Now Robert and I started to laugh out loud. I started to kick him, knowing we'd be in trouble if we didn't stop. "How do you know that?" I asked.

"Because the Bible says so," Miss Lynn answered.

"I know," Robert said through his laughter, "I'm going to write a book that says that I lived to be 1000 years old and break the record for the people that read it hundreds of years from now!" The whole class started laughing.

"No," I said, "because I'm going to write a book that says I lived 2000 years!" The class was out of control and in an uproar as kids started giving me high fives for beating Robert.

Miss Lynn got up and took our hands, and guided us to two chairs in the corner of the room. "I'll not have your silliness regarding the Word of God," she said.

Now I was a bit worried. Would Miss Lynn tell my mom and dad how we had acted in class? If so, it could be trouble. I decided to just cool it for the remainder of the class.

———————•———————

Mrs. Kaan was teaching us about the cavemen in fourth grade. I was nine years old. Wow! This was interesting stuff for me. I raised my hand, eagerly expecting a number of answers.

"Mrs. Kaan," I asked, "did these guys live to be 900 years old?"

She started laughing. "Of course not! At the time of the Revolutionary War, only a couple hundred years ago, the average life span was 40 or 50 years. Cavemen lived even shorter lives. Today we far outlive our ancestors. Where on earth would you get such a thought?" she asked.

"From Sunday school," I replied.

There was total silence for what seemed like an eternity.

Mrs. Kaan seemed frozen. Her face flushed.

"Well," she stammered, "some people have different beliefs. Perhaps you should address this question with your Sunday school teacher or your parents. But the history I need to teach you shows increasing life spans due to advances in medicine and health, not decreasing life spans."

What I Learned About Learning

One of the most important things I've learned is that the best way to study is not always at a school or institution. For me, I learn much more quickly and thoroughly by going directly to the sources and learning as much as I can from as many people as I can. And

I've learned that people can be wrong. Even esteemed teachers. They are human, and their teaching is based on what they know. Now, looking back, and having been a teacher at all levels from high school to university, I understand the limitations of teachers. Sometimes they are called to "do their best with what they've got." In other words, they may not be specialists in an area, yet they know it well enough and teach it the best they can—sometimes without the latest information. Other times, teachers are so focused on a single area that they miss the big picture. (Later in my life, I found this to be the case with many scientists, who had "tunnel vision" and were not inclined to study fields of science other than their own.)

———●———

In Sunday school the stories seemed to border on the ridiculous. We were told about Adam and Eve, of people living to be 900 years old, of a worldwide flood, the parting of the Red Sea, and the resurrection of Jesus. I remember thinking to myself, *Why doesn't the public school talk about such important things?*

TV didn't talk about the amazing Bible stories either. How could a snake talk to Adam and Eve? How did we know Jesus ever existed? Why couldn't Sunday school people answer my questions? After all, to me (at age nine) they seemed old and very smart. By then, I already knew that a lot of books were written that were not true, such as *The Cat in the Hat* and *Green Eggs and Ham*. This made me wonder if the Bible was basically a "fun" book for adults. I also wondered if Jesus was simply another "Santa" or "Easter Bunny" belief for adults, one that they were trying to get us children to believe.

Certainly church and Sunday school were anything but fun. Oh, how I dreaded the weekly services! The organ, the robes, the old-sounding songs, the standing up, sitting down, reciting things...It all was very boring and seemed somewhat morbid. Church didn't have any answers for me. The minister seemed to just assume that everything in the Bible was true. He provided no evidence like school did. If the Bible and Jesus were "fun" pretend things for adults, with church a "fun" place to go, then I really didn't want to become an adult.

I also wondered why we never talked about the Bible or Jesus at home. Were my parents hiding something? We talked about Santa at home—a lot. And we talked about the Easter Bunny. After all, even the school got involved with Santa and the Easter Bunny, along with witches and monsters at Halloween, but it never talked about Jesus—not at all. Why were the Bible and Jesus a Sunday-only thing if they were so important and true? And why did adults seem to go out of their way to make church *not* fun, not even interesting? It was a mystery for me.

———•———

By the time I was nine, the seeds of agnosticism and doubt had already been sown—even though I didn't know that agnosticism meant uncertainty about God. I was bright enough to grasp a lot of information at an early age, and there seemed to be a huge credibility gap between what I learned at school and through television versus what I learned at Sunday school and the church that bored me to death.

At school, even at my grade level, things were explained, reasons were given, facts seemed real. In comparison, Sunday school and church seemed like fantasyland—and the Bible seemed about as real as an adult comic book might be.

The public school didn't talk about incredible events like Adam and Eve, Noah's ark, or the parting of the Red Sea. The public school never said that God had created anything. Although the word "God" was included in the Pledge of Allegiance, the public school didn't acknowledge that God even existed.

2

Watering the Seeds of Agnosticism

It was the first day after my thirteenth birthday. I spent all day making concoctions with my new chemistry set. I was upstairs getting a glass of water when I heard my father come into the driveway at precisely 5:00 P.M., as he always did. Something was obviously bothering him.

"Dinner time!" Mom yelled a bit later.

The five of us sat down for dinner at 6:00 right on the button, as usual. "Whose turn is it for grace?" (We three boys always took turns saying a simple rote grace.)

"Rick's turn!"

"No, I said it last night, it's Ralph's turn!"

"No, I was the night before! It's Tom's—!"

Mom interrupted. "Tom, would you say grace, please?"

Tom sped through it. "God is great, God is good, and we thank him for our food. Amen. Pass the potatoes, please!"

"Meat, please!"

"Could I have the peas, please?" We were a very polite family. Constantly disciplined about proper etiquette. (I wonder how I lost that part of my upbringing?)

After we had all filled our plates and mouths with food, we started the inevitable small talk. "How's school?" My father always asked when he knew it was report-card time.

We then went through the usual ritual. Our report cards were reviewed by my parents. They always gave glowing remarks to my younger brother, Rick—who always got straight As—and some criticism to me for not applying myself, even though I had gotten nearly straight As. The truth was, I cared a lot more about sports than school. And "eggheads" were regarded as "geeks" by the athletes back then. I didn't want to be known as "smart." I wanted to be "cool." And my brother Rick couldn't even throw a football or shoot a basketball. So, secretly, I couldn't have cared less that his grades were perfect.

The conversation finally turned to my father's rotten day at work. Apparently he was mad because his boss had told him he had to talk to a lady tomorrow about going around and talking to everybody about Jesus, or something like that.

"Those darn Jesus freaks!" he muttered. "All they do is go around telling everybody that they're sinners. I'm a sinner. You're a sinner. Everybody's a sinner! Are you saved? Gotta get saved! Everybody saved! Saved! Saved! Don't they ever have anything else to say?"

"Free speech—isn't it, Dad?" my brother Tom said flatly.

"Well, not when it upsets the workplace. And we've had some complaints. Now I've got to deal with it and all I'll probably hear tomorrow is how much of a sinner I am."

My father had been a trustee in the church for several years, so I figured he knew almost everything there was to know about church and Jesus. *These Jesus freaks must be pretty bad,* I thought— my father hardly ever got upset about anything (except us). I'd never seen a Jesus freak though, except maybe once in New York City. There was a person standing on a box yelling to the people in the street something like "Repent, the return of Jesus is near!" Everybody just walked by him, though, so I thought it was no big deal. *Was this lady one of them?* I wondered.

Oh well, our family had more important things to do than to talk about Jesus. We had our vacation to discuss.

———————•———————

By age 13, I viewed church as a kind of club. Even though I was regularly attending the youth group, of which I later became president (setting up the first annual ski trip and other "club" events), I now strongly questioned nearly everything about the Bible and

God. Later I even joined the church, still thinking of it more as a club. If someone asked me if I was a Christian, I'd say yes because I knew that was the "right" answer. If anyone had asked *how I knew* I was a Christian, I'd have answered, "Because I belong to a Christian church."

The only time I remember praying in earnest was when my grandfather was dying. And that didn't work. He still died. So with a shaky belief foundation, my agnosticism only became stronger. And of course the rote grace my family said each night was absolutely meaningless to all of us.

———————•———————

I often laugh now at the "Jesus freak" incident. Even after many years of intensive research regarding the truth of the Bible, I remember still feeling awkward when I first saw my name in a church bulletin. I thought, *What will my friends think? Am I a Jesus freak?* The same thing happened when I first walked into a Christian bookstore. I was petrified of the kind of people I might find there, of being attacked by someone who wanted to "save me." Or would my friends see me and think I was some Jesus weirdo?

Words were very powerful to me as a developing young person, especially words about hard-to-define issues such as God. The home I was raised in unknowingly pitted Sunday school against regular school because we didn't talk about Jesus at home. In that battle, especially with no Sunday school capable of providing evidence supporting the Bible, the five-day-a-week public school won easily. For a belief, some evidence, some basis in truth must exist. *And any belief that has no basis in truth can, will, and should be called into question.*

Faith

The Bible commands its followers not to take anything on blind faith (see 1 Thessalonians 5:21). With no defense of the faith from home or church, with no evidence—the public school wins.

Today I often get challenged about the importance of faith. Of course faith is important. So are facts. (Both are included in

Hebrews 11:6, and both are alluded to in the greatest command-ment.) Sometimes, to allow the heart to be open to God, enor-mous intellectual barriers must be broken down. That's how it was with me. I (and my older brother Tom, a previous agnostic) let the evidence and facts fall where they might, let them break down bar-riers, even if it meant changing my belief system.

God provides evidence. Lots of it. We just need to seek it. But if we rely solely on blind faith, there's a great risk of being intro-duced to a false faith.

———•———

The huge, Fort Knox–like 2-ton doors groaned as they began to open into what we referred to as "Siberia." Rob Blaine and I were on the loading dock, awaiting the normal blast of arctic air, about to enter the freezer of Richmond's Ice Cream factory just outside Woodstown. In this frozen cavern we used 500-pound steel carts to load hundreds of pounds of ice cream for the delivery trucks' next-day routes. Because the temperature was always 60 degrees below zero inside, we could work only 45 minutes until we were required to take a 15-minute "heat break." But we were young and competitive (Rob was 19, I was 18)—and perhaps kind of crazy—so we created a game to stretch our breaks as long as possible. Besides, nobody was around at two o'clock in the morning anyway. We called our game "beat the clock," and we kept a tally of various record times for our "runs" in the warehouse. We always laughed a lot and made fun out of the drudgery of piling heavy 5-gallon tubs of ice cream, ice-cream bars, Popsicles, and other items on the large, racked carts.

As the doors slowly parted and thick clouds of condensed vapor poured out into the warm August night, we readied ourselves, like bobsledders, to get the heavy cart moving. *On your mark, get set...go!*

The doors had parted just enough for us to pass through. Freezing air seemed to pierce my face like sharp icicles as I pushed with all my might. Then the inevitable blast of cold wind from the fans that kept the chill to minus 60—it always seemed to find every small seam in my clothing.

We had our game down to a science. I pushed. Rob steered. Once we got the heavy cart moving, we could build up tremendous speed down the straightaways, and then Rob would nimbly turn down the appropriate aisle. We had to be careful to allow enough space to stop, though. The inertia built up with the tremendous weight, especially when the cart was filled with ice cream, and this caused us to have more than one crash at the end of an aisle when we didn't stop in time. While this didn't damage the cement walls, it ruined our game because ice cream was inevitably scattered everywhere, killing our timing.

"Can't you push any harder than that?" Rob shouted. No matter how fast we were going, he always tried to goad me on.

"If I thought you could steer better, I would!" I retorted.

We made it around to the vanilla aisle—a good aisle to get a lot on the cart at once. Rob barked out the number of tubs we needed. With German like precision each of us worked a side of the cart, grabbing one of the large containers in each arm and placing them two at a time on the cart in the easiest locations at the top. Even though this tended to make the cart top-heavy, it helped our speed because the bulkiest, heaviest items were placed in the most accessible area quickly. Vanilla done. We quickly turned into the chocolate lane. Hearts pounding. The 5-gallon containers started getting heavy when we were moving so many so quickly—I couldn't wait to get to Popsicles! Whoops! One tub covered with frost slipped through my grasp and landed on my toe. I swore.

Rob started laughing. "You need to work on that arm at the gym!" Faster, faster, down the aisle…

The strawberry lane. Multiflavors. We were whipping around corners with reckless abandon. Laughing and giggling like we were at an amusement park. In the next lane, Rob reached high for a couple boxes, and one ripped open, sending a rainbow of Popsicles over his face. We finished the aisle, scrambling to pick up the final items and head for "home." We both knew a record run was inevitable.

Entering the main straightaway, I pushed with all my strength to get maximum speed, with only one corner to round for home. The cart was moving faster than I could ever remember. As he'd done so often before, Rob reached up to grab the door-control rope just before we rounded the last curve. Timing was always perfect—the doors would open just enough to give us plenty of space to get through by the time we had turned the corner and traveled the final distance.

"Go, Rob!"

"Push harder, weakling!" he shouted back.

"Yeeehaaw!" We both knew we would beat the record by as much as 15 or 20 seconds. Rob was at his best, pulling the front of the seemingly lead-filled cart around the last bend.

The next fraction of a second has been frozen in my mind ever since.

As Rob yanked the top of the cart to steer it home, he cut the corner too closely, and the cart rode up over the edge of the corner pallet. The cart was moving at breakneck speed, and the combination of speed, the bounce, and the leverage from Rob pulling and me pushing caused the cart to tip and Rob to fall—with the cart headed straight at him.

As if it were in slow motion, I could see Rob looking up in terror as the huge cart tumbled over with only his head to stop it. His eyes wide as saucers with fear. I could see death in them.

The heavy 5-gallon tubs were falling.

Popsicles scattering.

It looked inevitable that the cart would crush Rob's head or decapitate him against the support columns. He had no time to move. A direct hit was imminent.

The floor shook as the steel cart slammed down with tremendous force.

There was deathly silence that seemed to last forever as I shuddered at the sight before me.

Somehow, a couple of rock-hard tubs of ice cream had become wedged between the cart and the ground, causing the cart to stop only inches above Rob's head. We both just remained still for a few seconds—in shock—before Rob slowly edged his head out. We both were shaking—but now it was not from the cold.

We left the freezer, deciding to fix our mess later. On the dock outside, we climbed up to our favorite resting spot, on top of about ten feet of stacked cardboard, and just lay on our backs to calm down.

Minutes of total silence passed.

"You almost died, man," I said.

"Yeah, I know," Rob replied.

A few more minutes of total silence.

"What do you think happens when you die?" I questioned him.

Rob turned to me with a stare that would freeze the most hardened criminal, and in a cold voice said, "Nothing. Absolutely nothing. You're gone. Kaput! Dead! And that's the end."

His words cut through me like a knife, and I stared into space, knowing exactly what he meant. He didn't believe in God, or anything else that went along with God. *There was no God.*

———•———

The Foundations

Rob Blaine's statements didn't turn me into an atheist; a lot more was required than that. But the foundation of agnosticism had been laid, and I was building a logical and philosophical basis for why God didn't exist, which demonstrates the incredible power of peers in formulating beliefs. Beliefs that may be right or wrong. Beliefs that may need to be "undone" later.

True atheism is one of the rarest "faiths" in the world (only about 4 percent of the world's population is estimated to be atheists). That's because there is far more evidence, even intuitively, for a God—some God—than for none at all. A true atheist almost has to *want* to become an atheist. And many do—choosing to reject God out of hand rather than face the possibility of being accountable to some higher power. (Agnosticism, or uncertainty about the existence of a God, is much more widespread—about 16 percent of the world's population.[1])

So where did I get the foundation of agnosticism that led me to atheism? From where you've seen—largely from my experiences at church and Sunday school. Combined with the teaching in schools and the media and my lack of religious teaching at home, these experiences made me a prime candidate for agnosticism. Yes, I still called myself a Christian…because that's what I was told I was. But by nine years old I doubted everything in the Bible. I had a hard time differentiating Sunday church and the Bible from pure fantasy.

———————•———————

Finally, as we relaxed on our cardboard hideaway, Rob and I had spent enough time for the jitters of his brush with death to subside.

"Rob," I asked, "aren't you afraid *not* to believe in God?"

"What do you mean?"

"Well, suppose you really died...and suppose there really is a heaven and a hell...and suppose there is a way to get to heaven that you've never figured out—wouldn't that frighten you?"

"Not if it's wrong," he stated coldly. (He seemed back to his old self.) "Besides, I'm not a bad person. And how would you prove anything about God anyway?"

"Some people think the Bible has the answers—I'm not saying I believe in the Bible, of course—but I do know that it says believing in Jesus is the key to heaven," I responded. "Aren't you ever afraid the Bible *might possibly, somehow be true?* If it is, then not believing in Jesus could be a real problem."

"In what way?"

"Well, the church people say the only way to eternal life is by believing in Jesus. What if that's true? What if the Bible is right? What if you had died from that cart falling on your head? Maybe by just believing that Jesus rose from the dead you would've been okay. I mean really...that doesn't seem like too much to do, does it? I think of it as 'death insurance,' which might be really, *really* valuable someday."

Rob, seeming annoyed, said, "But if the Bible's not true, what difference does it make?"

"It sounds like you're starting from the assumption that it's *not* true, aren't you?" I probed. "Doesn't that make you very prejudiced—unable to objectively evaluate the truth either way?"

Rob's previous assurance seemed to falter at this point. He had clearly started with a position that the Bible must be untrue. (This was my opinion too, but I felt that a little "death insurance" of intellectually believing in Jesus was a smart thing to do, just in case.) Now Rob was being cornered regarding his obvious prejudice. And I was starting to enjoy the mental challenge of the argument.

"Can *you* prove that the Bible is true?" he retorted.

"Of course not. It seems like a big fairy tale to me. But what if it *is* true? Wouldn't you take a safe approach and just believe—just in case? My parents make me go through the motions in church. I don't really believe any of it. But I figure I might as well try to believe in the Jesus part, just in case the Bible is right, and just in case there is a God."

Rob was slowly getting angry. "I'd rather be smart and dead than stupid and eternal!"

I wondered what he meant. His statement made no sense. *Perhaps stupidity is better,* I thought. Anyway, the competitive spirit was in me now. Even though Rob raised some good points that made the Bible seem ridiculous, I also knew that taking a safe approach was only logical. Also, I wasn't about to have Rob beat me in this argument.

"Rob," I said, "you almost died in there! Without a little luck, your head would've cracked like a walnut between that concrete floor and that 500-pound cart! I'd be scraping your brains off the floor right now! I agree the Bible is hard to believe. But isn't it all we've got? You just faced death—you just faced the difference between a 'possible nothing,' as you put it, and something much worse! Maybe even hell—with burning, stinking flesh, molten sulfur clinging to you, worms, horrible screaming, and your worst nightmare beyond belief!"

I started to feel strong, almost as if my argument was beginning to make sense. I didn't know what to believe, but I wanted to win this battle of minds. "If the Bible is wrong, you're no worse off since you would go to 'nothing' either way. But if the Bible is *right,* considering the downside, you had better believe whatever it tells you to believe! They say you either go to paradise or to a God-awful pit!" My words started feeling like they had power.

"Rob! Buddy! You were almost *toast!* Kaput! Done! Forever, and ever, and ever! Doesn't it make sense to at least consider anything that might take you out of absolute nothingness, or the pit of horror, of death, and of ultimate *defeat?*" (I knew my final appeal to "defeat" would help me win the point.) "Death, Rob! Horror, Rob! Defeat, Rob! And you were almost there!"

Rob paused a long, long time. I noticed a tear in the corner of his eye as he replied rather weakly, not with the same confidence he had had before. "Death is life that's finished. Done. We've got to face it...Nobody, not you nor the Bible, not the whole idea of Jesus—not a thing can ever change it."

Rob sounded really depressing. Were his ideas really right? Where did he get them from? It sounded as if all human beings were born for some unknown reason that only resulted in eventual nothingness. It didn't make sense. But on the other hand, I didn't have any reason to believe otherwise. I shuddered at the prospect of death without hope. And I felt tears starting to well in my eyes too.

———————•———————

A spider was winding its way up an endless silklike string toward the dirty, splintery beams in the warehouse ceiling. Rob and I had just made another ice-cream "Siberia run" and were again lying on our backs on our usual cardboard "tower" ten feet off the floor. The spider cast eerie shadows on the walls as the light seemed to magnify its size. And the strands of the web glistened like thin strands of glass as the light reflected off them. It was a fascinating, incredible sight.

Rob had just come back from his first year in college. I was about to go to the University of Colorado for my first year. Although we hadn't known each other much in high school, we both had a lot in common. We both loved all kinds of sports and played on the basketball team. In fact, I chose the University of Colorado by drawing a 50-mile radius around each good engineering school and counting the number of great ski areas within it. When a recruiter told me that Colorado was the best on my list, it was a no-brainer—that was the only school I applied to.

Rob and I both received the "Academic Athlete" award during our years in high school. We laughed a lot about the award and compared it to "kissing your sister," since athletes in those days didn't want to be associated with academics. But still, I realized Rob was smart, and I also figured a year in college could only make him smarter. So I didn't mind talking to him about things that I wouldn't dare talk to other athletes about.

"Funny," I said, "how a stupid spider knows how to spin a web, catch a fly or two, eat it, and start to spin a new web as soon as you and I attack its nice new web-home with our 'cannonballs' of rolled-up trash."

"Life is like that," he said. "Even the simplest creatures seem to inherit basic instincts that help them survive. Think about it. If spiders seem interesting, how about birds? Somehow they just 'know' how to fly. Kind of amazing, isn't it?"

"Rob, how do you think life gets going in the first place?" I asked.

"Are you kidding? Don't you realize by now that evolution is the master plan? If a creature can't hack it, it doesn't survive. It goes into the bottomless pit of creatures that fail."

"I'm not talking about survival, I'm talking about getting started in the first place."

"Well, I'm sure you're familiar with Stanley Miller's famous experiment that created life," Rob stated matter-of-factly.

"Miller didn't create life, just a few amino acids," I corrected. "Besides, after that there's still a long way to go. After you have all the stuff together, how does something come alive?"

Rob seemed to be growing impatient with the questions. "I don't know! But if we can start creating life, you can bet we'll find out sooner or later. Maybe it gets zapped with electricity or something. Heart patients can be brought back to life with electrical shock."

"Yeah, but it still seems like a miracle. Have you ever seen a close-up of a bug's antenna? Besides, how do you know for certain evolution is right?" I asked.

"Are you crazy? The *whole world* knows! Didn't old Rumpy teach you anything in biology class?"

I was getting embarrassed over sounding so stupid. Rob seemed to know what he was talking about. My thoughts started to drift back to high school—my sophomore year in biology class.

3

The Beginning of the Death of God

"Evolution is fact! Simply fact!" Our biology teacher, Mr. Rumpy, slammed his textbook on the desk to get our attention. "At one time it was called into question, but now we have ample evidence. There is no doubt that man evolved from the lowest form of life, which came together by chance." (This was 1966—I was 15 years old—and it was still four years in the future that the electron microscope would be able to detect atoms.)

Mr. Rumpy was a short, dumpy-looking teacher who had been around for a long time, and students accepted his teaching as fact. He based his statement about evolution on several points of evidence.

First, he pointed out the evolution of body parts. In illustration, he showed pictures of the elbows of various creatures ranging from frogs to bats to humans and described in some detail how they simply evolved into better, stronger structures through the "survival of the fittest." It sounded pretty logical to me. But it didn't compel me to accept evolution yet. After all, the strongest joints would certainly have belonged to the dinosaurs, whose fossils I had seen in the Smithsonian Institution. And the dinosaurs didn't survive. I remained very skeptical.

Then he reinforced the survival-of-the-fittest model with hard evidence. A species of moth—the peppered moth—was observed to consist of an abundance of white moths and only 2-percent black moths at the time when the bark on the trees of a village in England was covered with a white lichen. Birds could easily find and eat the black moths on a background of white lichen, which left an abundance of camouflaged white moths to procreate. Naturally the gene pool tended toward white. When industrial pollution arrived, the lichen died and the tree bark showed black. The population of the moths then shifted to 98-percent black—and only 2-percent white, which was now easier for predators to find and eat. Rumpy claimed that this demonstrated improvement in the species, since only the genetically best survived and produced similar, superior offspring. He finished that story by telling us that, when the industrial pollution was later cleaned up and the white lichen returned, the moth population again shifted, back to 98-percent white moths. Okay, chalk up a pretty good argument for evolution.

Rumpy also stated that the fossil record helps prove evolution. His favorite example was a fossil called the archaeopteryx, which he described as a reptile–bird. The pictures in our biology text showed a reptile with wings and feathers to fly, yet with claws on its wings and with teeth and a tail—things not found on birds (I thought) but on reptiles. It certainly looked like a missing link to me by the way Rumpy described it. But I wondered why there were so few archaeopteryx fossils and why they didn't have partially formed feathers. I was still skeptical. Rumpy quickly dismissed my question by making me feel stupid, saying that fossils are hard to find and that certainly we wouldn't have many of any particular fossil.

About midway through our teaching on evolution, Rumpy turned to the development of the human embryo itself as evidence of evolution. He showed us pictures of the embryo in various stages and pointed out that humans displayed evidence of their early ancestry, pointing to gill slits on the sides of the embryo that indicated our heritage under water. Likewise he pointed to a yolk sac that indicated, perhaps, a reptilian ancestry (eggs?). And he pointed to a tail that humans have before birth. It all seemed to make perfect sense at the time. Clearly, we had parts of our own bodies that didn't seem to belong there, which looked like parts of other creatures.

The "smoking gun" evidence for me was Stanley Miller's 1953 experiment, in which Miller created, in an early-earth environment, the first building blocks of life—two necessary amino acids.

Although I was just learning what an amino acid was, I knew it was vital to all living cells. Our textbook had pictures of the lab setup, which looked very technical and certainly must have been developed by people who knew exactly what they were doing. *Yes, I decided, if man can demonstrate how the chain of evolution can get started in the first place, there must be a way to "energize" life into it. Then all the other evidence starts to fit into place.* I could understand how Rumpy came to his conclusions. Evolution must be fact. And it didn't seem like God was necessary for anything.

The Choice

Any theory for the chance origin of life, such as the theory of evolution, is the "killer of God" for any religion associated with the Bible (which includes Judaism, Christianity, and Islam—over half the world's population). Essentially, if life originated by chance, then there is no reason for a "God" who would be creator of the universe and life—everything would have started randomly. Eastern religions, however (for example, Hinduism and Buddhism), are compatible with chance origin because in such religions god is not defined as a personal Creator—just as an impersonal force. But anyone claiming to believe a biblical religion must choose between Genesis 1 and chance origin. They can't both be right if one honestly and literally reads the words, *because they directly contradict each other*—which is underscored when the Bible is read in the original language of Hebrew.

By definition, someone who embraces a theory of chance origins, such as evolution, must support atheism, because that person would believe there was no Creator—and this is key to the definition of God. The only alternative is to change the definition of "God" to some *thing* that didn't create the universe or the life in it, some thing that neither cares about nor interacts with humans. Such a god would be

- totally impersonal (would have no personal interest in human beings)

- limited in power (would lack ability to create everything)

- limited in presence (would not be able to completely control everything)

All this would place "God" in the same category as a force of nature. Why not regard electricity as a god? Or gravity? Or heat? Or magnetism? After all, many peoples have worshiped such forces as gods.

"Rob," I said to my friend as we continued our break-time conversation, "no doubt evolution is right. Do you believe there is any chance whatsoever that there could be a God anyway?"

Rob started to chide me sarcastically, as we'd both done to each other many times before. "It's possible, I guess, but face it—if he didn't create us for a purpose, why would God care about us? If he doesn't care about us, he wouldn't interact with us. And if he doesn't interact with us, then why should we care about God even if he *does* exist?"

He continued. "The answer is so simple and obvious. First, God doesn't interact with us. If he did, why wouldn't he just boldly display himself in the sky? Or why not just come and talk to us? Second, God doesn't care about us because he would never allow all the suffering in the world if he did. And third, God doesn't care about us because God didn't create us in the first place. We already know that from evolution. But the simplest reason behind God's not interacting and not caring is that he doesn't even exist. Things all just happened randomly according to the laws of physics. 'God' is an invention of man to give an intellectual species some hope."

It sure sounded like Rob's reasoning was strong, and deep inside it reflected my own conclusions despite my arguments. "Oh well," I sighed, "I'll just look forward to some good skiing in Colorado."

At that point—as an 18-year-old agnostic—I was fearfully confident that God simply didn't exist at all.

4

Atheism at
the University

"We'll be arriving at Stapleton Airport in 26 minutes," the captain announced over the intercom.

Soon I would be on a new adventure, my education in the School of Engineering at the University of Colorado in Boulder. I had never seen the campus, but it looked good in the brochures. And these brochures all reminded me that Colorado was great for skiing.

I had been talking to a guy named Jim in the seat next to me. He was about my age and was going to his home in Fort Collins. I asked him about the city of Boulder, and he gave it glowing accolades. It sounded like a great place where I could have a lot of fun, ski, and maybe even squeeze in a bit of education.

"How far is Boulder from the airport?" I asked.

"About 30 minutes to an hour, depending on the traffic."

"What's the best way to get there? Does the university have a shuttle bus? Or should I take a city bus? Cab? Airport limo?"

"Are you kidding?" he said. "No university bus. City buses are infrequent, cabs cost a fortune—there is really no good way. Do you mean you actually got on this plane for your first trip to college without knowing how you'd get up there?" He made it sound as if I was really stupid.

"Yep," I responded. "I guess I thought of it being a pretty easy thing." I had always been adventurous. I traveled alone a fair amount in high school, including a trip to South America—

Chile—when I couldn't speak a word of Spanish. Somehow it always worked out.

"Tell you what," Jim said. "Let me ask my parents if they would mind swinging by Boulder on the way home. It's not that far out of the way, and besides, we haven't been there for a while."

I was genuinely grateful for the offer, not realizing the predicament I'd gotten myself in—I didn't even have much money with me. When we landed, I met his parents, and we headed off to Boulder. It was the fall of 1969. The days of summer jobs at Richmond's Ice Cream were nearly over, and Rob Blaine would soon be a memory. A new chapter in my life was about to begin.

———•———

My roommate, Bill Naples, was also enrolled in the engineering school, but it quickly became apparent that he didn't intend to stay. Bill identified himself with the environmentalists and the Vietnam War protests and all of the things relating to that intense era. As a naïve "straight" kid, I received shock treatment one day during our first few weeks when Bill invited me to join him and some buddies for a little "fun." He took me to a dorm room where a group of guys were hanging out. After a lot of chitchat and jokes, a closet was opened in which were growing marijuana plants, with leaves draped over the closet bar to dry. I was not only stunned but literally frightened. For all their shortcomings, my small town and my family had done a good job of scaring me about drugs. How could I escape? I was 2000 miles away from anyone. Far from safety. In a world of my own, at college.

I watched as they carefully crumbled the "weed" into cigarette paper. After they'd twisted both ends, I watched nervously as they began to pass the joint from one to the next. What would I do when it came to me? I was new at the university and didn't want to be uncool.

Finally it was my turn. I had tried cigarettes only a few times in my life before, and I knew I couldn't stand them and would choke. In fact, just the thought of smoke in my lungs made me want to cough. So when the joint was passed to me, I decided to suck the smoke into my mouth and just blow it out—because I knew I literally couldn't inhale, and besides I was afraid of the drug yet didn't want to look stupid.

This was the last and only social event I ever did with my roommate. At the university I saw several other acquaintances have horrible experiences with LSD and other drugs, so I quickly realized how devastating the consequences could be. Although I was able to avoid illegal drugs and was generally able to avoid getting caught up in the anti–Vietnam War movement and riots, my encounters with experts in the sciences and also the arts—I studied fine arts at the same time as engineering—brought me into considerable spiritual conflict.

Engineering school was, understandably, quite conservative. However, the professors in the required science courses clearly did not believe that a God of the universe could possibly exist. They accepted that Darwin and other scientists since had essentially proven evolution to be fact. The professors also seemed to chastise any individual believing in God for being uninformed and ignorant. Essentially such a person was considered less intelligent.

Perhaps the most important point in my development came when I was sitting in an advanced course in nuclear physics. The professor was highly esteemed. (Boulder, Colorado, is known for the presence of the National Bureau of Standards and the National Center for Atmospheric Research, so we had access to some of the top scientists in the world.) In one lecture, the professor made the point that so much had been learned in the fields of both theoretical and experimental physics that if a highly intelligent person were taught from birth straight to age 50, he or she still would not begin to grasp the knowledge we had achieved in the field to date. He went on to articulate how recent advances (this was in the early 70s) seemed to indicate that the more we learned, the more we saw that the laws of physics held the clues to our development as a species and that a "God" was not necessary. In other words, naturalistic origins and random chance could account for everything. The professor was obviously brilliant and gave what seemed to be good reasons for his arguments. I certainly didn't have enough information to challenge him at the time—*nor did science itself.* (For example, the field of molecular biology was still in its infancy. Neither had theories of chance origin been subjected to rigorous statistical analysis.)

Nor did I want to challenge this professor, since I was already convinced that naturalistic evolution was true. I wasn't interested in considering any alternatives. As far as I was concerned, he just supported the arguments I'd been making all along. He was just another very highly educated person who supported evolution.

————•————

Even engineers had to take some humanities courses. Though I never took a philosophy course, all of my humanities teachers seemed to be "philosopher-wannabes." Consequently, we had crackling discussions about whether or not a "God" could exist. Inevitably, the professors directed our reasoning down the same path, which happened to be especially in vogue then because of the Vietnam War. They would say, "If a God really existed, he must be either not all-loving or not all-powerful. Why? Because," they would continue, "if he were both all-loving and all-powerful he would not allow suffering to exist; he would stop it. So either he is not all-powerful, or he is not all-loving." They called it a logical fallacy for people to believe in the Christian God. This philosophical approach made great sense to me when combined with the science I was learning which seemed to indicate that God was not necessary anyway.

This intellectual atmosphere was not unique to the University of Colorado. My brother Tom was learning the same at the University of Virginia; my brother Rick was learning the same at Yale and Columbia. (Others, such as author Patrick Glynn, have written about the exact same experience in such institutions as Harvard.[1]) Is it any wonder that generations of people, including me, had turned away from God?

Intellectual Life at the University

Universities can create an atmosphere that leads students into agnosticism or, as in my case, pure atheism. I believe it is unintentional. Professors (now I am one) and other instructors tend to think they are on an intellectual plane above most people, especially students. They learn how to communicate forcefully, how to debate, and how to present their arguments in a compelling light. Professors also learn to defer to their peers, whether in the sciences or in the humanities. Often they simply agree with the findings of a peer rather than investigate issues for themselves. Consequently, a theory like evolution can be passed on for decades by those who make a livelihood from it—simply because others don't question it.

———•———

For me, higher education made an absolute mockery of the religious teaching that I had already been barely hanging onto. After two years of college, I would have felt like a complete idiot to believe in God. And significantly, I had accumulated the ability to argue with others *against* belief in God. The only recourse I seemed to have was to make a brief investigation of non-Bible-based religions. So I decided that, whenever an opportunity presented itself, I'd ask questions so I could see what others thought.

Hippie Theology

One day, Tom, a friend of mine who was active in the hippie groups in Boulder, took me to a place called the "Hill." There we encountered a bunch of people dressed in robes, pounding on tambourines, and chanting "Hare Krishna!"

"Hare Krishna, Hare Krishna, Hare Krishna." Incense was burning. Tambourines clanging. I had never seen anything like it. But I was curious about religions, especially since the Bible seemed to be false.

One man, tall, bald except for a braided piece of hair coming off the top of his head, asked me, "Do you know the *true godhead?*"

I certainly did not expect this question and was dumbfounded. Thinking quickly back to my "Christian" upbringing, I replied, "Uhh…yes, the Father, the Son, and the Holy Spirit."

"How do you know?" was his reply.

Now I was lost. I didn't know how I knew, and the flood of childhood uncertainty started flowing through me again. The Hare Krishna went on to explain to me in some detail why "Brahma, Vishnu, and Shiva" were the three gods of the godhead, and that Krishna, the eighth incarnation of Vishnu, was superior to Jesus. I'd never had it explained to me like that at all before. Did these people who looked so strange somehow know something?

Going back to my usual skeptical self, I asked for evidence of their belief, and the Hare Krishna simply told me that it was in the Bhagavad Gita, a book I should read. There was no indication of what I would find nor how I would know it was from God. He seemed pretty convinced, but I decided that, before I would jump into any religious thing, I would check its sources for evidence, since I'd already been "burned" by a Bible that people seemed to think was true. I did discover that the Bhagavad Gita was a Hindu holy book, and that Hare Krishnas had a belief based in Hinduism. After reading portions of the book, I saw no substantive evidence that its claims were from any real, historically existent "god." As far as I could see, it was just a philosophical story.

———————•———————

Another time, my roommate Bill (who was deeply involved in "saving the environment") took me to a meeting where a few environmental engineers got together with some people from New Age religions. These people believed that God was somehow connected to the environment. Similar to the Hare Krishnas, they all began chanting words of peace and invoking the protection of "Mother God" before they assumed a lotus position and began to meditate Yoga-style. Well, I couldn't begin to get into a Yoga position—talk about feeling out of place, tied in knots like a pretzel. And the chants…I had no idea what they meant.

"Mmmmmmmmmmmm."

Finally I pulled the leader aside and asked him what it was all about.

He explained to me that "all was one" in the universe and that we needed to be in touch with our "inner selves" before we could be truly part of this "oneness." By now I was pretty suspicious of any religion. I asked him for evidence that his belief was the one true belief. His response just seemed like a bunch of words—it was something like this:

"You know you are one because of the eternal power that resides in your soul and the souls of all living things…That is the nature of the true god that nourishes, protects, and provides hope…and with this eternal power, you can become one with nature…"

It sounded even worse to me than church and Sunday school combined.

———•———

In my teen years I had been intrigued by Muhammad Ali's conversion to Islam, though I knew virtually nothing about the Muslim faith. In college I did a modest amount of research about Muslim beliefs, largely because of my inspiration from Ali and my disappointment with every other religion that I was seeking. I read a good deal of the Qur'an, the holy book of Islam. In the end, I found virtually no evidence for the faith other than the claims that tied Muslims to the Christian Bible (which I had already rejected anyway).

However, the Muslim faith seemed much more real and viable than the beliefs that were based in Hinduism, Transcendental Meditation, or the New Age—popularized most notably by the Beatles. But the evidence for Islam was still somewhat biblically based (Islam believes in revised versions of the first five books of the Bible, the Psalms, and a version of the Gospels.) So just like the Jewish and the Christian beliefs, Islam remained unproven, and worse—a fantasy—in my mind. Nor did I find evidence for God in the Qur'an, which in fact seemed somewhat aimed at attacking Jews and Christians.

———•———

By this point I'd made at least a cursory survey of several religions and had heard a lot of professors and peers present logic against a God or religion in general. It was lack of evidence of God, combined with rational arguments from scientists and philosophers, that convinced me that atheism was the only reasonable and intellectually sound "faith" to have.

Objectivity

Many people place total faith in human achievements and knowledge, thus from the start excluding the possibility of the miraculous and a Creator God. But if we don't even consider God as an option for explaining all that is around us, especially in light of growing knowledge that seems to support his existence, we are not applying good science—we are not being objective. Though this is changing in most universities there remains a presupposition that only "natural" events are real and that other dimensions beyond those we can observe (where God might reside) simply don't exist. Hence a shift of thinking towards atheism has been inevitable. However, as scientific knowledge continues to accumulate, it is the shift toward *naturalism* that requires more faith than does belief in something supernatural. Think of belief in evolution, for instance, as naturalism, a rejection of anything supernatural. Opening the doors to consider evidence for God would mean breaking down the barriers that have been so firmly entrenched—barriers that exclude any consideration of other dimensions, or miracles, or God.

Many atheists or agnostics are so "comfortable" (as I was for years) that they don't even want to consider breaking down these barriers that are obsolete. And the many people whose livelihood depends on a commitment to evolution–naturalism have no desire to break them down. But I have yet to find someone who would do the same in medicine—who would hang onto ideas from, for instance, a time before we even knew what germs were (Darwin's time). Or someone who would still cling to mid-nineteenth-century technology. In the end, if eternity is in the balance (as I became convinced of), barriers must be broken down to allow people to consider God. After all, wouldn't eternity be far more important than anything discovered, invented, or theorized in the last 200 years?

At this point in my life, I was a hard-core atheist. I rejected the existence of any kind of being that matched Webster's definition of God:

> A being conceived as the perfect *omnipotent*, omniscient *originator* and ruler of the universe, the principal object of faith and *worship* in monotheistic religions.

I felt equipped to debate the issue of the existence of God. I had a knowledge base from which I rejected God as *Creator* (evolution–naturalism), as being *omnipotent* (philosophy—why didn't he stop suffering?), and as worthy of *worship* (no evidence for his interaction with humans, whereby he might help or harm us). Nobody seemed to be able to present a meaningful case *for* God. Yet, my scientist and philosopher friends would certainly speak out *against* God. Though I would listen to the beliefs of various religions, I saw no evidence whatsoever for any belief in a Deity. My thoughts moved from God to my career, which was about to begin at Procter & Gamble, in marketing. Any real consideration of God would take a backseat for many years. Perhaps when I wanted a moral "church club" for my children I'd reconsider. Otherwise, the idea of God provided only a bit of entertainment when I encountered "Jesus freaks" and had some fun "beating the Bible."

Bible-Beating Atheists

How do atheists "beat the Bible" for their cause? I wouldn't have known had not someone pointed out that I was doing just that. From about 1975 to 1985, I made a game of being a "Bible-beating atheist" in situations where I couldn't be negatively affected. How? It was simple. An occasion would arise in which an "unimportant" person would make a comment about God, the Bible, or Jesus, or just religion in general. (Essentially I would "set them up.") Once a comment had been made, I would challenge him or her to defend the comment (which inevitably was in favor of God). Nobody ever could. Then I would counter with a litany of evidence against the God of the Bible (or against Jesus) and ask for a reply. For a person as arrogant as I was back then, it satisfied my pride that I could out-argue others in the most important question of life. It was like the arguing games I used to enjoy with Rob Blaine on top of the cardboard "tower" at Richmond's Ice Cream factory.

Spreading the "Faith"

Once someone is committed to atheism, it is virtually no different than with any other cause. A person will support it according to his or her own level of commitment and belief. And if that commitment risks offending others, that's a consequence each person must evaluate. To me, expressing my viewpoint was okay as long as I was very careful not to let "religious matters" interfere with my business or family life.

One time when I was working for Hills Brothers Coffee, I had a discussion on a business trip to Dallas. The person next to me on the plane indicated he was a pastor in charge of evangelism for a large church. Before I knew it, I was in a conversation regarding the methods of church in general and how boring it had been for me as a child.

"Wasn't the message of hope inspiring to you as a teenager?" the pastor asked.

"No," I replied flatly. "It was boring and meaningless."

"Didn't you feel close to God when the choir sang their songs of praise?"

"No, I couldn't stand their robes and the somber melodies."

"Well, what *did* you like? And why did you keep going?"

"I liked nothing, and my parents made me go," I replied. "By the way, how do you know for certain that Jesus rose from the dead?"

"The Bible makes it clear," he responded.

"How do you know the Bible's accurate and historical?"

"Because the early church handed it down to us in today's form."

"How do you know the early church didn't change it to meet their doctrinal objectives?" I asked.

"Well," he stumbled, "there is no evidence of any changes."

"So you admit you assume history from a book that you can't clearly prove to be historically accurate?" I continued: "What evidence do you have for any of its miracles?"

"Of course, nobody could ever prove a miracle," he said. "People just have to believe on faith."

"How do you know your faith is better than any other religion's faith? They claim miracles too."

"Because we have history to prove it."

"What history?" I pressed.

"Well…ummmm…the Bible."

"That sounds like circular reasoning to me," I said. "You just stated that we need to believe a miraculous story based on faith. Then you claim the Christian faith is superior to other religions based on history. Yet you conceded that the basis for history is the Bible—a book you admit you can't prove is historically accurate or hasn't been changed. It doesn't make sense!"

The pastor was caught in an embarrassing position with no good answer. Discussions like this happened over these ten years and built up my disbelief in the accuracy of the Bible. Nobody—absolutely nobody!—could explain why ordinary people should believe the Bible.

Looking back, I'm amazed at how ill-equipped many churches, pastors, and others were to defend the Bible (see 1 Peter 3:15). Even today, few churches teach people to defend the God of the Bible. Is it surprising that all my years of church and Sunday school allowed the seeds of agnosticism to sprout into atheism?

5

The Challenge

One day in about 1984, I was having lunch with Jack Mores, an advertising agency representative from Portland, Oregon, and a friend of his, "Bob," who was in the advertising promotions business. We were simply enjoying the day and the position of being executives in the advertising world, which in those days allowed long lunches, great food, and lengthy talks. Somehow the conversation turned to the topic of God. I started pontificating about the philosophical need man has for a God as a "therapeutic" idea, claiming that modern knowledge indicates the nonexistence of God.

"What is the alternative to God?" Bob asked.

"Nothing," I responded. "Why does there need to be a 'God'? And if he really existed, why would there be so much suffering in the world?"

"Well then, how did everything we see come to be?" he questioned me.

"That's simple," I said. "Evolution is responsible, not a 'God'!"

"How can you prove evolution?" he asked.

"Well there are a vast number of evidences. I could take up this entire lunch. But give me a break—virtually every scientist believes it, and they make a living out of studying it. Evolution clearly shows that a God is not necessary."

But Bob went on. He described how Christians had "hard" information to support their beliefs.

"Come on!" I said sarcastically. "I've been talking to Christians for years and nobody has any strong support for either the Bible or for Christianity."

"Perhaps they just haven't researched it themselves," he said with a smile. "I could talk about it for hours, but that is not the purpose of this lunch."

Then Bob challenged me to sincerely research the Bible in the same way that I criticized it. He said that if I did an honest job of researching the Bible, I would find it 100-percent accurate—even regarding creation versus evolution. I thought he was completely out to lunch. Yet I was too arrogant to turn down this challenge. In my mind I replied, *Give me two weeks and a library and I'll put this Bible accuracy claim to rest forever.*

"You're on, Bob," I said. "Let me gather some facts, and you'll see how utterly ridiculous it is to think that a God exists. But once I prove it to you, the next lunch is on you."

"Lunches are always on me, aren't they?" he said. "After all, I sell promotions and you guys buy, right?" We all started laughing.

———•———

God used my arrogance and skepticism to prod me to research his existence extensively. Although I believed that I would disprove God and the Bible within a couple of weeks, instead my research lasted many years. (I don't recommend this for anyone. I was a tough sell and had no intention of accepting a false God.)

I think back to that casual conversation with Bob as the most important point in my life. Yet it didn't seem that way at the time. I never saw Bob again, and I've long since forgotten his real name.

Somewhere out there, "Bob" may read this book and recognize the impact he had on me.

Thanks, Bob. I owe you lunch. And certainly much more.

Where Do You Go to Find God?

I sat bolt upright in my bed, covered with sweat. My heart was racing. The Krishnas—where were they? The robes? The bald heads? The leader with the ponytail? I slowly realized I had been dreaming. Then my thoughts drifted back to the events of the past day, and I started to see why my mind was full of old memories of

Krishnas, gurus, Yoga, and the things that were popular when I was in college.

Earlier that day I had been working on a project with Jack Mores and an exceptional creative team—husband and wife Bill and Marcie Barkley. As usual, we first reviewed the project's status at the ad agency office, then left to have lunch together as we continued to discuss strategy and the next steps.

Something special always seemed to come out of ad agency lunches. And with Bill and Marcie, usually it was some great creative concept. Sure enough, as we brainstormed while eating, some intriguing ideas came up. Bill proposed a provocative idea and indicated they had done some similar things for another client. He could either bring the work to the office sometime to show us, or I could swing by their house if I wanted to see the work right away (he and Marcie worked from home).

I was pretty excited about the ideas and in no rush to drive the hour-and-a-half commute to get home, so I agreed. Upon arriving at the Barkley's, I felt like I had stepped backward in time. Their modest house was meticulously decorated in the style of the late '60s to early '70s. The cotton hangings on the walls looked to be tie-dyed. The rug on the floor appeared to be specially woven in a "Middle-Eastern" pattern. There was art all over—art that appeared to be from India or thereabouts. And the pungent odor of incense.

Bill brought out a few videotapes, and we looked intently at the "magic" he and Marcie always seemed to bring to corporate America. As usual, I was amazed at their creativity. Then I noticed an unusual picture on a wall in the next room. It was a man with a long beard, who appeared to be a guru or something. After working with Bill and Marcie for several years, I had developed an excellent relationship with them and felt comfortable asking some personal questions.

"Bill, I'm kind of curious," I said matter-of-factly. "Who is the person in the picture?"

Marcie gave Bill one of her special looks, with a smile and a twinkle in her eye. Bill looked back at her smiling, as if they were both communicating without a word. Marcie answered, "He's 'Rashij…'" It was some Indian-sounding name I couldn't remember for more than two seconds. "Bill and I are into Yoga, and he's our teacher."

"Yoga, huh?" My thoughts raced back to college, where my engineering buddies and I had come to the conclusion that anyone involved in that sort of thing was a kook. "What caused you to start Yoga?" I asked.

"Bill and I went to a conference where he was teaching," Marcie explained. "He taught us how to get in touch with our 'inner souls.' It's really incredible."

"You'd be amazed," Bill added. "Once Marcie and I started, nothing in our life has been the same. It's improved our work, our relationships, even our intimacy." Bill sounded very serious.

"How do you do it?" I asked.

"First you need to get into a lotus position," Bill offered. "Marcie, why don't you show him?" Marcie assumed a lotus position that it seemed only a double-jointed person could do. She and Bill went on to explain that they each had their own personal "mantra," which was a word that they said over and over again as they remained in a state of meditation. They indicated that they often did this for an hour or more at a time!

"How do you know it's doing anything for you?" I asked pragmatically. (The skeptic in me was coming out, although I would never want to hurt my friends.)

"You can *feel* it," Marcie said excitedly. "It's like your soul is *one with the God of the universe.*"

"And it's relaxing too," Bill said. "When I have a tough day with a client, I come home and meditate and it brings a peace about me like you wouldn't believe!"

"Tell me about the 'God of the universe,'" I asked. "Is he the person in the picture?"

Bill and Marcie started laughing. "Of course not. The God of the universe is a force that is present in all of nature. It pervades everything," Bill said.

"How do you know?" I asked.

"Well, you just know," Marcie stated. "I think if you were to try it you'd see what we're talking about. In fact, another conference is coming up next month."

"Yeah, Marcie and I would love to have you join us," Bill volunteered.

"Interesting," I said. "Let me think about it." We resumed discussing the project until it was time for me to leave. I thanked them and left, wondering about this "mystical" religion they believed.

————•————

Bill and Marcie caused me to wonder if there was any statistical evidence for a specific "God." Certainly they offered none for their mysterious thinking that God was a force in everything.

I had no idea of what test could be applied so I could really know for certain that God did or didn't exist. What evidence could I provide to win my point with Bob?

Part II

Standards of Proof

6

Definitions of Proof

At first I thought I would simply go to a library and disprove the God of the Bible through direct contradiction by facts and information. But I quickly realized that I was not dealing just with the issue of the Bible being correct—I was dealing with the issue of whether "God" was real. Defining "standards of proof" would be necessary.

Thinking the way an engineer with a background in philosophical debate would think, I decided that, if I was really going to answer the question of the existence of God (and as importantly, the question "Who is this God?"—if he existed at all), I would have to impose rather strict standards of proof. I felt very confident that God couldn't be proven. After all, I'd heard "God can't be proven" many times from both skeptics and theologians alike. On the other hand, I decided that if God were real, he wouldn't be so mysterious that he wouldn't give evidence for his existence in a form that humans could understand. Otherwise, he would be no different than any myth or other human invention. So I decided to apply the commonly accepted standards of proof in my search for God. *My expectation was that God would fail in all tests.*

Yet, to be intellectually honest, I decided if I could find convincing evidence that a God did exist, I'd seek out more information about who this God was, and I'd present my case to others. I decided I would search for evidence that was consistent with the three commonly accepted human standards of proof:

1. analytical

2. statistical

3. legal

1. Analytical Proof

It has been said that "outside of mathematics, nothing can be proven." In a literal sense that is accurate, because only in mathematics do definitions of relationships of numbers form the basis for "proof." Such proofs are unchallengeable because the definitions are stated as absolute in the first place. We even define the word "prove" in mathematics so that it can never be wrong. For example, we define a numerical system (for instance, what "1" means, what "2" means, and so forth) and then define their relationship (for example, "2+2=4"). Absolute proofs can be based on these definitions. Indeed, far more complex mathematical relationships can be proven using the *analytical* method.

As an example, one basic algebraic law taught in high school is

$$(A + B) \times (C + D) = (A \times C) + (A \times D) + (B \times C) + (B \times D)$$

This law has been proven analytically through the definition of the components and the conventions of symbols like parentheses and order of computation.

The above law is simple compared to the types of mathematical proofs in physics that led to Einstein's breakthroughs. Proof through mathematics can be difficult and complex, but it is *"hard"* proof. In other words, it cannot be challenged because the method of proof is *absolute*—by virtue of the definitions that were created in the first place.

"Hard" and "Soft" Evidence

"Hard" proof is also found in the field of statistical analysis. Analytical and statistical "hard" evidence enables hard proof in such sciences as physics (especially), applied mathematics, chemistry, and to some extent microbiology. Hard evidence can be measured. It is defined. Or repeatable experiments can verify it. It represents the strongest evidence within science.

"Soft" evidence is evidence that is gained through systematic study or observation. Many of our greatest advances come from it. For example, simple observation of herbs used in traditional medicine have led to important modern pharmaceuticals. Through further experimentation, such "soft" evidence can lead to a "hard" probabilistic and predictable outcome. Many other things, like Teflon, for instance, have come from simple soft-science observation. So did microwave ovens. But we must recognize its limitations. Soft science has also led to many mistakes, such as the long-held belief that the sun circled the earth. Until observations can be established as fact—through hard, predictable science, they provide a degree of evidence that is less precise and dependable. The soft sciences—the sciences of observation—generally include anthropology, geology, general biology and botany (nonmolecular), and so on.

Here's a final example of the difference between hard and soft science. Wouldn't it be great if we could predict with virtual 100-percent accuracy, as with the law of gravity, where we could drill a well to produce oil? Or where we would find gold? We can't. Geology is a soft science—a science based on experience and observation. In contrast, physics (for example, gravity physics and astrophysics) is a hard science—measurable, precise, and highly predictable. For instance, we can know for certain when a solar eclipse will occur. We should be careful to distinguish between those categories. As you will see, hard science (analytical and statistical proof) and soft science (legal proof) played different roles in my search for "proof" of God and who he is.

Here's how analytical proof related to my search for God. Instead of using numerical definitions, I used word definitions. Here are some examples.

———————— • • • ————————

- If a car requires an engine, and that engine requires (by definition) a designer, the car implicitly requires a designer.

- If a computer requires a printed circuit, and a printed circuit requires a designer, then a computer implicitly requires a designer.

- If a baby requires DNA and RNA (both far more complex than a car or computer), and DNA and RNA require a designer, then the baby requires a designer.

———————— • • • ————————

How Does Analytical Proof
Relate to the Existence of God?

Analytical proof first requires a *definition*. The most accepted basic definition of God is "the originator and ruler of the universe" (Webster). Focusing on only a tiny piece of the universe (the first living cell), I could analytically prove no need for a Creator God if some natural mechanism could be shown to be able to bring "first life" into existence. On the other hand, an "originator" would have to exist if I could prove that the only other alternative—random chance (for example, naturalistic evolution)—was impossible. By definition (Webster), I would call that originator "God" if naturalistic evolution were to lose.

The challenge then became, how could I ascertain whether naturalistic origins were viable or impossible? After all, I presumed that all the world accepted this, mainly through evolution. So to disprove or prove God analytically, I would want to use hard science if at all possible. In other words, just a bunch of dead bones, such as the lack of transitional fossil species (Bob had talked about this at our lunch), wouldn't be enough to convince me. And at this point in my life, I had swallowed naturalistic evolution hook, line, and sinker and thought I would never be able to disprove it.

2. Statistical Proof

The second commonly accepted type of proof is proof by *statistics* or probability. For example, scientists have essentially proven that gravity exists. I doubt that anybody will be able to refute this. Many other laws of physics have also been proven, based on tests that indicate the probability of the law is so high (regarding cause and effect) that any other explanation is deemed virtually impossible.

On the other hand, do we know for *absolute* certainty that these laws are true? No! But as a result of massive experimentation, we know that the odds of denying the laws of physics are absurdly small. Many experiments involving dropping things have determined that gravity exists beyond any doubt. People accept it as fact. Scientists commonly accept statistical experiments as proof. And nobody (at least nobody I know) would jump off a cliff trying to prove that the law of gravity is wrong. All laws of physics that we commonly accept today, on which are based everything from the design of airplanes to the safety of our bridges, are founded on statistical proof.

In a sense, everyone's daily actions are also based on statistical, or "probabilistic," proof. Becoming acquainted with such everyday proofs teaches us to avoid doing ridiculous things like jumping in front of speeding trucks (force = mass times acceleration, a Newtonian law of physics); standing in a bathtub and sticking our finger in an electrical socket; or remaining in the path of an advancing tornado. All of these situations carry a probability of a disastrous consequence based on proof of the laws of physics. *None* are proven to 100-percent certainty. Yet all key laws of physics are proven to a degree of certainty exceeding 1 chance of non-occurrence in 10^{50}. That means that there is less than 1 chance in 100,000,000,000,000,000,000,000,000,000,000,000,000,000,000,000,000 of any of them *not* being right.

In other words, the odds of gravity *not existing* are absurdly small. Gravity is essentially absolute fact. Yes, a hardcore skeptic might claim that gravity is "still unproven." However, I have yet to find a skeptic willing to challenge the proof of gravity by jumping off a cliff.

● ● ●

Statistical proof is probably the most common proof we use in the daily course of our lives.

- Every time we enter a freeway we have some probability of suffering a fatal auto accident.

- Every minute we have some probability of being hit by a meteorite.

- Every time we eat we have some probability of choking to death.

- We depend on the proof of gravity for the stability of everything from our homes to large buildings and bridges.

- We depend on the proof of the laws of physics for such things as heating and refrigeration, electricity, and the structural soundness of, for example, dams.

- We depend on the proof of chemistry findings for medicines and thousands of other substances.

━━━━━━━━━━━━━━━━━━━━━━ ● ● ● ━━━━━━━━━━━━━━━━━━━━━━

Statistical proof is not 100-percent certain. But it is *highly reliable* through repeated observation and experimentation. Again, the standard benchmark is that anything with a probability of less than 1 in 10^{50} is impossible or absurd (without the intervention of an outside force); therefore humans accept such probability as "proof."

How Does Statistical Proof Relate to the Existence of God?

It seemed to me that a God of the universe would provide some statistical "proof" that he exists. I just needed to know where to look and how to find it. After all, I had learned to trust everything from medicine to airplanes to electronics based on statistical proof. Why not rely on it in my search to determine the existence of God?

As an atheist, I wanted to do my own thing. It would be contrary to my thinking to accept a God who might try to take control away from me. I needed hard evidence. I needed empirical findings—I needed statistical probability (like the statistical proof of gravity, the first law of thermodynamics, or other laws of physics). Otherwise, it would be much more convenient (and much more attractive) for me to simply dismiss God as being unable to reveal himself.

Soon I discovered that there *was* a statistical test. Certainly nobody can "test" God by a repeatable experiment. However, I could test the probability of his existence by testing for something that only God could do…*I could test for his ability to foretell the future with perfect precision and accuracy.* I wondered if any person, god, or holy book had ever predicted the future like this. I chose to use it as a critical test for God.

3. Legal Proof

The third commonly accepted type of proof is *legal* proof—proof beyond a reasonable doubt, just as in a court of law, for a historical event.

When it is claimed that something has happened in history, be it the beginning of mankind, the flood of Noah, the resurrection of Jesus, or a murder last week, the only way of proving it is by legal evidence. Courts of law have defined this standard: judgment by peers based on evidence, the best that is available. Hence there is often uncertainty with legal proof, because an event can't be repeated. So in a sense this is soft proof, in the same way that geology is a soft science. Yet soft proof in either field can turn into hard proof *if ample statistical evidence supports an event.* For example, an overwhelming number of core samples within a given area that show underlying granite can statistically assure a scientist that the bedrock is granite in that area. Likewise, an overwhelming number of consistent and credible testimonies about an event can move the evidence into the area of hard proof.

Legal evidence includes

- eyewitness testimony

- hostile-witness testimony

- corroborative reports (reports other than the above in regard to an event)

- circumstantial evidence (surrounding factors that support or refute an event)

How Does Legal Proof Relate to the Existence of God?

At first, legal proof seemed to me to be the weakest proof of all. After all, it is essentially proof by observation of an event or by circumstantial analysis. By contrast, analytical proof is by hard definition. Either God existed as Creator, or he did not. The theory of naturalistic evolution would have to be tested in a reasonably hard, scientific (probability-based) way—leaving the only possible alternatives as either the existence or the nonexistence of God. Also by contrast, statistical proof would require hard *empirical* evidence (that is, evidence that could be verified or disproved by observation) and the use of the same standards of probability that we apply to laws of physics. I would have to apply them in the same way to justify the existence of God. So how would legal proof fit into the picture?

It became apparent to me that if I rejected the existence of God analytically and statistically, then legal proof would not carry much weight. On the other hand, if by those same means I discovered that God existed, then I would be faced with the issue of *who God was.* By then I realized that the many religions that exist have many different ideas. Philosophy-based religions like Hinduism, Buddhism, Shintoism, and so on have one type of idea. History-based religions like Judaism, Christianity, and Islam have quite another. It became obvious to me that, if God existed, then knowing who he, she, or it really was—finding a definition—was of extreme importance. Otherwise I could be listening to, or worse, worshiping, something totally untrue, perhaps even offending the nature of God.

What is the "best" legal evidence? I asked myself. Clearly, eyewitness testimony and hostile-witness testimony. Corroboratory and circumstantial evidence could also play a key role. A "smoking gun" with a bullet whose markings matched that gun's barrel, owned by the accused and in his possession at the scene of a crime, could be strong evidence. But even that would pale in comparison to evidence from witnesses, especially several of them who actually had seen someone say or do something like shoot someone.

I wondered what religions provided legal proof, if any. Could I support the claim that a religious leader was God by the same standard that a court of law convicts criminals? If not, why not? Wouldn't a God of the universe provide some legal evidence of his existence?

———◆———

Starting My Research

The competitive spirit was in me to win the challenge from Bob. Having been competitive and skeptical all of my life, I would have felt ashamed to have some Bible-beating fanatic beat me in a battle of minds. Yet I certainly didn't want anyone to think I was a Jesus freak or, worse yet, a "God freak." So I didn't let anyone know I was beginning my research, not even my own wife.

Basic research was difficult in Oregon (which is where we lived at the time) since all the good bookstores and libraries were in the city of Portland. This limited my research time to the days I traveled the 30 or so miles from our home in Salem into the city to visit the ad agency. However, we soon moved to southern California, which made my research easy. A great library was right on the way home from work, along with many excellent bookstores. By that time I had essentially forgotten about Bob. I was in it for myself, and I started talking to people about evidence of God when I was traveling, instead of playing the "Bible-beating atheist." I started reading a lot. Basically, I was seeking God—methodically, somewhat objectively, but very skeptically.

Until my pride caused me to accept Bob's challenge, I didn't give the idea of God a chance. But when I began to investigate God, I did it with intensity, as if my life depended upon it. As it turned out, it did—and so may yours.

Part III

Analytical Proof of God

7

Dice or God?

The origin of the very first life form was the obvious place to start to disprove God. All I needed to do was demonstrate a mechanism for development of "first life" that didn't require God, and by definition God would not be necessary for the creation of life. God would be dead in my mind since he would have no purpose for existence. I believed that all the esteemed scientists who seemed to support evolution must have the information I needed, and I was quite confident I could find it.

Secondarily, I would seek evidence of other planets that could support life. If there was a high probability of the existence of such planets, the idea of a God-of-the-earth-only would be diminished. In my search to disprove or prove God, I would try to find as much hard evidence as I could.

Definition of God

My process of analytical proof, it seemed, had to start with the definition of "God" and "no God." The next issue would be the testing of these definitions. I chose to start small (the idea of God could always be expanded.) I chose to simply define God as the *originator of first life,* an "intelligent designer." "No God" I defined as the *origin of first life without a specific creator.* It would mean that first life came about through natural causes, in other words, naturalism.

First life had to have only one cause, either God or a natural, random process. Therefore if I could prove one to be true, the other would be false. On the other hand, if I could prove one to be false, the other must be true, since I saw no alternatives to these two choices. Here is the way I charted my thinking.

• • •

Definitions

First life	= The first living, reproducing cell
Random chance	= Origin of first life randomly (naturally)
Evolution	= Process of developing first life by random chance
Intelligent design	= Creation of first life by purposeful design
God	= The intelligent designer—the originator
Fact #1	• First life existed. (Life exists today, so there had to be a "first.")
Fact #2	• First life came about by random chance (naturalism) or intelligent design. Only one is true.
Conclusion #1	• If first life came about by random chance, evolutionary origin is true. If not, some concept of God is true.
Conclusion #2	• If first life came about by intelligent design, some concept of God is true. If not, evolutionary origin is true.

Word Equations

If first life occurred by chance:	Evolution = cause
If first life required design:	God = cause
If God = cause:	God = real

• • •

Beginning to Analyze God and the Creation of First Life

I went back to the dictionary to make sure my simplified definition of God was still consistent with an accepted general definition:

> A being conceived as the perfect omnipotent, omniscient originator and ruler of the universe, the principal object of faith and worship in monotheistic religions.

At this point, I didn't want to complicate my definition by placing all of the parameters on God that Webster did ("perfect," "omnipotent," "ruler of the universe," "object of…worship"). My starting definition could include *any* intelligent designer capable of producing that first living cell. I could always do more research to define God more exactly. But to begin to disprove God I had to first prove there was a reasonable degree of certainty that we could determine the way first life could have originated without God.

I certainly expected to disprove a Creator God fairly quickly. All I had to do was disprove his actions as Creator (that is, by proving evolution). I smiled as I recalled my high-school teacher Mr. Rumpy exclaiming "Fact! Fact! Fact!" regarding evolution. I was looking forward to building my case against God.

So I started my attempt. *There must be far more evidence now than I learned about in high school and college,* I thought. *And with the new facts I'll dig up in textbooks and by talking with others, I'll have enough evidence to bury the notion of a Creator God forever.* I smiled, thinking how pleasant it would be to get some new facts I could use to argue with when I met "Bible beaters."

On the other hand, I realized that if evolution failed, and new evidence showed it to be impossible, I'd be forced to acknowledge that some form of Creator God had to exist. But what were the chances of that? I chuckled to myself. *On the other hand, it might be nice having a God around,* I thought sarcastically.

I was confident back then, even eager to present hard, logical evidence to all the "uneducated" people who didn't believe in evolution. Though I assumed that "we" (evolutionists) had all the modern scientific facts on our side, I still had a somewhat open mind. I thought that if, by some quirk, the hard evidence suggested that a Creator God had to exist, the issue of the existence of God would be answered. The remaining step would be to find out more about who or what that God was. It seemed to me that, if there were a God truly powerful enough to create life, I had better attempt to determine who he was and what he wanted. But first things first.

The theory of evolution, or more broadly, naturalism, was the "killer of God" for me. Just like many educated people, I assumed that "evolution specialists" would know the facts, and I didn't want to look stupid by contradicting my peers. I was embarrassed to admit to anyone that I was looking for scientific data to prove or disprove God. I thought I'd be ridiculed. (I think that's a major roadblock for many people seeking God today.) For me, it was easier to dismiss even thinking about a God at all by assuming that evolution was fact.

But then I asked myself, "Where did I learn about evolution?" It was, first, from textbooks written by evolutionists, and second, from the media. And where did the media get its information? From the evolutionists. I realized it was a *closed system of thinking and promotion*. I saw that, if evolutionists claimed the theory was fact, and changed the theory each time a scientific breakthrough disproved portions of an earlier version, the whole thing could become a self-perpetuating fantasy. It would be believed only because those with a vested interest—the "experts"—were continually promoting it as fact. After all, even scientists tended to rely on their colleagues, often assuming that they had "proven" evolution. Therefore, I admitted to myself, evolution education was inherently inbred—and I personally was a product of such inbred thinking!

Creationists with Evidence

No longer could I simply assume that the evidence for evolution was overwhelming and would shut out contradiction. This was plainly unfair and unscientific. Since something as important as God was "lying in the balance," I felt compelled to thoroughly investigate both sides. So I began to find and listen to creationists to see if they had any cold scientific responses to evolution. I didn't expect them to, but in the interest of objectivity, I was determined to listen.

It seemed to me that the whole idea of God and creation was illogical, dreamed up by people desperate to hope for something. Religion! I hated it. My scientific peers were on the same bandwagon. As Rob, my co-worker at Richmond's Ice Cream, had once said, "If God were both loving and omnipotent, he wouldn't allow suffering. Therefore, God must not exist." Evolution seemed to support that idea of uncaring random chance bringing about life. Yet if I was going to be fair in my quest, I had to start looking for answers. Where would I find a Christian, Jew, or other religious person who understood the evidence for evolution and could provide yet stronger evidence for the existence of God?

A week later I had my first chance to talk to a person who could shed some light on why creationists believed what they believed and—finally—could tell me where to look so I could examine creationist ideas. On a short airplane flight back to Los Angeles, I was seated next to a person avidly reading the Bible.

"Tell me," I asked, "do you believe that a God created life like the Bible says, or do you believe in evolution?"

"Well, I believe in creation, of course. Why do you ask?"

"Let's just say I've been taught evolution all my life, and all the evidence I've seen seems to back it up," I said. "What makes you believe so strongly in creation when all the top scientists in the world reject it?" (I expected the normal non-answer—"because the Bible says it's true." To me, the Bible was anything *but* true.)

Instead my seatmate responded, "First, you're incorrect. Many leading scientists in the world are now rejecting evolution and believing in creation as a form of 'intelligent design.' On top of that, many others are at least considering it. Secondly, you were taught a lot of misleading things in school."

"Wait a minute!" I exclaimed. "Isn't that being somewhat presumptuous? How do you know what I was taught in school? And how do you know it was wrong?" I asked, somewhat irritated. (I wasn't used to having someone counterattack my leading questions—especially someone with a Bible in his hands!)

"First, because I can tell by your question that you went to a secular school. Second, because I also went to secular schools all my life. Third, because I have children in secular schools right now and therefore have years of seeing the evolution science that is being taught," he responded. "Furthermore, I have made it a point to investigate the truth of evolution." Then he smiled. "After all, I don't want to waste my time reading a book"—he tapped his Bible—"that may have major errors any more than anyone else."

"Give me an example of something that contradicts the science you think I've been taught," I challenged, expecting to have a chance to shoot holes in somebody's pet theory.

"Well, evolution literally means 'change,' but regarding creatures, there are two kinds of evolution. One is *microevolution*, or change *within* a species. This would be like a human being who can be tall or short, blue-eyed or brown-eyed, and so forth. The other type of evolution that has been theorized is *macroevolution*, which is a change *from one species to another that's entirely separate*—for example, a fish to a frog," he stated matter-of-factly. "Now really, forgetting evolutionary claims for a moment, how do you expect a fish and a frog to mate?"

He certainly made a point about the fish and frog mating. But I wanted to get back to the issue of micro- and macroevolution. "I don't remember ever hearing those two terms," I remarked. "In fact, it seems what you describe as 'microevolution' fits perfectly into Darwin's survival-of-the-fittest model. I clearly remember reading about the peppered moths that were something like 98-percent white and only 2-percent black when white lichen covered the trees around a village. Since white moths were better camouflaged against predators, they passed on their favorable genes in greater numbers. When pollution came along, killing the lichen and exposing the black bark of the trees, the proportions reversed—proving Darwin's survival of the fittest. Species naturally improve as gene pools shift," I stated confidently.

"I know your example well," he replied. "That's a great example of microevolution. And nobody doubts Darwin's observation of the survival of the fittest—including the Bible. Understand that the color variation between moths would be like the color variation between people. One could even conclude that such incredible variation within a species is part of God's miracle of design that allows it to survive. Yet there still have been no documented accounts of changes *between* reproducing species."

"How about the fossil record?" I asked. "I remember reading about a combination bird-and-reptile that they found."

"You're referring to the archaeopteryx," he noted. "A few scientists still cling to this old idea. However, most scientific journals and texts have now updated the information to classify it as simply an ancient bird. Everything I've read indicates that all its feathers were fully formed. And some unusual features, such as the claws on its wings, are found on several species of birds today—all for a purpose. To me, if evolution were fact, we'd find some reptiles with partially formed feathers."

"How did you find all this information?" I asked.

"Mostly by reading and going to lectures," he replied.

"Where do you find out about books and lectures that try to refute evolution?"

"Do you live in southern California?"

"Yes."

"There are great programs of apologetics at both Trinity Law School (which used to be called 'Simon Greenleaf') in Santa Ana and at Biola University in Fullerton," he said as I quickly wrote down the information.

"What is 'apologetics'?"

"It means 'defending the faith'—in this case, the faith of the Bible. So you'll be able to find answers to your questions about creation and how it fits with science. There are also some other great organizations in southern California. There's an organization called the Institute for Creation Research near San Diego. They have a museum and a wealth of information. Some scientists are critical of them, though, because they are 'young earth.'"

"What's 'young earth'?" I asked.

" 'Young earth' describes theories that attempt to fit the entire creation event into six 24-hour days, which the Bible seems to indicate if you read it literally. Of course, if God is God, presumably he could do it in any time frame he chooses. But the young-earth view requires several somewhat controversial answers to scientific findings. For example, how do you explain the apparent age of the universe with stars hundreds of millions of light-years away? How do you explain the dating of dinosaur bones? How did Adam name the millions of species of animals and plants in a single day? And there are many other questions. The Institute seems to have an answer for everything, however. Many of the answers rely on a cataclysmic event—such as the worldwide flood. But even if you don't believe all of their conclusions, they do provide a lot of really good insight.

"Then there is also Reasons to Believe, a group out of Pasadena that is 'old earth.' As you might guess from the name, it provides evidence of how the Bible fits precisely, even amazingly, with the known scientific record—meaning they believe that the age of the universe is about 13 to 15 billion years. Scientists seem to love Reasons to Believe, and are astounded at how the Bible and science seem to be in complete accord. In fact, many scientists and others, like myself, have become believers in the Bible based on the strength of the evidence they have gathered."

"Come on!" I said rather loudly. "The Bible's *filled* with myths. How do you account for 900-year-old men, or Jonah living in the belly of a whale, or any of the 'miracles'?"

"First," he replied, "who's to say that miracles couldn't be caused by a God who could create the earth and life in the first place? So that's a good place to start."

For once I agree, I thought. *I was hoping we'd have a chance to get into creation.*

"Moreover, the more we learn, the more we find evidence of miracles that could easily have been performed by God—perhaps using his own creation. For example, ancient Babylonian and Chinese writings indicate long lifetimes as well. From science, we know that about the time of the great flood of Noah—when life spans started dropping—a cataclysmic cosmic event, the Vela Supernova, occurred. Some scientists believe this event is responsible for a very large percentage of the radiation the earth now receives and will continue to receive for many years to come. Since we know radiation causes aging, and the supernova occurred at the time life spans started decreasing, there is reason to think (though no absolute proof) that the two are related.

"Regarding Jonah, there have been two accounts in modern history of humans being swallowed and living for extended periods, in one case more than a day, in the belly of a whale or large fish. But a God outside of time and space could do *anything* in this limited time–space domain. Certainly it's nice when we can have logical support for miracles of God from scientific evidence, but frankly, it's not necessary. God would still be God, and we would still be humans. Therefore, any God who could create the heavens and the earth could certainly perform other 'easy' miracles, such as giving humans long life spans.

"Also, you need to consider the dozens of scientifically correct insights in the Bible that were recorded 2000 years before science knew of them."

"Such as?" I questioned.

"Well, things we take for granted today, like principles of quarantine and waste disposal, and even amazing things like insights into physics such as thermodynamics."

The flight attendant broke in with an announcement of our final approach to the airport.

"Listen, my name is John," he said, "and I've really enjoyed talking to you, but I have to finish reading this for a Bible class I'm teaching tonight. I'd suggest you simply go to a good Christian bookstore and get some basic reading material. They have entire sections on this kind of thing."

"John, I'm Ralph," I said. "I appreciate your insight. I've got a long way to go before I believe any of this stuff, but at least you've given me a place to start."

If half of what John had been saying was true, there would be a lot more to this investigation about God than I thought. For the first time in my life I began to think that maybe somebody, somewhere, at least *thought* they had some evidence supporting the Bible and refuting evolution. But if the evidence was so strong, why wasn't everyone talking about it? Why didn't people, like all my Sunday school teachers, even know it?

The plane touched down. I was eager to start digging into the resources John had recommended.

8

What It Takes to Randomly Assemble Life

It seemed to me that analytical proof of the existence of a Creator God depended largely upon disproving naturalistic evolution. As I had decided previously, I chose to look first at only the origin of first life. After all, if life couldn't get started naturalistically in the first place, the rest of the theoretical evolutionary process would be of no consequence. By default, it would mean that life had started supernaturally—that a Creator God of some type would have to exist. I broke down into five basic steps the complex events that would be necessary for the chance origin of life.

• • •

Random Chance Model
To Produce First Life—

All steps must be completed well within the time frame of the Universe (only 15 billion years are available)

1.	2.	3.	4.	5.
Reproductive cell components must be gathered	Correct specifications of all components must appear in the same place at the same time	Correct components must be properly assembled	Destructive elements present must not overwhelm cell assembly	Cell assembly must be energized with life

The Complexity of a Single Living Cell

As I came to understand the vast complexity of a single cell, this was my first clue that there might be some technical and mathematical problems with naturalistic evolution. Here is what I discovered.

A single reproductive cell (a cell capable of reproducing itself) is the smallest living creature. Cells can very in size from the smallest bacteria, which are 1/50,000 of an inch, to the largest—the yolk of an ostrich egg. There is also wide variation in shape, variety, and function of living cells (for example, cells in plants, or in muscle, blood, nerves, and so on). We can put the size of an average cell in perspective by figuring that about 1000 cells would fit within the period at the end of this sentence. (For additional reference, 25,000 bacteria-sized cells would fit in the same space.)

Despite their differences, virtually all cells do certain functions. In fact, these functions are so complex that a single cell is far more complicated structurally than the most advanced factory in the world. All cells "breathe," eat, get rid of waste, grow, reproduce, and eventually die. They are essentially miniature organisms; in fact, there are many single-celled creatures. (One of the most well-known single-celled creatures is the amoeba, often studied in biology classes.)

But the true complexity of a living cell cannot be fully appreciated until the vast number of the individual parts of its structure are considered. While there are an enormous variety of cells, there are several parts that are common to most.

Following is a brief description of just a few of the common parts of a cell. (The diagram on the next page is a highly simplified representation of how these parts might be likened to a typical factory.) Remember that *each individual component is made up of many substructures,* and only a small fraction of the total "factory systems" are represented here. Keep in mind also that cellular activity takes place in a space that is usually a thousandth of the size of a period—sometimes less.

DNA. DNA is like the master computer—the essential part of every cell that dictates all actions of the cell. Though an entire chain of DNA

A Simplified Schematic of a Very Basic Cell

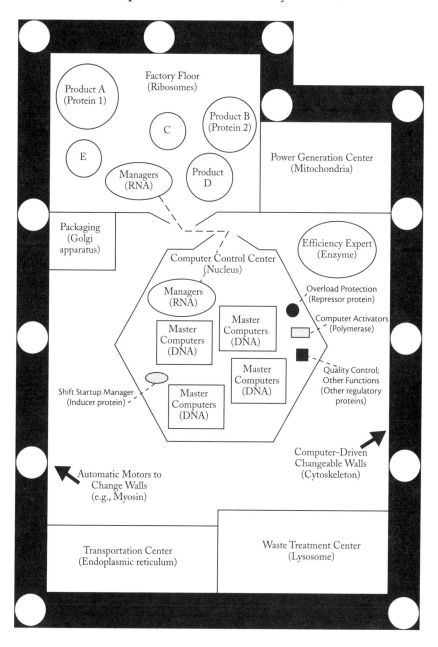

uses only six essential ingredients, the tiny chain is enormously long—often containing billions of parts. To illustrate, if you were to take the amount of DNA in a single human body, straighten it out, and place it end to end, it would stretch out for *50 billion kilometers* (it would literally extend from the earth to beyond the limits of the solar system)![1] The amount of information in a single strand of DNA is obviously enormous.

It is the information encoded in the DNA that separates a human being from, for instance, a spider (and the DNA will be observably different). The ability of DNA *genes* (sections of DNA that correspond to traits of an organism) to generate various numbers of protein products also differs greatly within species. (This was an important issue confronting me regarding evolutionary change from one species to another. What mechanism would change—in fact, "improve"—the DNA?)

DNA does an incredible number of things in tiny fractions of a second, managing information beyond human comprehension. In each cell, it gives instructions regarding how each part of the cell should work, including such typical "factory" functions as

- generating power
- manufacturing a great quantity and variety of products (proteins)
- designating the function and relationship of these products (proteins)
- guiding final destination of key parts (molecules)
- packaging certain products (molecules in membrane-bound sacs)
- managing transfer of information
- assuring a level of quality (one far beyond any human standard)
- disposal of waste
- growth
- reproduction

One single human DNA strand collectively contains *3.2 billion* base pairs—like the rungs that make up a ladder—in its structure—now well-known as the "double helix." So with 46 such structures—called chromosomes—in a human cell, there are 147.2 billion base pairs of information in a single cell—all in an amazingly tiny space.

Also important is the makeup of the genes, the groupings within the DNA strand. Current estimates indicate about 30,000 to 40,000 possible variations, with more complexity and "splicing" (recombining) alternatives than once thought. Hence, the possible combinations of DNA information on the "production floors" (the ribosomes) are virtually endless.

RNA. RNA is the substance that carries out the instructions of DNA. It also has six basic ingredients—the same ones as DNA except for a different sugar and one of the four "bases" (more on this later). The easiest way to think of RNA is as a "reverse copy" of DNA that travels from the cell nucleus (where the DNA is—the "computer center") to the "production floor" where instructions for manufacturing the vast array of proteins are carried out.

Nucleus. The nucleus is like the "computer control room." It is where DNA is located, and where information is transferred from DNA to RNA.

Ribosomes. Ribosomes are essentially the "production floors"— where RNA instructions are received and various types of protein are manufactured depending on the RNA code. A human body requires literally thousands of different types of proteins. The manufacturing job, dictated by DNA (then copied and carried to the "production floor" by RNA) in the ribosomes is amazing. In a single cell there may be many ribosomes producing vast numbers of different proteins.

Mitochondria. These are sites of energy production through cell respiration. A cell may contain *hundreds* of these sausage-shaped mitochondria to provide all the energy it needs to survive.

Lysosomes. Lysosomes process and rid the cell of destructive waste products, essentially digesting waste materials and food within the cell. Digestive enzymes (a kind of protein—one of the products the cell produces) break foods down into basic elements.

Endoplasmic reticulum. This is essentially a transportation network for molecules in the *cytoplasm* (the liquid substance of the cell), moving the molecules to specific final destinations.

Golgi apparatus. This is a type of "packaging center." It takes certain molecules and packages them into sacs to be targeted to various locations in the cell "factory," or even to be distributed outside.

Enzymes and regulatory proteins. Many of the proteins produced by the cell are for the operation of the cell itself. Enzymes dramatically speed up certain activities of the cell. Some regulatory proteins (polymerases), in a sense, turn genes "on" or "off"—permitting RNA replication or not—depending on the needs of the cell. Many other regulatory functions are also accomplished by certain proteins, including operation of the cell's built-in "proofreading" system. Without it, a cell might have a DNA-copy error rate of 1 in 10,000. However, thanks to the error-control system, the occurrence of copy errors *(point mutations)* ranges from only one in a billion to one in a hundred billion.[2]

Cytoskeleton. These are the walls of and the "scaffolding" inside the cell. A far cry from normal factory walls, they can change and adapt amazingly in many ways, based on DNA instructions. For example, one key role of the cell walls is simply the holding of the *organelles* (the "organs" of the cell—all the above parts) in place. But the cytoskeleton must also be able to move with growth and reproduction. This is enabled by many types of proteins in the cytoskeleton. (Once such "cellular motor" is *myosin.*)

My Conclusions About Living Cells

I had just scratched the surface of molecular biology in what we looked at above. The sheer complexity in even a simplified cell structure caused me to wonder how these billions of parts could randomly come together in just the right way, at just the right time. And that would be just the first step of naturalistic evolution. When I considered further that there are about *75 trillion* cells in the human body, with about 210 cell types,[3] I started to have my first doubts about evolution. The sheer numbers of parts and changes, and the specialization, seemed almost too incredible to believe. As I had done so often before, I assumed that scientists must have good reasons to believe evolution though. I decided I'd research more to find out why. I asked myself the following questions:

● ● ●

1. How would a correct individual component "know" to arrive?

2. How would all the components "know" to assemble properly?

3. How would the cell's surface (including the cytoskeleton) "know" to somehow cover the cell to protect it, allowing it to work?

4. How would something of such complexity all happen at once? (For instance, I reasoned that just having mitochondria [cell "lungs"] by themselves would do nothing—without the presence of DNA, RNA, and protein.)

5. Where would the information as to how all the cell components should work come from in the first place?

6. What would initially energize life?

● ● ●

Many of the textbooks I consulted speculated on the idea of change (suggesting evolution), yet none answered these questions. I decided to ask others how they got around such problems.

Revisiting Evolution

As I went back to biology books and magazines, I found little fundamental change in the neo-Darwinism I had been taught in high school and college. The only difference was a plethora of new theories sprouting up to address the rapidly changing world of biochemistry. The electron microscope, "wet chemistry" that could "map" DNA, other new microscopic techniques, and "laser tweezers," along with a vast number of research projects using such new technology, were helping us understand cell structure and the human genome (human DNA) like never before. All my reading pointed in the same direction: We are far more complex than we have ever conceived. And the simple idea of random chance originating first life seemed to be giving way to much more bizarre theories. Moreover, the idea of a "primordial soup" containing just the right ingredients, possibly energized by heat, and creating just the right environment for the first protein–DNA beginning of life was now called into question by biochemists.

Now that I had gained much more information on cells and DNA molecules, I didn't just accept the theory on face value anymore. And I was troubled by the point that my seatmate John had made on the airplane flight—that the peppered moth phenomenon was an obvious stretch to take ordinary, basic genetics into an explanation of the chain of evolution. Was he perhaps right?

I decided to follow John's advice and see what the Institute of Creation Research (ICR) had to say. Their museum had quite a few exhibits that clearly explained what they saw as apparent misconceptions of science. They showed how, with a cataclysmic event like a great flood, a number of seemingly predictable factors could change—factors on which much scientific measurement is based. Though a lot of what they said made sense, I was shocked when ICR asserted that the universe is only 10,000 years old.

Wait a minute! I thought. *It sounds like they are simply trying to make science fit the Bible, using the flood as an excuse.* I purchased some of their literature to see what they had to say, reminding myself that my purpose was to see how creationists defended the existence of a God. I had just gone through a lot of biochemistry that had me reconsidering God. Then I remembered what John had said on the airplane about "young earth" and "old earth" creationists. I recalled him saying that scientists would have a problem with some issues in the young earth point of view—but that God could do anything in any time frame. I concluded that I might be able to prove evolution statistically impossible with biochemistry, but I doubted that I could ever accept this 10,000-year-old universe idea unless I accepted the English translation of the Bible hook, line, and sinker. *Not likely,* I thought, *considering the many translations since the original text.*

When I sat down to review the ICR books, the first things I found seemed to make a lot of sense. Biologists had discovered that the human embryo's "gill slits" once thought to be vestiges of "fish ancestors" are actually the early formation of our inner ear. Likewise, what was thought to be an ancient tail remnant was shown to be our tailbone muscle attachment—vital for important bodily functions. Finally the yolk sac was discovered to be the early blood cells needed for growth. Chalk one up for the creationists.[4]

The issue of common body parts, like an elbow existing in a hamster, a bat, and a human (implying some ancient common ancestry) was pointed out as a weak argument. A good designer (that is, a Creator) would certainly use a successful design for similar purposes in different systems. I learned that in engineering school when we used wheels in all kinds of designed systems. Chalk up a no-brainer for the creationists.[5]

The lack of transitional fossil evidence was also stressed. Actually, I had heard this from evolutionists as well. As an evolutionist myself, it had always troubled me that anytime a fossil was asserted to be transitional, it always had fully formed parts—never a *partial* eye or a *partial* feather, for example. Besides, after learning about the complexity of cells, I was much more concerned about the mechanism of building the first cell than with making soft-science conclusions about a bunch of bones.

The peppered-moth issue was explained exactly the way John had explained it. The survival of the fittest was simply the adaptation of a single species' DNA within the limits of a variable genetic code. I had learned from my early molecular biology study that it would not mean a change *between* species. I couldn't help but wonder why these examples were still used in some textbooks as "evidence."

Discouraging News

Then I started reading about my favorite piece of evolutionary evidence, the Miller–Urey experiments. I knew that proteins use 20 *life-specific* amino acids and that Miller had produced several in the lab in 1953 (I have heard recently that they have all been synthesized). The literature I obtained from ICR and elsewhere pointed out many concerns.

1. Even if every one of the elements of a cell could be "manufactured," all attempts have been made in an artificial laboratory environment. Clearly, the early earth was hardly such a controlled environment.

2. In all experiments attempted, even when some of the life-specific amino acids were produced, a far greater quantity of other, life-*destructive* elements

was produced (98-percent of the by-product was destructive tar).[6]

3. Biochemists have recognized that the presence of oxygen in the early atmosphere would be a problem. The building blocks of life would be destroyed in the presence of abundant oxygen. On the other hand, if there was no oxygen, then there would have been no protective ozone layer, and life would have been destroyed by intense radiation.[7]

4. The process of creating amino acids is reversible. In other words, the same energy source that creates new amino acids can even more efficiently destroy the newly created ones. (Miller and Urey recognized that problem and created a "trap" to capture the "good" elements and preserve them from destruction.)

At this point I was very discouraged. I had expected to find some breakthroughs in the Miller–Urey experiments that would give me some firm ground to stand on. What I discovered was more problematic than helpful. I now realized the idea of the naturalistic origin of life was far more difficult than I had ever dreamed, since even simple life has the appearance of intricate design. However, far from defeated, I still reasoned that if we could create the initial building blocks, someday we should be able to reconcile it with an environment or a process. To me the biggest hurdle was still the supercomplexity of a single cell, and how it all came together at once in such a perfect package.

Continuing with the First Step

One day I was playing golf with a business associate. He brought a friend with him named Mark. When I discovered that Mark taught biology at a local college, I asked to ride in the cart with him. By the third hole he had affirmed that he strongly supported the theory of evolution, and I knew this would be a great round regardless of the score I shot that day. On the fourth hole, his drive sliced wide right. Mine too.

"Mark, how do biologists explain that the first cell came into being, recognizing its extreme complexity?" I asked. "With more than 3 billion base pairs of DNA distributed among the 46 chromosomes, along with the ribosomes, the mitochondria, and all the other complex things in such a tiny space—how did it all get there in just the right way? And at just the same time?"

"That's a good question," he said. "I can see you've been studying this. The point you're missing is that you are thinking of a highly evolved cell—one similar to what's in your body. Human cells—in fact, most animal and plant cells—are called *eucaryotic* cells, which means they have a true nucleus. And most eucaryotic cells also have dozens of different kinds of parts, some of which you mentioned.

"But the earliest form of life was very simple," he continued. "The first form of life was a single-celled bacterium, which falls into the category called *procaryotic* cells. They are far simpler. In fact, scientists believe that the first cells were essentially a relatively short string of DNA and an RNA transfer component, along with a protein structure."

"So if I was going to challenge the construction of that first cell, I'd need to start with just a pair of DNA chains, some protein chains, and some RNA—realizing that amino acids are the building blocks of protein and are contained within the needed material as well," I responded.

"Essentially you're right, but it may have been just a single strand of DNA reproducing by a simpler process called *binary fission*," he said. "Obviously since bacteria are living creatures, even the earliest ones would have had to have some means of eating, digesting, and moving. But we don't know if they were identical to today's bacteria or were more simple. The earliest fossil record we have of any living thing is of a bacterium existing about 3 $^1/_2$ billion years ago."

"But even if we took the absolute simplest bacterium cell back at the beginning of the earth," I asked, "DNA would still be an essential thing, wouldn't it? Wouldn't we still be talking about millions of rungs in a double-helix ladder?"

"That's an area of considerable debate among scientists," he replied. "In bacteria of today, we know that a single genome, or strand of DNA, has a few million symbols. [A symbol would be defined as any of DNA's six parts—the phosphate, the sugar, and the four bases.] I'm sure any ancient bacterium would also have had to have considerable DNA structure, probably nearly the same as we find today."

Mark hit his second shot on the green. I landed short.

"Just so I'm clear on this, even the simplest bacterium of the first form of life would have had to have a DNA molecule that would contain probably several million symbols, which would equate to at least a few hundred thousand base pairs?"

"Yes," he replied. "There's a bottom limit necessary for the function of even the simplest bacterium."

"What would be the lowest limit of base pairs for the very first bacterium, being conservative?" I asked.

"It would be hard to image a functioning bacterium with fewer than 100,000 base pairs."

"And along with such an ancient DNA chain, there would also need to be corresponding protein chains that would be able to connect to the DNA, or to the replicating RNA?"

"Yes."

"And furthermore, the ordering of the base pairs that form the genes, along with the order of the protein chain, would be essential to the function of the cell?"

"Yes," he said as I chipped up and one-putted. He two-putted.

"So proving that a 'God' was not necessary to start life would be as simple as showing that it was possible for these molecular particles to come together to form the simplest bacterium."

"I never thought of it quite like that," he said, "but I guess that's right."

We continued our game, and I gleaned a lot of additional information about biochemistry. Now I started to see how evolution might begin. We were *not* talking about the complex cells I had been studying. The first cells were very simple. I almost couldn't wait to get home to run some numbers to calculate probabilities.

At least now, I started to believe I might have a basis on which to combat creationists. I could mathematically show them that, with lots and lots of time, all these things could come together, and somehow electricity—or something—would bring it to life.

9

The Molecular Anatomy of Life

Nagging in the back of my mind was another huge problem. Even if it was possible by a wide margin to obtain that first little bacterium, there would be an enormous amount of random change and mutation that would then have to take place to develop all the species of the world, including human beings. I knew we had a lot of time. But was there enough? After all, that would be a lot of change! I decided to remain focused on the project at hand—getting to the very first cell.

———•———

As I delved further into DNA, RNA, and protein functions, I discovered the following things.

If we were to "unravel" a DNA helix, we would find a basic ladder-type structure with phosphates and sugars on each vertical column. The "rungs" which attach to the sugar–phosphate sides are combinations of these two bases: either thymine (T) plus adenine (A); or guanine (G) plus cytosine (C). Those paired combinations are always TA, AT or GC, CG. No other combinations exist. (The diagram on page 91 shows the structure of such an unraveled DNA molecule.)

But DNA is used to produce *many* necessary proteins. Any protein chain is made up of a few hundred amino acids. There are twenty kinds of life-relevant amino acids (out of the more than 80 amino acids found on earth)—each one is only about 10 to 30 atoms in size.[1] Yet any protein chain can have many of each different kind. Hence, *the order of the amino acids in a protein determines its function*. In other words, all these factors are needed:

- the right amino acids, along with

- the right grouping of amino acid clusters, and

- the right order

All these are extremely important. *None can be random for the protein to perform a function.* These proteins match up with DNA bases (via the RNA transfer mechanism), thus determining the function of the cell. The bottom line is, the formation of the proteins required for life is extremely complex and very precise.

The proteins in any multicell life are the primary ingredients that determine what structure each cell has and what each cell does. Since our bodies, and those of plants and animals, are made up of cells, we can conclude that it is protein, built according to the instructions of DNA, that determines what becomes hair, skin, bone, and all the organs of one's body. It also determines whether we will be a plant, a human, or a toad.

Therefore, the process of instructions built into the DNA molecule is essential, as is the process of "telling" the ribosomes—via RNA—what proteins to manufacture. Simply put, the process works essentially as indicated on page 91. The DNA helix splits. Since the combinations are always in pairs (that is, TA, AT or GC, CG), when "pieces" of RNA then attach to the single half of the DNA molecule, they always make an exact map of it. (Note that in RNA, ribose is used as a sugar instead of deoxyribose—hence the "R versus the D"—and uracil takes the place of thymine.) The completed RNA molecule splits away and moves to the ribosome where a protein is produced according to the instructions carried by the RNA, which it received from the DNA. The DNA "knows" what the cell (or creature or plant) needs next.

Could Evolution Produce Such Amazing Complexity?

Every *second* of every day, our human body is organizing about *150 thousand, thousand, thousand, thousand, thousand, thousand* amino acids into carefully constructed chains.[2] Our body is vastly more complex than all the manufacturing facilities in the entire world.

Structure of DNA and RNA How Protein Is Produced

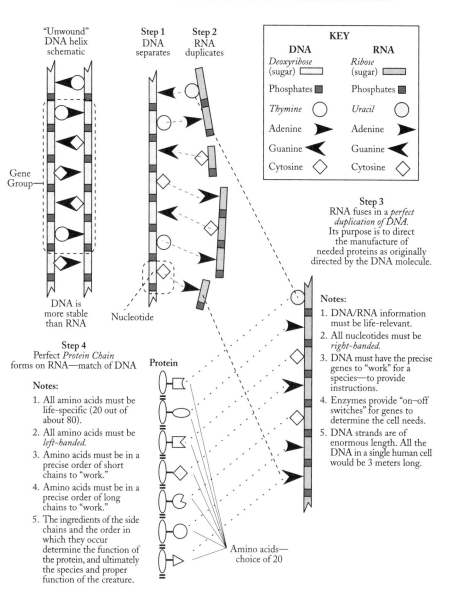

"Unwound" DNA helix schematic

Step 1 DNA separates

Step 2 RNA duplicates

KEY

DNA	RNA
Deoxyribose (sugar)	Ribose (sugar)
Phosphates	Phosphates
Thymine	Uracil
Adenine	Adenine
Guanine	Guanine
Cytosine	Cytosine

Gene Group

DNA is more stable than RNA

Nucleotide

Step 3
RNA fuses in a *perfect
duplication of DNA.*
Its purpose is to direct
the manufacture of
needed proteins as originally
directed by the DNA molecule.

Step 4
Perfect *Protein Chain*
forms on RNA—match of DNA

Protein

Notes:

1. All amino acids must be life-specific (20 out of about 80).
2. All amino acids must be *left-handed*.
3. Amino acids must be in a precise order of short chains to "work."
4. Amino acids must be in a precise order of long chains to "work."
5. The ingredients of the side chains and the order in which they occur determine the function of the protein, and ultimately the species and proper function of the creature.

Amino acids—
choice of 20

Notes:

1. DNA/RNA information must be life-relevant.
2. All nucleotides must be *right-handed.*
3. DNA must have the precise genes to "work" for a species—to provide instructions.
4. Enzymes provide "on–off" switches for genes to determine the cell needs.
5. DNA strands are of enormous length. All the DNA in a single human cell would be 3 meters long.

DNA can automatically change its protein production, based on the needs of any cell or the entire creature, by turning "on" or "off" the genes along its length. Genes are essentially groupings of base pairs that determine some characteristic. These on–off signals are referred to as "hormones" or "regulatory proteins." Polymerase is a typical example of a regulatory protein.[3]

Scientists Attack the Random Origin of Life

At first it seemed to me that the estimated 4½-billion-year age of the earth would be plenty of time for a worldful of atoms tumbling around to "get lucky" and form the first DNA and RNA molecules, the first proteins, and from them the first bacterium. Yet I began to have doubts when I started hearing and reading of scientists stating the incredible odds *against* the random-chance origin of the first cell. For example, British astronomer Sir Frederick Hoyle, a highly esteemed mathematician, calculated this probability, assuming only "left-handed" amino acids (just one of many necessary criteria). He ignored many other more complex problems—and still concluded that

> the likelihood of the formation of life from inanimate matter is one to a number with 40 thousand naughts [zeros] after it. It is enough to bury Darwin and the whole theory of evolution. There was no primeval soup, neither on this planet nor on any other, and if the beginnings of life were not random they must therefore have been the product of purposeful intelligence.[4]

A Master Statistician Analyzes the Probability of Evolution

Sir Frederick Hoyle later went further in his analysis of random life formation using calculus and differential equations to develop models of both single-celled and multicelled creatures' ability to change species within various generation-to-generation timetables. He incorporated evolutionist mutation theories into his models, recognizing the counterproductivity of negative mutations as well as the contribution of positive ones. He concluded after extensive analysis,

When genes are tied to each other, as they are when reproduction from generation to generation follows an asexual binary fission model or a budding model, there can be *no positive evolution.* Rarer advantageous mutations are *swamped by more frequent deleterious [injurious] mutations.*[5]

And Hoyle's analysis of more far more complex multicelled creatures arrives at essentially the same conclusion—even very small genetic changes "cannot arise spontaneously."[6]

Microbiologist Dr. Michael Denton viewed the random assembly of first life from the perspective of the minimum protein development necessary (far less than what has actually been observed):

To get a cell by chance would require at least one hundred functional proteins to appear simultaneously in one place. This is one hundred simultaneous events, each of an independent probability which could hardly be more than 10^{-20}, giving a maximum combined probability of 10^{-2000}. Hoyle and Wickramasinghe in "Evolution from Space" provided a similar estimate of the chance of life originating, assuming [the development of] functional proteins to have a probability of 10^{-20}.[7]

Harold Morowitz, also a microbiologist, calculated the odds of a cell randomly assembling under the most ideal conditions to be 1 chance in $10^{100,000,000,000}$. Although some point out that there are a few exceptions to the "perfect sequencing" that Morowitz assumed, astrophysicist Dr. Hugh Ross counters by noting that Morowitz was conservative by not taking into consideration the selection of only bioactive (life-relevant) amino acids with the right *orientation* (*chirality*—see page 95). Also, says Ross, "destructive chemical processes operate at least as frequently as constructive chemical processes." Therefore, Ross concludes that "the bottom line is the odds for the assembly of the simplest living entity *actually grow worse* as more details are figured into the calculation."[8]

Astronomer Michael Hart, presenting an apparently extremely conservative model, said,

> For each of 100 different specific genes to be formed spontaneously (the minimum number of genes needed, formed over ten billion years) the probability is (10^{-30}) x 1/100 = 10^{-3000}. For them to be formed *at the same time, and in close proximity*, the probability is *very much lower.*[9]

Why were all these scientists (and others) saying it was so impossible that life could even get started by random chance? I'd been to the museums. I'd seen the pictures of the chimp turning into a man. I'd argued the "fact" of evolution to the nonscientific community for a long time. Could I have been wrong all those years? My intelligence and pride were at stake. I decided I wouldn't accept a few scientists' statistical claims against random origins unless I could understand why and how. Again, I was skeptical.

Some of the basic problems with what I was taught about evolution had been easily exposed by my early investigations (for example, microevolution versus macroevolution). However, just because I had been taught with faulty evidence in some areas didn't mean that everything was wrong. Again, I reasoned that *the core issue had to be at this molecular level*, so frequently mentioned. So I went back to the basic questions:

- Was it possible for life to start randomly in the first place?

- If so, was it conceivable for life to mutate into all the species in the world—with all the parts necessary within each species—in the time frame since the beginning of the world?

- Finally, was there a satisfactory mechanism I didn't yet know about to make all this happen?

After all, to me, all the interest in dinosaurs and fossils was only speculative soft evidence based on observation. I leaned toward hard science—mathematically calculated probabilities. As I saw it, facts are facts, and guesses are guesses.

By that point I realized what extreme precision was necessary for DNA to form in a manner that would work. Likewise I realized that the bonding proteins virtually always had to be in a very specific order to make sense. These facts alone started to indicate considerable difficulty for theories about the random origin of life.

Then I came face-to-face with something troubling. Very, very troubling. It is a simple biological phenomenon that is seldom discussed in much detail in biology textbooks and is almost never addressed by evolutionists. It opened my eyes with the straightforward facts.

Chirality

Chiral is the term used to describe molecules that are "handed"—that is, they come in "right-handed" and "left-handed" versions (technically, *dextroform* and *levoform).* I found that the *chirality* of certain molecules used in the building blocks of life was a critical factor. Why? Because *every single nucleotide* (essentially, basic section) in the DNA chain must be of one orientation— right-handed—in order for the entire chain to work. One mistake cannot be tolerated. Likewise, virtually all amino acids in proteins must also be of one orientation—left-handed—for a protein to work. (See Hoyle's comment on page 93.)

These orientations of both nucleotides (in DNA and RNA) and amino acids (in proteins) are absolutely necessary. Otherwise the entire basic process of the cell—the sequence of manufacture from DNA to RNA to working protein—fails (see figure on page 91). Hence, for first life to be properly assembled, I saw that a perfect mix of both proper *nucleotide orientation* (all right-handed) and *amino-acid orientation* (all left-handed) had to occur. Furthermore, I needed to keep in mind that the chains of both DNA and protein are extremely long.

However, in startling opposition to what I now knew was needed for first life, all amino acids occur naturally in *equal* proportions of right- versus left-handed (a *racemic mixture).* I also discovered that researchers, after years of study, have not found *one single means* of "purifying" such a mixture—or substantially increasing the proportion of left-handed amino acids to right-handed ones. (The same problem, though more complex to explain, exists for nucleotides.)

It hit me like a ton of bricks. To create the first cell, not only would all of the hundreds of thousands of the right kinds of amino acids in the hundred-plus functional proteins required for the first cell have to suddenly show up at exactly the right place, at exactly the right time, *but they would all have to be left-handed.* The same would hold true for the first DNA and RNA chains, except the components would all need to be right-handed. Even before I started calculations, I recognized how vast the problem was.

The Random Origin of First Life— Estimating the Probability

After I had carefully considered the many things that had to all happen in a precise way at a precise point in time to allow the random origin of first life, the extremely small probabilities given by prominent scientists started to make sense to me. I could see my argument against a Creator God starting to slip away. I decided to summarize some of the main problems and limitations I had become aware of.

● ● ●

1. The first bacterium had to have a *bare minimum* of at least 10,000 amino acid "connections" (a minimum of 100 functional protein chains, each with a few hundred amino acids—far below what has been actually observed in nature.)[10]

2. The problem repeats for the nucleotides, except the DNA chain is much longer. For the first bacterium, I assumed a chain of only 100,000 base pairs. (Current observations of the simplest bacteria show about *500,000 base pairs*—and each base pair is made up of six parts, for a total of 3 million components.)

3. All connections had to happen at the same place.

4. All components had to arrive at the same time.

5. There was only so much time available.

6. There was only so much matter available.

7. There was only so much space available in which interactions could occur.

8. There is a reasonable limit to the number of interactions between particles at a given point in time in a given place.

9. In addition to all the above, the order of and connections between amino acids and nucleotides had to be correct.

———— ● ● ● ————

I focused first on the problem I had recently encountered—the issue of chirality. If this couldn't be resolved by a process of random chance, then naturalistic evolution simply wouldn't work. My objective was to estimate the probability of getting all the correctly oriented components together at once (all the necessary left-handed amino acids, all the necessary right-handed nucleotides) for the simplest conceivable bacterium.

RNA

In my calculations about resolving the issues raised by chirality, I deliberately omitted an additional complicating factor. In reality, components for assembling the first RNA molecule would also have had to be present at the same time and place as the DNA and protein components, substantially reducing the odds of "success."

———— ● ————

A theory first proposed in the late 1980s suggested that it could serve all the purposes of DNA, RNA, and proteins combined— thus perhaps allowing for the random origin of life. Some experiments had shown that RNA was capable of performing a tiny fraction of protein functions. However, such an RNA molecule would still need to contain all the information of DNA and perform all the necessary functions. It would therefore be an extraordinarily complex molecule.

———— ● ————

Before 1986, researchers and texts had asserted for 20 years that RNA had successfully been synthesized in the lab. In that year, Robert Shapiro exploded the myth in a public forum of the International Society for the Study of the Origin of Life (at Berkeley, California). No one challenged Shapiro then, or has since.[11] This demonstrates how incorrect or old "evidence" can be perpetuated.

Using the "coin-flip analogy," I needed to calculate the probability of flipping 10,000 consecutive "heads" (analogous to the probability of getting 10,000 left-handed amino acids together without a single right-handed one). The fact that all nucleotides needed to be right-handed ("tails") greatly compounded the problem and lessened the odds substantially. Mathematically, I needed 10,000 correct amino-acid "flips" times 100,000 correct nucleotide "flips"—at a *minimum*. So combined: 1 billion consecutive "flips" exactly right, none wrong, at a given point in time. The calculation was easy. Each flip carried a probability of 50 percent—1 out of 2. So the probability of all flips occurring in a row was 1 chance in 2 multiplied by itself 1 billion times. In other words $\frac{1}{2}^{1,000,000,000}$. (This number is so small that virtually all computers attempting a direct computation simply display it as zero, or incalculable. See "For Those Who Like Math" below for an easy way to have a computer calculate it using algebra and trigonometry.)

Converted to scientific notation (log 10), the probability of assembling 10,000 left-handed amino acids and 100,000 right-handed nucleotides is—

$$1 \text{ chance in } 10^{301,029,996}$$

Incredible! The odds of winning a typical state lottery with a single ticket are about 1 in 10 million, or one in 10^7. So the odds of assembling simply the correct molecular orientation for the first bacterium (using a very conservative number of base pairs and amino acids) would be like winning more than *43 million* state lotteries *in a row* with the purchase of a single ticket for each! Just to write that number down would fill 100 encyclopedia-sized books and would take almost ten years, if you wrote at a pace of a digit a second.

For Those Who Like Math

Using algebra and logarithmic functions, you can make a computer provide an answer to 1 chance in $2^{1,000,000,000}$ in scientific notation.

$X = 2^{1,000,000,000}$

$\text{Log}_{10}(X) = 1,000,000,000 \times \log_{10}(2)$ [because $\log(X^{11}) = n \times \log(X)$]

$\text{Log}_{10}(X) = 30,103,000$

$X = 10^{301,029,996}$

There would be 1 chance in "X," or in regular numerals, 1 chance in about 1 with more than *300 million zeros* after it!

Time and Matter

It was more than clear to me that the issue raised by chirality alone placed the odds for the random beginning of first life at essentially zero. But the problem of assembling the first bacterium went far beyond the necessity of correct molecular orientation. The correct amino acids had to be selected, as well as the correct genes (portions of DNA) in order for the message to make sense. Otherwise it would be like scrambling millions of letters together and hoping to come out with a book. And the margin for error in the millions of components of even the simplest bacterium would be virtually zero.

Now I knew why many of the most knowledgeable biochemists and statisticians were starting to speak out against evolution. Considering the vast improbability of the random assembly of only the first living cell (not to mention the vast parade of changes that would have to follow to fill the earth with so many species), it was hard for me to see why other scientists didn't see the mathematical improbability. But after all, I had thought the same way only a few years ago.

Even so, a 15-billion-year-old universe filled with atoms still seemed to be a lot of time and a lot of matter to work with. But was it enough to compensate for the incredibly improbable scenario of getting so many things right at once? I decided to use the numbers

I had already found, ones provided by experts in various scientific fields. I would estimate whether there had been enough time and matter to randomly assemble just the first bacterium. I reminded myself to forget about all the ensuing transitions. If first life couldn't have arisen randomly, then there must be some kind of God. I felt that I was fighting against myself.

1. I allowed the entire time since the beginning of the universe for the formation of the first bacterium, conservatively assuming it could have developed away from the earth and traveled here. So I assumed the commonly accepted time frame of roughly 15 billion years, which equates to about 10^{17} seconds (the numeral 1, followed by 17 zeros).

2. I took the commonly accepted amount of matter in the entire universe and broke it down into the tiniest subatomic particles. That gave a total mass in the universe of about 10^{84} *baryons* (a baryon represents some of the smallest parts of atoms).

3. I assumed the maximum conceivable number of interactions between these tiny particles as 10^{20} per second (as also assumed by Drs. Parker and Morris[12]).

So this very conservative model, in which I accounted for all of time, all of matter, and a nearly inconceivable frequency of interactions throughout the entire universe—meant that the total maximum number of interactions since the beginning of time would be

$$10^{121} \ (10^{17} \times 10^{84} \times 10^{20})$$

I then divided the number of possible interactions by the estimated probability of a random-chance beginning of life, using Dr. Harold Morowitz's estimate of the probability of all components getting together at the same time and place for life to arise. (This estimate now seemed very generous based on the points made by Dr. Ross—see page 93[13]). When I put it into the form of this equation,

$$\frac{10^{121}}{10^{100,000,000,000}} = \frac{1}{10^{99,999,999,979}}$$

the resulting figure was inconceivably small—so small that I knew any mathematician or scientist would tell me it was *just plain zero!* My conclusion?

———————————————• • •———————————————

> *It was absolutely impossible just to get the parts*
> *together to start the first simple bacterium, let alone*
> *all the amazing changes that had to happen after*
> *that so human beings could finally evolve. Random*
> *chance could not possibly assemble the first cell.*

———————————————• • •———————————————

So all the talk about fossils and everything else was essentially moot.

How Do Scientists Defend Evolution?

I decided to study how evolutionists attempt to defend chance origin of life. First, I found a few that still have the century-old idea of an infinite universe. But I knew from physics that discoveries by Hubble in 1929, and later Penzias in 1964, when reconciled with Einstein's general relativity formula, showed that the universe had to have a beginning. And I found that general relativity has been experimentally tested to a precision level of 10^{14}, which means it is as close to a scientific law as virtually anything.[14] So the old analogy that declared that a room full of monkeys typing randomly for infinity would eventually produce the works of William Shakespeare was now proven incorrect. Infinity couldn't be used to explain the process of evolution anymore.

I found that there were many other theories. Fanciful theories. Some attempted to get around the problem of chirality with an outer space "chaos theory," for which I could find no meaningful basis in fact. Others tried to explain life by hypothesizing parallel universes that somehow brought alien life to this planet. But every idea presented was fantasy. Sheer fantastic theory. Nothing, absolutely nothing, had any evidence—hard or even reasonable soft evidence—to support it, as far as I could discover. However, now I had hard evidence of the most basic form for why the chance origin of life could *not* have occurred.

10

Back at the University

One night I decided to test my new analytical belief out in the "real world"—at one of the top biochemistry institutes in the United States, a mecca for evolutionary thinking—the University of California at Irvine (UCI). This would be a final chance for some expert to draw me back to evolution.

Over the course of two evenings, I attended lectures at UCI given by Michael Behe, author of the book *Darwin's Black Box*.[1] I was fortunate enough to have lunch with him earlier on the first day of the lectures and discuss the ideas he had presented in his book. An associate professor at Lehigh University in Pennsylvania, Behe viewed the issue of evolution from an academic viewpoint. He dealt primarily with transitional evolution, not the origin of first life; he said there was an enormous problem for transition between species in evolutionary theory.

Many intricate changes would have to take place simultaneously to produce even a partial change in a species (analogous to the many events that would have to occur to cause a single bacterium cell to develop into the complex cells found in the human body). Behe's argument, founded on a concept he called "irreducible complexity," went into great detail. He spoke not only of change in single cells, but of entire biochemical systems that would need to change *all at once*. This seemed to contradict Darwin's conclusion about the need for *gradual* change over time:

> Natural selection can act only by the preservation and
> accumulation of infinitesimally small inherited modifi-
> cations, each profitable to the preserved being.[2]

Some evolutionists today have also been tending away from "gradualism" because they too recognize the impossibility for a "part of something"—part of a system—to provide any benefit (or even any function). They have theorized that there were great, sudden bursts of evolution of species that took place within a very short time. A viable mechanism for this has not been proposed since all observation has shown that necessary parts (for example, eyes and feathers) appeared in their complete form all at once. (This sounded more like creation to me.)

Behe used a simple analogy of a system—that of a basic mouse-trap. One might envision the mousetrap's base—the block of wood—somehow gradually developing, but it would be of no use without the spring. And those two parts would be of no use without the latch. And then a trigger mechanism would be neces-sary...and so on. And all the parts would have to be formed simul-taneously. They would all have to be assembled. And for the entire system to work, energy would have to be applied to set the trap.

Behe went on to point out how simple a mousetrap is, com-pared to the intricacies of such systems as the human eye—or even the simplest bacterium. And these systems are "irreducibly com-plex." In other words, if they are "reduced" by a few parts, or even one part, they are no longer a system—they are useless. The odds of everything happening at once to make an eye "work"—the parts, the assembly, the "know-how," and any necessary energy—are small beyond reason. How could someone ignore the basic statis-tics? Perhaps only if they saw the implications, and were absolutely refusing to even consider God. But Behe's approach was an appeal to basic reason, not to believe in a "God."

The presentation at UCI was to a large room with few cre-ationists but with a very large number of biochemistry students and evolutionists. There was such tension in the room you could cut it with a knife. After the lecture, when questions were allowed, the anger and hostility erupted in a few cases—with students bent on defending evolution, yet unable to make much of a case against

Behe's argument. I remember how one angry student hammered Behe with question after question without giving the professor a chance to answer him. I was impressed with Behe's calmness. Eventually the harassing student was booed, even by his own peers. It gave me some insight into how emotionally charged this issue had become.

That night after the lecture, the aggressive student was trying to make his case to his peers in the lobby. *He was making his case against the Bible.* Strange—evolution apparently wasn't the issue, the Bible was.

The following evening a different incident happened. After the second lecture by Behe, there were several small groups of students around the foyer discussing what they had heard. But there was quite a large group assembled outside, and a professor was standing on a landing about three steps above them and was speaking to them. He was obviously trying to explain why Behe's argument could easily be dismissed, and was taking questions from the crowd.

I raised my hand and asked the professor, "Are you a professor of microbiology here at UCI?"

"Yes, I am," he proudly responded, making sure I understood his credentials. I'm sure he was wondering why an older man like me was hanging around to ask questions among a large group of students, most of whom were quite a bit younger.

I said, "You've been discussing Behe's lecture, but let me ask you a far more basic question. Would you agree, if random development of the very first living cell did *not* happen, then Behe's argument, mutational change, the fossil record, and all the other transitional issues of evolution make absolutely no difference? In fact, wouldn't they become moot? After all, any kind of supernatural intelligence necessary to create the first cell could presumably create other life as well."

"Well, of course you need a starting point," he pondered out loud, wondering where I was leading.

"Then let me ask you one of the basic biochemistry questions that has been studied for years," I continued. "What evidence is there to overcome the high statistical improbability of the optical purity (left-handedness or right-handedness) necessary for the development of the very first living cell?" (See pages 95–100 in regard to "chirality" and the issues it raises.)

"Oh, there's an enormous body of such evidence," he chuckled in a somewhat condescending way, as if he'd answered my question and was ready to move on to the next. But I'd been a skeptic too long and had been involved in too many battles to let him off the hook so easily. I also knew that a common tactic to quell subsequent discussion is to try to make others feel uninformed and uncomfortable.

But by now, I felt *very* informed, even to the point of being somewhat comfortable in this setting and questioning a well-respected professor with far better credentials. What I really wanted to know was, did he have any answers I didn't know of?

"Professor," I continued, "can you provide me with one single name, or with a hard experiment or journal article that clearly demonstrates a method of satisfying the origin-of-life chirality problem?"

Again he laughed. "But there are so many of them, I wouldn't know where to start!"

There was a dead silence as students were wondering what would happen next.

"Again, sir," I replied, "I'm not asking for many of them. I'm just asking for *one* name, hard-evidence experiment, or journal article—something that proves a solution to the chirality problem. Just one, please. I really want to know."

Now the professor started to fidget, and the students sensed that something big was at stake. Some started snickering.

"Look, experiments have been going on for years on this subject—many experiments," he said in a very short, firm tone as if to put me in my place for asking such questions.

I replied, "So surely someone as knowledgeable as you can at least come up with *one single* example that provides a solution so that I can look it up, can't you? An issue that important would not be something an esteemed professor in your field would forget, would it?"

The professor glared at me. His steel-cold eyes seemed attached to my stare. I didn't blink. I was a "well-trained skeptic," and I was not about to let this chance to evaluate the truth escape. Obviously he was embarrassed in front of his students—something he wasn't used to. "Well, why all this talk about chirality anyway! There are other things that are more important!" He threw up his hands rather indignantly, turned, and left. By now a lot of students were laughing. I had my answer.

As he stormed off, I turned to the students and said, "Yes, I know there are other problems. But are they more important? I don't know. Hopefully you guys are finding out some answers for people like me interested in evolution or creation. There are enormous statistical issues involved in correct biogenetic sequencing or simultaneous DNA mutation in germ cells. Add to that the addition of life itself to inanimate cells, and the theory of naturalistic evolution is statistically far less likely than a tornado assembling a junkyard into a Boeing 747."

The students were staring at me. I went on: "Frankly, if this single basic problem of chirality can't be resolved, *all of the other enormous problems in evolutionary theory make little difference.* By the way, don't be afraid to ask your professors to provide you with hard evidence when important claims, such as those about chirality, are made. The academic world spreads false rumors just like everyone else.

"In fact, for 20 years scientists believed that RNA had been synthesized in a lab. It was even in college textbooks. Finally Robert Shapiro checked it out and found it to be a rumor spread entirely from a single ambiguous paper drafted in 1967. His announcement was a bombshell at the 1986 conference of the International Institute for the Study of Origin of Life at Berkeley. Random development of RNA in the environment of early earth has been shown to be impossible.[3]

"Digging, digging, digging has shown me how poorly I was taught about the origin-of-life issue. It has also shown me that, sometimes, highly controversial subjects can be better taught if self-taught."

The students started laughing and applauding.

I certainly had no intention of embarrassing the professor, I just wanted the truth. Months of poring over the available literature and talking to others produced not one single reasonable explanation to the chirality problem—which was just one of many fundamental problems. By pressing the issue within the setting of such a well-educated, hostile (certainly noncreationist) crowd, I assumed I'd get my answer one way or the other. Either I'd glean a shred of hard evidence or not. The outcome was as I suspected.

The Only Hope for Chance Origins

The only real hope for a theory of chance origins would be infinite time. As the staunch evolutionist Richard Dawkins said in his book *The Blind Watchmaker*, "Given infinite time, or infinite opportunities, anything is possible."[4] But we now know time is not infinite! As I discovered, the verification of general relativity, combined with the experimental physics of Hubble in 1929, Penzias in 1964, and Smoot in 1992, taken all together demonstrate that time and space had a beginning.

Furthermore, several methods of measuring the age of the universe have confirmed a finite age of 13 to 15 billion years. (To confirm this, since the early 1990s, the edges of the universe have been mapped more and more thoroughly. Millions of data points have been added each year.) Even if we use an outside estimate of 20 billion years for the universe (4.5 billion years for the earth), that amount of time is virtually nothing considering the time necessary to randomly resolve just the issue raised by chirality.

If there's not anywhere near enough time to "flip amino acids and nucleotides" so they would work for first life, think of the added problems of

- selecting only life-specific amino acids (there are more than 60 none-life-specific ones)

- having them placed in combinations (like letters into words) that work

- having them placed in chains (like words into sentences) that work

- doing the same with nucleotides in the DNA chain

- and lastly, *making the cell come alive*

All of this for one single cell!

Just for a single cell to appear, infinity would be necessary. And this presumes there is some natural means to add life to basic matter ("spontaneous generation"). This is something that has never been observed, nor do human beings have the slightest idea of how to add life to matter. So even if there had been infinite time to allow the first cell to be put together, we know of no way that evolution could bring such a cell alive. And in the absence of a naturalistic theory that relies upon random chance, the only alternative is some form of intelligent design—supernatural creation—or what is commonly defined as "God."

11

I Start to Investigate God

For me the chain of evolution had been broken, which led me to the only other conclusion—that there is some kind of intelligent Creator of first life. In addition to the whole chirality issue, I had run across a number of the other serious flaws in the evolutionary chain:

● ● ●

- *Irreducible complexity.* It was necessary for trillions of simultaneous mutations to occur just to achieve a change in one single system (for example, to add an eye).

- *Contradiction of the first law of thermodynamics and general relativity.* The first law indicates that matter and energy can be neither created nor destroyed. But general relativity, along with supporting observations, indicates that there was clearly a beginning of everything. They can't be reconciled without supernatural intervention.

- *Lack of any proven mechanism for transition from lower to higher life forms.* (Theories of positive mutational change have been shown to be statistically impossible.[1])

- *The fossil record.* It doesn't support evolution.

● ● ●

I felt betrayed by the "men in white coats" who had taught me evolution based on old science—from before we even had the ability to view detailed cell structure. Though in awe of science and its achievements, I was amazed that many held onto neo-Darwinism in the face of obvious evidence.

However, my months of research had also shown me that many leading scientists had already come to the conclusion that evolution is fatally flawed from a sheerly scientific perspective. But it seemed that the world was just slow to catch on. It had taken me a lot of effort just to try to discover the hard evidence to rebut creationists. And eventually, embarrassingly, I had to change my mind.

I thought of the angry responses I would get—people telling me how wrong I was to change my opinion of evolution versus creation. But were they willing to use an objective statistical approach to determine what was true? The issue was emotional for me too. God versus atheism. But I could find no strong rebuttals to the statistical problems from the evolutionist community because there was no hard evidence. It was that simple.

As I saw it, naturalistic theories were relying increasingly on fantasies and contradictory evidence. As a skeptic, I was astounded how soft-science observations and speculations somehow took on more importance than hard science. Perhaps it's because it's easier (and more enjoyable) to "look at a dinosaur bone" than to face the implications of the formula for general relativity. Yet after learning what I'd learned, it looked like it would be intellectual suicide for a soft-scientist evolutionist to debate a knowledgeable astrophysicist and a molecular biologist about the origin of life. The hard scientists would understand where the facts lie.

Why were intelligent scientists not facing reality? Then it struck me that, for many people, "God" was getting in the way of good science. One day I stumbled across the words of George Wald in the May 1954 *Scientific American* article "The Origin of Life." To me, they summed up the real reason behind years of scientific deception and explained the continued existence of theories about the chance origin of life.

> When it comes to the origin of life there are only two possibilities: creation or spontaneous generation. There is no third way. Spontaneous generation was disproved one hundred years ago, but that leads us to only one

other conclusion, that of supernatural creation. We cannot accept that on philosophical grounds; therefore, we choose to believe the impossible: that life arose spontaneously by chance![2]

How that opened my eyes! All those years I had idolized scientists for what I thought was their firm commitment to objectivity. Now I had found at least one scientist honest enough to admit that he'd rather seek the impossible (deceiving himself and others) rather than believe in a supernatural Creator. I wondered how many other scientists felt the same way. I could see how evolution had become the accepted norm—taught to me and millions of others in school.

Positive Evidence for God

Now that it was obvious to me that naturalistic evolution of first life was statistically impossible, I began to wonder if there was any positive evidence of supernatural creation. Certainly the intricacies of the cell—DNA, RNA, proteins—seemed to show abundant evidence of design—the design of specific traits and characteristics that make human beings human, and that make each of us the specific individual we are.

Was there any other evidence apart from biochemistry? I decided to investigate more of the resources that my seatmate on the airplane, John, had recommended. I started to get information about the Reasons to Believe organization and classes and seminars at Simon Greenleaf College (now Trinity Law School) and Biola University.

———•———

"The odds of finding another planet in the universe that could support life are nil!" remarked Dr. Hugh Ross in a lecture at Simon Greenleaf College of Apologetics and Law. "It's as if God designed this planet earth specifically for human beings, along with allowing for a maximum number of other life forms."

I had enrolled in a class called "Science and the Bible," hoping to learn if there was any hard scientific evidence to support the Bible's claims, which I had rejected so long ago. Dr. Ross, the professor, was a highly qualified astrophysicist and cosmologist—and the founder of Reasons to Believe. His credentials included not only a B.S. and M.S. in physics, but a Ph.D. in astronomy; and he was involved in extensive research on quasars and galaxies as a postdoctoral fellow at the California Institute of Technology (Cal Tech). This satisfied my need to find a highly qualified "hard-science" person to ask the questions that most troubled me about religion and science. Although this course offered credit for advanced degrees, I signed up for no credit. I had no interest in writing papers for grades, and I felt I had enough degrees. I just wanted to know if the existence of a God—even the God of the Bible—really could fit with science.

"Dr. Ross, please explain that to me," I said. Still the skeptic—even though I had already been convinced that biochemistry provides very hard evidence that evolution is impossible—I wanted to see some positive evidence of a God as well.

I continued, "I realize that there are maybe a billion stars in our galaxy. And I also understand that there may be about a billion galaxies in the universe. Is that true?" I'd done some studying on these issues and had even read some of Dr. Ross's books.

"Yes, that's about right," he said.

"Well, with all those stars in all those galaxies, doesn't it seem likely that another planet such as earth could exist?" I stated.

"It could," Ross said, "but one has to estimate the probability—which is virtually zero."

"Please explain," I replied.

"We know there are certain parameters necessary for life," Ross began. "An obvious one is the distance of the earth from the sun. If we were slightly closer we would receive too much heat from the sun and life would burn up. If we were slightly farther away, we would freeze to death. That's one of the simplest examples. There are many, many others that we never think about. For example, the mass of land in the Northern Hemisphere versus the mass of land in the Southern Hemisphere allows for a flowing blanket of air that keeps the planet temperate. The difference in heat retention and flow between land mass and water—which obviously is more prevalent in the Southern Hemisphere—allows circulating of air between the two hemispheres."

Ross continued, "Today, we know of a few dozen such parameters. Only the slightest change in one of them would make life impossible. And every year more are being added."

Since the time I took that basic course from Dr. Ross, I have contacted Reasons to Believe to find out the latest data concerning the likelihood of another "planet earth." The latest findings now show 153 specific parameters that are necessary for life to survive on a planet, none of which are believed to have a random chance of occurring of higher than 10 percent. Many parameters have an estimated probability of only 1 percent or $^1/_{10}$ of 1 percent. (See appendix A for a listing of 128 of these parameters.)

Ross estimated that the number of potential planets in the entire universe may be 10^{22}, which is a lot of planets! (This number appears reasonable since it comes not only from an expert in the field but is within the range of statistics derived from the observation of extrasolar planets.)

Yet, when we calculate the probability of all the events listed in appendix A occurring to provide conditions for life (using the same mathematical, hard-science means we used to calculate the probability of the random beginning of first life), we find the odds of a planet like earth randomly occurring are

$$1 \text{ chance in } 10^{166}$$

This means that the odds of any of the 10^{22} planets having an earth-like capability to support life are

$$\frac{10^{22}}{10^{166}} = \frac{1}{10^{144}}$$

The result of $1/10^{144}$ would be considered *just plain zero* by any statistician or student of applied mathematics.

My Conclusion from Analytical Proof

From analytical proof, it is impossible that random chance produced even the first cell of life, let alone the parade of evolution that is said to follow it. I was saddened to learn that, in fact, I had been taught a religion in school—the religion of atheism—because the theory of evolution had ruled out any basis for the existence of God. And I was angry to learn that this religion of atheistic evolution was based on obsolete, incorrect science. Only people ignorant of astrophysics and microbiology, or those with an agenda would permit the perpetuation of 150-year-old science. Moreover, I was angry that the government (through the schools) was essentially forcing the teaching of bad science and the religion of atheism by not acknowledging the latest research. Certainly the schools succeeded with me. They turned me into an "intellectual atheist."

And then I wondered why the *anthropic principle* (the fact that earth alone is so precisely suited for human beings) was not taught. What was the school system afraid of? Facts are facts. Education is education. It was all true, and was entirely independent of teaching students what God to believe in.

I was embarrassed to admit to my peers that I was wrong, especially after being so outspoken for so long. I wondered why I had to learn the truth on my own—not in my educational system? (My response to the concept of "the separation of church and state" is that it can breed "separation of *truth* and state" if taken to an extreme. Maybe there should be more latitude regarding what is taught in schools, provided there is *hard evidence* for the truth for any specific hypothesis.)

In summary, I had concluded that there is "microproof" for the existence of God because modern knowledge of biochemistry shows naturalistic development of the very first living cell to be impossible. Second, I had "macroproof" that the odds of the occurrence of a planet capable of supporting life would be impossible without a designer—in other words, "God." In both of these areas—from the heavens above to the DNA we are made of—I felt satisfied because the proof was in the hard science of statistics and mathematics. It was not based on a conjecture made from the observation of old bones. It was based on facts, not guesses or presumptions. And so my analytical proof conclusion was—

● ● ●

Some form of a Creator God exists.

● ● ●

I finally acknowledged that God must exist.
The next question was, who or what is this God?

12

Who Are You, God?

"You're crazy!" I yelled at Steve Conoman, who had just tried to convince me that the flood of Noah had actually covered all the mountains of the world—even Mount Everest. "Do you have any perception of how much water that would require? And where did it go? And how? Don't you have any sense of reason?"

"You're the one that's the idiot for not checking it out!" he responded. "They've actually found shells on tops of mountains. And scientists think the mountains used to be much lower."

I laughed sarcastically. "We can't survive a simple 8.5 earthquake that moves the earth only a few inches, and you're telling me scientists believe Mount Everest was created in a few hundred years? Now that's *real* believable!"

———————•———————

I had moved to southern California to become president of a small design firm, which quickly grew into a major firm doing advertising. We also started making a lot of money. I had purchased a family ski condo at Big Bear, California, which I also offered to the company's top people for creative sessions. Steve, Keith Tomkin (the original owner of the company), and I had been working on a project and were always very open in the way we spoke to each other. Dinner was finished, and as often was the case, we had been drinking too much, which only added to the intensity of our discussion. While my mind-game days of fighting against God were over, I was not about to be pushed around by the ridiculous ideas of a "Bible-beater"—Steve, who professed to be a Christian.

———————•———————

"What do you think?" I asked Keith.

"Well, I don't believe in everything the Bible says," he replied. "But basically I've been through years of Bible study and kind of select the parts that make the most sense. But I certainly believe in God."

"Yeah, Muncaster," shouted Steve. "Do you even believe in God?"

"Actually I do," I responded.

"Well, what kind of God? Who is he?" Steve pressed.

"I'm not sure," I replied. "I suppose I think of God as some kind of a 'force' that could create everything. Are you telling me you believe in absolutely everything the Bible says?"

"Yep!" Steve emphatically replied, with a sense of pride.

"Adam and Eve?"

"Yep!"

"900-year-old people?"

"Yep!"

"Parting of the Red Sea?"

"Yep!"

"Jesus' resurrection from the dead?"

"Most importantly!"

"Well, I must say I admire your convictions, if not your brain," I muttered.

"I know where you're coming from, Ralph," Keith admitted. "I was there too. Then about the time I got married, I went to church a lot. I also joined the Masonic Lodge and did a bunch of things."

"I didn't know you went to church!" I replied.

"Well...not so much any more," Keith admitted. "I've pretty much heard it all, so I really don't need to. Besides, I didn't like the way they were always hitting you up for money."

"But Keith, you've got plenty of money. So what?"

"That's not the point. I earned it, and I should determine what to do with it."

I knew that both Keith and Steve loved to enjoy their money. And so did I. Actually it was Keith who had taught me to enjoy all the things money could buy, I recalled as I reflected back on the beat-up old cars I used to drive even as a young corporate executive, and our underfurnished houses. But now, all three of us always had to have the most expensive we possibly could afford of anything. Keith and I drove top-of-the-line Mercedes, and both of us owned gold Rolex watches. I'll never forget the day we each blew $300 on a single pair of sunglasses. While Steve didn't have that spending power quite yet, he spent what he could when he could, and it was visible to everyone.

Then I thought about two very dedicated and humble Christians back at the office—Vern and Ron—who diligently worked very hard for us, often long into the night. They were two of our best employees. Soon these two would leave the company, partly, I believe, because of our arrogant displays of materialism. I didn't even imagine my path would cross with Ron and Vern again, in the distant future.

———————●———————

"So tell me again about this 'force-type' God," Steve goaded me.

"What I can say with certainty is that *some* God created the heavens and the earth with meticulous precision that is beyond human reason," I replied. "What I can also say with certainty is that the account in the Bible, which you say is so true, is absolutely absurd."

"How can you be so sure?" he asked loudly, with a condescending look on his face.

"Okay, Mr. Genius, tell me how the plants were supposedly created on day three, then survived the very first day without any sun yet for photosynthesis? After all, doesn't the Bible say the sun was created on day four?"

"Don't you think that a God who could create the plants to begin with could keep them alive for a day or two?" he hurled back.

"Well, how did we even know when a day actually was, if we didn't have a sun for a reference point?" I asked.

"Hmmm…well, maybe God was the reference point!"

"God's spirit was 'over the surface of the deep,'" I said gloatingly. "God was at the earth…Don't you read your own Bible?"

"Well, maybe some other reference point," Steve said.

"But do you really think everything happened in six 24-hour days?" I asked, calming down a bit. I was beginning to feel the old mental competitive urge.

"Of course," he stated a bit pompously. "The Bible makes it very clear."

"Look, enough of that," I said. "Let's have some fun. I have another question, somewhat off the topic. What is the very fastest you think you could count to a hundred?"

"Heck, I don't know," he said. "Maybe in 30 seconds."

"Keith, what do you think Steve could do? Thirty seconds sounds tough to me, but he might make it. Anyone up for a little wager?"

"I'm in," Steve said, throwing a buck on the counter.

"Attaboy, Steve," I said throwing mine in too. "What about you, Keith? You can get in just by betting against whichever person you think is wrong."

"You know I hate these things." He paused for what seemed like an eternity. "I guess I'll go with Steve doing it." He threw his buck in.

If Steve did it, I'd be out two dollars. But more importantly, pride was at stake between the three of us—though I had an ulterior motive.

"All right—let's do it, guys!" Steve said. "On my mark—get set—go!" And he started slobbering off the most horrendous counting in the English language that we'd ever heard. Keith and I couldn't contain ourselves. We both broke up laughing.

"Ni-eight, ni-ni, dred—done!" Steve proudly proclaimed himself the winner, quickly grabbing the money from the counter as he saw the stopwatch marking 27 seconds. By now all three of us were silly with laughter.

As calm finally settled over us, I said to Steve, "Well, you beat me, I guess—if you want to call that English," which caused another round of chuckling.

"But let's go back to the Bible for a minute," I said. "As I recall from reading Genesis, on day six Adam was assigned the task of naming all the living creatures of the world. Now, I read that passage carefully, and he didn't even have a full day, because he wasn't formed until some other creatures had been made before him. But let's give old Adam the benefit of the doubt, that he had a full 24 hours. Do you remember reading that, Steve?"

"Er…yes," Steve hesitantly replied. I wasn't certain if he did or not.

"Keith, do you have a calculator?" I asked.

"Yep," he said, as he reached to the table beside him and tossed it to me.

"Okay," I said punching some buttons, "it's easy to calculate that there are 86,400 seconds in a day. Now guys, I'm not lying to you, I've been doing some research on this lately. Scientists have identified 1.4 million *species* in the world, not to mention the many subspecies. They speculate there are many more. So even if Adam had an entire day to work with, he'd have to slur his words *eight times more*—he'd have to go eight times faster—than Steve just did, and do nothing else that day, just to name the animals. And I might add, 'hippopotamus' is a bit harder to say than 'three.' "

Keith started to break up with laughter again.

"Now what, Keith?" I asked, starting to laugh myself.

"Oh, it's just what you said…about doing nothing else," he managed to get out. "Can you imagine someone waiting for a mate…then getting Eve, the perfect woman…first time he'd ever laid eyes on her…and then just sitting on a rock, doing nothing but slurring out the names of animals—like Steve here?"

"And think of what Eve must have thought, coming to life and seeing her husband…some babbling idiot…going on with these names for hours on end…" I added.

After more laughter, calm finally settled in.

"Steve, do you see why I have such a problem with some of what the Bible says?" I said.

"Yeah, I guess that's why I don't buy it all myself," said Keith.

"I'm telling you guys, everything in the Bible is true," Steve said. "And Muncaster, I bet if you really checked it out you'd be shocked to see that it's all true."

Huh, I thought. Hadn't I heard that before? Of course—Bob, in Portland. I didn't tell the guys yet that I had already started studying about the Bible for that very reason. But I still had a long way to go, and at this point I needed much better proof that the God of the Bible was the real God.

Part IV

Statistical Proof of God

13

Could I Develop Statistical Standards for Determining God's Existence?

By definition—analytically—I was now convinced that a God existed. Even statistically, the evidence for a God passed both the "macro-test" (the statistical evidence for the uniqueness of planet earth—designed just for humans) and the "micro-test" (the first living cell's amazingly complex design and the impossibility of random chance assembling it). It was statistically impossible for there not to be a God. However, as I had told Steve and Keith, I was still far from accepting any "God of the Bible." Yet I was determined to take the search for statistical evidence of God a step further. Who was this God whose existence I was now convinced of? Did any religion have any statistical evidence that he was real? If so, what was that evidence? And how can I be confident that the evidence wasn't contrived?

Bob and Steve had both challenged me regarding the Bible. And I'd heard so many people declare that the Bible was inspired by God. Could it be proven? Certainly you would think that if God really inspired the Bible, he would have provided some statistical evidence. *But,* I wondered, *how might I find it?* I decided to search the Bible for evidence that I could test statistically.

God Comes into Our Family

Throughout my courtship and the early part of my marriage, God was certainly not very high on my scale. He didn't even rate, except as an occasional game to break my boredom while I was on frequent business trips. My wife, Jan, didn't talk much about God either, except from time to time to suggest perhaps we should try a church. Early in our marriage, I thought a church might actually be "good for the kids." (We eventually had three sons—Joel, Jason, and Justin.) After all, I actually did enjoy one aspect of my childhood "church club"—the church youth group, where we had a lot of fun as teenagers. We had had a lot of fun with the skiing, camping, and other adventures I had designed during the two terms I served as "youth president." The group had all my friends in it. I reasoned that some church influence and "nice" friends could be only a good influence for my boys.

Jan and I had been scheduled to be married in a mainstream Protestant church—the same denomination I grew up in—only in Colorado, where Jan lived. However, the church had a change in leadership just after we had sent out invitations and they changed their minds and would not let us get married there without going through Christian "premarriage counseling" first. It was too late for that, and besides, we had no idea what it meant.

The new leader of our wedding site wouldn't budge. So we ended up finding a Unitarian church that would agree to let us hold the wedding there.

The Unitarian leader simply said, "So you need a building for your wedding, eh?"

"Yes," I responded. We put some money down, and we were in.

It really was unusual. Here we were, calling our entire wedding list, telling them that our service had been changed at the last minute from a prestigious Protestant church to a Unitarian church (Unitarians reject the authority of Jesus and the Bible). And our service had something of a Catholic flair—because of Jan's desire to honor her mother. Incidentally, our videographer friend was probably a Muslim. I guess you could say our wedding had God "covered."

Jan and I never seemed to do anything "normal" anyway. When I first saw Jan, she was working in a grocery store. I boasted to the friend I was with that I would ask her out. Naturally I had to build a relationship first. So I shopped that store almost every day, making a point to go through her check-out line and talk to her. After two weeks, with a houseful of food, I decided the day had come. So that evening I purchased $200 of groceries—a lot back in the early '70s—so I could buy some time to work up the courage to ask her out. Fortunately, Jan accepted my invitation to a date.

Ironically, about a year-and-a-half later a new employee showed up at Jan's store and said to Jan, "I remember you! I was in line here a year or two ago, and some jerk had the gall to ask you out! Aren't you the one?"

"Yes," Jan sheepishly replied. "Now he's my husband."

————————●————————

"Look at this!" Jan exclaimed as she held up a flyer from a church proclaiming a "new form of worship." "Debbie Boone's going to sing at their next service. I think this is the same church we went to a while back in Laguna Hills." Jan seemed to know not to push me too hard to get me to go to "church things."

I took a look at it and replied, "Yeah, maybe."

After all, I was getting pretty interested in really trying to understand who "God" was now, and I decided that maybe we should start getting more serious about finding a real church. In southern California, we had gone to a few churches on a widely spaced basis, starting in about 1985 in Laguna Hills.

We decided to go to the "Debbie Boone service" at Saddleback Valley Community Church and I actually enjoyed church for once. The pastor, a man named Rick Warren, gave a highly relevant message that seemed to use the Bible as a tool rather than a stick. The people were warm and friendly and, except for my disbelief in Bible miracles, everything seemed to make sense. I remember thinking, *This would be a good family church. I hope the real God is the one this church believes in.*

We started attending Saddleback Church fairly frequently. A few months later, the church had a speaker from the Institute of Creation Research. I was really impressed. This was a church that didn't expect people to check their brains at the door. Perhaps I would be able to get some real questions answered there.

No longer did I feel uncomfortable about letting my wife see me reading religious literature. I still didn't want anyone to think I was a Bible fanatic, though. So I kept a lot of my Bible reading private. One Sunday at church, the topic of daily Bible reading came up, and after that I felt a bit less afraid of looking like a "Jesus freak."

I was reading the Bible on an almost daily basis, looking for clues to how I could either prove or disprove God's existence through what was written in it. Still, to me all the stories bordered on fairy tales. Yes, I'd gotten some explanations through the Institute for Creation Research and Reasons to Believe, but I had a lot more questions. I was looking for more answers—something, perhaps, that a God who transcends time and space had placed in the Bible that would show how it had been inspired by him.

God and Probability

I will always believe in statistics and probability. After all, *all of life is based on probability in some way* (see chapter 5).

It simply makes sense that if something is sufficiently improbable (like winning many lotteries in a row with a single ticket for each), in essence we know it to be impossible, barring some supernatural influence (or cheating). Many scientists hold to the standard that anything with a probability of less than 1 chance in 10^{50} (that is, 1 with 50 zeros after it) is absurd, or impossible. By taking this a step further, we might conclude that anything with a statistical chance of less than 1 in 10^{50} that happens anyway is of supernatural origin.

Developing a Statistical Test

I knew that a good statistical test must be quantifiable and meaningful. In other words, it must be based on a *sufficient sample* of *good data* in order to offer proof that any certain hypothesis is actually true. So in my search for God—the *right* God—I needed to find something I could

1. count

2. evaluate the significance of

3. authenticate

A statistical test doesn't need to be 100-percent perfect to fall within the bounds of statistical certainty. But, I reasoned, a perfect God could make it 100-percent perfect.

So what could I measure? Miracles? But they are claimed by all religions and are usually not verifiable. Then I stumbled on a verse in the Bible that made a lot of sense to me. The Bible wasn't afraid to let itself be tested. And it seemed to be urging the testing of other holy books and of people as well:

> Test everything. Hold on to the good (1 Thessalonians 5:21).

Since the Bible seemed so eager for people to test everything (including it), I decided to read more to see what type of test it suggested. After all, it did claim to be from God, even though I had rejected it.

The Perfect Prophecy Test

Searching the Bible, I found a test that seemed to be the ultimate test for God. Isaiah, recorded as speaking for God in about 740 B.C., said,

> Remember the former things, those of long ago; I am God, and there is no other; I am God, and there is none like me. I make known the end from the beginning, from ancient times, what is still to come (Isaiah 46:9-10).

This made perfect sense to me. Only a God of the universe would be able to perfectly know the end from the beginning. Could the God of the Bible live up to that? How about the God of other holy books? What about other people? Events thought to be miracles could be deceiving. But how could I doubt *cold, hard evidence of the perfect prediction of the future,* if the evidence was actually there? Upon further examination I found many biblical examples, and I found other references to using prophecy as a test:

> "Present your case," says the LORD. "Set forth your arguments," says Jacob's king. "Bring in [your idols] to tell us what is going to happen. Tell us what the former things were, so that we may consider them and know their final outcome. Or declare to us the things to come, tell us what the future holds, so we may know that you are gods" (Isaiah 41:21-23).

I also found commands from Moses (supposedly from God) in the books of the law:

> You may say to yourselves. "How can we know when a message has not been spoken by the LORD?" If what a prophet proclaims in the name of the LORD *does not take place or come true, that is a message the LORD has not spoken.* That prophet has spoken presumptuously. Do not be afraid of him (Deuteronomy 18:21-22).

And how serious is the Bible about false prophecy? I also found this in the law:

> But a prophet who presumes to speak in my name *anything* I have not commanded him to say, or a prophet who speaks in the name of other gods, must be put to death (Deuteronomy 18:20).

Apparently the Bible takes prophecy very, very seriously. *(Did other religions take prophecy so seriously?* I wondered.) Why would prophecy be such an indicator of the true God? I thought about it for a minute, then reasoned this way: If there was any means, other than through the words of a real God, of predicting the future with perfect accuracy—such as through psychics, Ouija boards, tarot cards, astrology, and so on—it would be making certain people consistently rich. Lotteries would be won by the same people—or by those using the same technique. Horse-racing would be dominated by them. Casinos would shut down. Any form of gambling would no longer be "gambling." But all types of gambling still exist, everywhere in the world. Therefore, there is obviously no sure way of predicting the future, unless the Bible should end up revealing a God who could do it.

Prophecy also ideally fit my needs for a statistical test. Prophecies from any source were quantifiable (I could count how many accurate prophecies were made if I looked only at historically verifiable ones). Prophecies could be evaluated. In other words, some would be more remarkable than others. And if several different holy books all contained significant prophecy, they could be readily evaluated against each other.

I was somewhat surprised by the Bible's arrogant-seeming boast about its God being *the* God, and that there were no others. I was surprised by the law that prophecy be 100-percent perfect. In probability testing only an acceptable degree of statistical significance is necessary to reach a conclusion—not perfection. But I reminded myself that a perfect God of the universe would be able to perfectly predict the future in any writing or person he inspired, just as the Bible had declared.

I decided, then, to use perfect prophecy as a statistical benchmark to determine what or who God is. Statistically significant prophecy (preferably 100-percent perfect prophecy) should exist somewhere, in some source, in some form, if God is real. If I found an authority containing such proof, I would need to seriously consider the possibility that it was "from God."

Since the Bible was the book in which I discovered this excellent test for God, and since the Bible declared that all prophecies from God had to be 100-percent accurate, I decided to start with the Bible to see if it could pass its own test—and *how well* it could pass its own test.

Prophecy Criteria

The specificity of any prophecy would play a large part in my evaluation of its significance. For instance, proclaiming that someone will meet a "tall, dark, handsome stranger" doesn't say much. One example of such a prophecy that I knew of was Jeane Dixon's prediction about John F. Kennedy's assassination.[1] In reality, her prediction in *Parade* magazine in 1956 said that "a Democrat" would win the election and would "die in office." This was far less specific. Just how amazing was this prediction?

First, the odds of a Democrat winning that Presidential election were about 50 percent. Second, the odds of a President dying in office—as of 1960—were about 40 percent. The combined probability of both events happening was 50 percent times 40 percent —20 percent. In other words, there was a 1 in 5 chance that the events would have occurred anyway. So was the prophecy remarkable? I didn't think so. Yet it catapulted Jeane Dixon into a successful career as a psychic. But, I found in my investigation, her career included many mistakes, such as

1. the prediction that World War III would occur in 1954

2. the prediction that Jacqueline Kennedy would never get married again (ironically, this prediction was made the day before she married Aristotle Onassis)

3. the prediction that the Vietnam War would end in 1966 (it continued until 1975)

If Jeane Dixon had made those prophecies in God's name in the Israel of biblical times, she would have been stoned to death! I was excited by the prospect of finding a source more reliable than Jeane Dixon by applying the prophecy test. Did the Bible or some other source contain anything that came close to such a perfect standard?

I decided to apply certain standards of specificity and authentication so that the prophecies I used would neither be moot nor contrived. Here are the criteria I developed to exclude what I considered to be meaningless prophecies and to provide myself some assurance of authenticity in their accurate fulfillment, no matter how ancient the occurrence (assuming that documentation could be verified).

Something that claimed to be a prophecy should—

1. *Be of sufficient specificity, and unlikelihood, that a cursory examination would lead a reasonable person to conclude a probability of 1 in 10 or smaller.* This criterion eliminates the "tall, dark, handsome" generalities and the "Democrat dying in office" prophecies that are not very remarkable. While 1 chance in 10 by itself is not that spectacular either, several 1-in-10 prophecies strung together—with none being wrong—would be. (For example, just eight correct 1-in-10 prophecies in combination would equate to 1 chance in 100 million.)

2. *Be authenticated by one source and confirmed by a separate source that would receive no* net benefit *from the confirmation of the prophecy.* This would eliminate contriving prophecies for someone's benefit. "Net benefit" is important, because in some cases there may be some perceived benefit that might prejudice the confirmation of the prophecy.

3. *Be based on reliable source.* The sources of both prophecy and confirmation must be reliable, or the prophecy becomes just speculation.

14

Thinking About the God of the Jews

Now I was very serious about finding God. Not only finding further proof of his existence, but finding out who or what this God was. As I proceeded, I recognized that the complete Bible is made up of two "testaments": 1) the Old Testament, or Hebrew Bible—the only part believed by the Jews (often called the *Tanakh*), and 2) the New Testament, which is used along with the Old Testament by Christians. As I saw it, the main difference between Jews and Christians is the Christians' belief in and acceptance of Jesus as the promised Messiah of the Old Testament, who suffered and died to save people from their sin.

I decided to examine each testament individually to see if either could clearly point to a God through 100-percent accurate historical prophecy. Furthermore, I wanted to see if the Old Testament really led into the New Testament via prophecy, as some of my Christian friends were saying.

Frankly, at the time my image of the Jewish people was about as diverse as could be. On the one hand, I had seen, in news stories on TV, devout Jews dressed in strange clothing bowing at the Wailing Wall in Jerusalem. On the other hand, there was Bruce, a good friend in college. He seemed to represent something very different.

———— • ————

"All religions are hypocritical!" yelled Bruce, our next-door neighbor at the University of Colorado. We had been discussing Bruce's beliefs as a Jew and our encounters with Hare Krishnas.

"I do the family stuff," he said. "The bar mitzvah, the weddings, the Passover celebration, and all of that. But I don't really know about the 'God' thing. I don't know if God is real or not."

"Isn't that key to identifying yourself as a Jew?" I asked.

"Naaah," he chuckled. "You're a Jew because you were born a Jew. We all know it. As far as religion goes, we're no different than any other religion. Some people go to synagogue and some don't. Some are really involved and others aren't. I'm not about to dress in dark clothes, grow long sideburns, and do all the stuff the orthodox Jews do just to prove I'm okay to God."

I knew Bruce led a pretty loose lifestyle and would probably not let any religion get in his way. "How about the Bible?" I asked. "What do you believe? Is it inspired by God or just another book?"

"I don't know," he said. "People call it inspired, but who could ever know?"

"Have you read it?" I asked.

"No."

I began to feel like I was back in one of my battles of the mind with Rob Blaine at Richmond's Ice Cream factory.

"Then how can you judge one way or the other?"

"I can't, but have *you* read it?" (It was a great countermove.)

"No," I responded rather sheepishly.

"Well, I really just don't care," Bruce said. "If I'm basically a good person, I assume that any God who is real would realize that and would let me enjoy life. Why should I read the Bible? What difference would it make?"

I thought Bruce had made a good point in assuming that being "good" meant getting approval from God. And if he'd already closed his mind to seeking God regardless of the nature of God, then what good would any holy book do? I had always assumed the Jews were really spiritual, perhaps because I had thought of them only in the spiritual context. I now realized that Jews were just like other people—some were very serious about their religion and others weren't. I decided to ask one final question.

"Suppose the Bible, or any other holy book for that matter, could demonstrate beyond a shadow of a doubt that it was inspired by 'God.' Would you pay attention to what it said?"

"I guess so, if it was really compelling," he laughed. "But how would you ever prove such a thing? It's impossible." At the time, I agreed with him. How could anyone possibly ever prove any holy book to be divinely inspired?

I Set a Background for Testing Biblical Prophecy

I already realized that the Bible had been written by many authors over many years. From the outset, I was suspicious that the Bible had been "designed" to meet the religious needs of the Jews. In short, I was very skeptical. But as I dug into research on the Jewish culture at the time of the recording of the Torah and the rest of the Tanakh, I began to see that there were good reasons to trust prophecy made and fulfilled over generations or in different geographical locales. I summed up my thinking.

• • •

1. *The Israelites were a theocracy (governed by God).* Their laws were recorded as holy Scripture, and anything regarding that Scripture was of extreme importance and not taken lightly. This was especially indicated in the precise way they copied Scripture for future generations.

Rules for Duplication of Scripture

- Only master scrolls were used for duplication.

- Scribes were highly trained and highly esteemed. They were held in training till age 30; only after they reached that age could they serve officially.

- Scribes had to ceremonially wash before copying Scripture.

- Any time the name of God was written, a sanctification prayer was said.

- The name of God was written with letters missing to ensure fulfillment of God's command to never take his name in vain.

- Although the scribes had memorized large portions of Scripture, each letter of each copied scroll had to be visually confirmed, one by one.

- A thread was often placed between letters to ensure separation and accuracy.

- Each letter in each scroll was counted, and the count was compared to the master scroll.

- Each word in each scroll was counted, and the count compared to the master scroll. (The Hebrew word for "scribe" literally means "counter.")

- The middle letter in each entire copied scroll was located and compared to the master.

- If there was a single mistake, the scroll was discarded as a master.

- When master scrolls were worn out, they were given a ceremonial burial.

2. *The Israelites memorized enormous amounts of Scripture.* Unlike today, many people could not read nor write. Education was heavily based on memorization, particularly memorization of holy Scripture, which was the law and divine guidance of the nation. Scripture—in particular the books of the law—was respected as God's word-for-word instruction to Israel. If anyone attempted to change Scripture, it would require changing not only a vast number of written copies but the memory of hundreds of thousands of people.

3. *Prophecy was seen as of utmost importance and was regarded as a criterion to test if something was from*

God. False prophets were to be executed (Deuteronomy 18:20). Hence, any prophecy that could be proven or disproven within a prophet's lifetime was of enormous importance. It is unlikely false prophets would have survived.

● ● ●

So when I considered the books of the Tanakh (the Old Testament), I needed to keep this point in mind: Although they were written by many different people over a long period of time (about 1500 years), I should consider valid any prophecy that was written in one book and fulfilled historically in another book, providing it could be

1. Found in different books of Scripture or at very different times or places, and

2. Verified by apparently objective people or by obvious historical events.

Why consider prophecies trustworthy that are validated by the same collection of books in which they were originally recorded? I boiled it down to two reasons.

- First, the Jews would have had no reason to deceive themselves regarding the definition of their God.

- Second, there would have been no method to totally change the historical record. After all, *all* scrolls containing differing information would have had to be destroyed, with the new, falsified scrolls taking their place. Furthermore, the memory of every person who had memorized Scripture would have had to be changed. This could simply never happen.

My Initial Findings About Old Testament Biblical Prophecy

I was stunned at the ease of finding prophecy in the Bible—and lots of it. I discovered that virtually every bookstore had some resources on biblical prophecy. I used many along with the Bible. As a skeptic, my job was to determine how valid each specific prophecy was. Was the Bible's prophecy specific enough and provable enough?

Early on I realized that many biblical prophecies were in the short term. In other words, the prophecy was made and fulfilled in the same generation and recorded by the same group of people that the prophecy affected. I realized why short-term prophecies must have played a key role in the development of Jewish Scripture. If the Hebrews believed that prophecy was the key test of something being from God, it seemed obvious to me that they would test their prophets with short-term prophecy. If the prophets failed, their words would not be included within holy Scripture.

In my investigation, I didn't consider the short-term biblical prophecies, even though they might have been true, because they did not meet my statistical standards of objective verifiability. *In fact, I ended up excluding nearly 100 prophecies* (see appendix C) as untestable, either because they were short-term or because they were too vague.

The Jewish Bible

The Bible of the Jews is identical in content to the Old Testament of the Christians. However, the organization is different. The Hebrew (Jewish) Bible has a traditional book sequence (believed by scholars to be the order of the canonization of the books). This differs from the sequence of the Christian Old Testament, which attempts to categorize the books. In addition, the Christian Bible splits several books in the Jewish Bible into two, for example, 1 and 2 Kings, 1 and 2 Chronicles, 1 and 2 Samuel, and others.

The Hebrew Bible is made up of three parts: The Torah (the five books of law, given to Moses), the Neviim (books of the prophets), and the Ketuvim (books of writings—history and poetry). The first letter of each section, put together forms the Hebrew word for the Jewish Bible: TaNaKh.

15

Testable Prophecies I Found in the Old Testament

After excluding so many prophecies with my standards, I wondered what would be left. The answer amazed me. There was still a vast number of remaining prophecies, all fitting within my strict standards—specific prophecies of people, places, timing, events. I began by focusing more closely on the prophecies about the Jewish exiles.

Prophecies of the First Jewish Exile

In 722 B.C., the capital city of the ten northern tribes was captured by the Assyrians. Those ten tribes were then taken into captivity by the Assyrians. However, the first exile was not complete until the successful siege of Jerusalem by the Babylonian king, Nebuchadnezzar, in 587–586 B.C. At that time the exile of the Jews of the southern kingdom was completed. *Eight* prophets correctly predicted this along with many specific details.

Moses (Deuteronomy 28:49-57). Moses prophesied about this exile in about 1450 B.C. (As a reference point, Lamentations was written by Jeremiah soon after the fall of Jerusalem in 586 B.C., confirming Moses' prophecy almost 900 years later.)

141

Prophecy	Fulfillment
A foreign nation would defeat the Hebrew nation.	History
Everything would be destroyed.	History
The invaders would have no respect for the elderly and no pity for the young.	Lamentations 2:21
They would lay siege to cities.	Lamentations 3:5
The Hebrews would resort to cannibalism.	Lamentations 2:20

Amos (Amos chapters 3, 5-9). In 760 B.C., almost 40 years before the Assyrian conquest and almost 200 years before the Babylonian conquest, Amos prophesied that Israel would be devastated for her sins. *Fulfillment:* History.

Hosea (Hosea 1:2-8). In 753 B.C., Hosea likens Israel to an adulterous wife that will be punished by God, then eventually restored. He prophesies that Judah will be temporarily spared. *Fulfillment:* History. Israel—the northern kingdom—was exiled by the Assyrians in 722 B.C. Judah was spared for another 130 years.

Micah (Micah 1:2-3:12). In 742 B.C. Micah prophesied judgment against Samaria (the capital of the northern kingdom) and Jerusalem. Many details were given, including a later reuniting of Israel. *Fulfillment:* History. When Samaria fell, the capture of the northern kingdom by the Assyrians was complete. Later Jerusalem was besieged and captured.

Isaiah (Isaiah 7:18-25; 9:8-10:4). In 740 B.C., Isaiah prophesied the defeat of Israel at the hands of the Assyrians and the captivity of the northern kingdom. He also prophesied a later defeat of Judah, the southern kingdom. *Fulfillment:* History.

Habakkuk (Habakkuk 1:1-11). In 612 B.C. Habakkuk prophesied that the Babylonians would sweep through and defeat Judah. Details given include the siege of various cities. *Fulfillment:* History.

Jeremiah (Jeremiah 5:1-19; 6:1-30; 7:30-34). In 627 B.C. Jeremiah prophesied many details about the judgment of the exile, including the devastation to come. He also predicted that the Ben Hinnom Valley would be named the "Valley of Slaughter." *Fulfillment:* History.

Ezekiel (Ezekiel 6:1-14; 7:1-27; 8:17-18). Ezekiel actually became a prophet in 593 B.C. after he was in exile (along with Daniel and others). He made many specific exile prophecies.

I concluded that the many specific prophecies of the first exile of the Jews, confirmed by history and archaeology, had a probability of coming true randomly of *much smaller than 1 in 10—each.*

Prophecies of the Exact Timing of the First Exile

Jeremiah specifically prophesied that King Nebuchadnezzar would begin the exile of the Israelites to servitude in Babylon. The prophecy was made in the first year of Nebuchadnezzar's reign, prior to his defeat of Judah (Jeremiah 25), and it specifically limited the time of the servitude in exile to seventy years (verse 12). *Fulfillment:* We find in history that the exile began in 606 B.C. (when Daniel and other key leaders were taken) and that the Jews were allowed to start returning in 537 B.C., 70 years later.

Later Jeremiah prophesied a second 70-year period of exile—the time from the total destruction of Jerusalem until the final return was completed—when the Temple would be rebuilt (Jeremiah 29:10-14). *Fulfillment:* History shows that the exile was complete after the capture of Jerusalem in 587–586 B.C., exactly 70 years later.

I concluded that the prophecies of the exact length of the Jews' exile—over two different periods, and as confirmed by history and archaeology—had a probability of *far less than 1 in 100* of being fulfilled randomly.

A Prophecy Naming the Person Who Would Allow the Return of the Jews

Isaiah prophesied in about 700 B.C. that a leader named "Cyrus" would allow the Jews to return to rebuild Jerusalem and the Temple:

> [The LORD] says of *Cyrus*, "He is my shepherd and will accomplish all that I please; *he will say of Jerusalem, "Let it be rebuilt," and of the temple, "Let its foundations be laid."*
>
> This is what the LORD says to his anointed, to *Cyrus*, whose right hand I take hold of to subdue nations before him and to strip kings of their armor, to open up doors before him so that gates will not be shut: I will go before you and will level the mountains, I will break down gates of bronze and cut through bars of iron. I will give you the treasures of darkness, riches stored in secret places, so that you may know that I am the LORD, the God of Israel, *who summons you by name* (Isaiah 44:28–45:3).

This is a very specific prophecy naming a future leader, "Cyrus," whom God would enable to defeat the Babylonians and whom God would summon by name to allow Israel to return to the land and rebuild Jerusalem and the Temple. Isaiah made this prophecy more than 100 years before Jerusalem and the Temple were even destroyed—about *160* years before Cyrus was born! *Fulfillment:* The Persians conquered Babylon. Cyrus became king and allowed the Jews to return to rebuild the city and the Temple precisely as prophesied.

Modern archaeology has even located an ancient artifact, the "Cyrus cylinder," which shows the actual decree Cyrus gave that allowed the Israelites to return to their land and rebuild.[1]

I concluded that this prophecy of the exact name of the person who would allow the Jews to return to their homeland—confirmed by history and archaeology—had a probability of vastly less than 1 in 100 of being fulfilled by chance.

These prophecies of the first exile really got my attention. What were the odds of these prophets correctly predicting by chance

- the total destruction of two capital cities
- exile of the northern kingdom by the Assyrians
- exile of the southern kingdom 130 years later at the hand of the Babylonians
- the exact length of the exile
- the name of the person who would overthrow Babylonia and decree the return of the Jews to their homeland?

Already I was overwhelmed by the statistical odds against just these prophecies. Now I was eager to proceed to see what else could be uncovered.

Prophecies of the Second Jewish Exile and the Survival and Return of the Jews

Several key prophecies I found indicated that the Jews would be exiled a second time, but that their identity would be maintained and they would later return to their homeland.

In that day the LORD will reach out his hand *a second time...* He will raise a banner for the nations and gather the exiles of Israel; he will assemble the scattered people of Judah *from the four quarters of the earth* (Isaiah 11:11-12).

Say to them, "This is what the Sovereign LORD says: I will take the Israelites out of the nations where they have gone. *I will gather them from all around and bring them back into their own land.* I will make them one nation in the land, on the mountains of Israel. There will be one king over all of them and they will never again be two nations or be divided into two kingdoms" (Ezekiel 37:21-22).

"To your offspring I will give this land" (God speaking to Abraham in Genesis 12:7).

"I will make you into a great nation and I will bless you; *I will make your name great,* and you will be a blessing. I will bless those who bless you, and whoever curses you I will curse; and all peoples on earth will be blessed through you" (God to Abraham in Genesis 12:2-3).

Fulfillment: History. In 1948, Israel became a nation, nearly 2000 years after the Jews had been dispersed from their homeland. *Never before in the history of the world has an ethnic group been separated from its homeland for more than a few generations and yet maintained its identity.* Not only did the Jews maintain their identity, as indicated in Genesis 12:2-3, but against all odds, they returned to the land God had promised Abraham through his son Isaac. And since that time, Israel has survived several attempts to destroy it—against great odds.

Concerning the prophecy that the name of Abraham—the father of the Jews—would become great, consider this: The Jewish population represents about three-tenths of 1 percent of the world population—in other words, 34 people out of 10,000. Yet we hear far more about the Jews than we do about many cultures, races, and religions of dramatically greater population size.

These prophecies about the Jews—confirmed by history and events that we can observe today—have a probability of being fulfilled by chance that is small beyond reason.

The statistical prophecy testing I was going through was hitting me like a ton of bricks. My rational mind told me it was impossible. After all, hadn't man written the Bible? Yet, something was quite amazing—almost frightening. How could books written centuries in advance predict the future? And with 100-percent accuracy? The evidence already looked overwhelming. How could all the details of the first exile be predicted so accurately? How could anyone know the exact *name* of a future ruler who would allow the Jews to return from an exile that hadn't happened yet, to rebuild a city and Temple that hadn't been destroyed yet? And that ruler hadn't even been born yet. But all this was predicted well over a hundred years in advance of the events! And finally, with absolutely no precedent, how could anyone even think the Jews would exist after 2000 years of exile, let alone return a second time to their promised land? The odds against these prophecies alone had to be overwhelming.

I had to verify the evidence. So I went to encyclopedias and to libraries, and used other resources to validate dates and events. I realized these resources would certainly not be biased in favor of the Jews. If anything, they would tend to dismiss prophetic claims. To my surprise, I found the events precisely paralleled the events as recorded by the Jews.

The only minor caveat I found was that ancient dating sometimes varied by a year or two. The reason is that ancient dates were usually defined based on the time of a particular ruler's reign, and different systems were used in determining when a particular king's reign started. What formed the most accurate basis for the dating of the kings of Israel (from 893–666 B.C.) was a very accurate account from Assyria that was discovered (the eponym lists). This archaeological find pinpointed the dates of Assyrian kings during that period and also made references to Israel and its kings, allowing us to verify those dates as well. All dates can be coordinated with the present because of an eclipse that occurred at the time—which we can confirm today. Then multiple references in different books of the Tanakh allow us to relate the Jewish prophets to the kings of their time.[2]

I found that archaeology had confirmed *many* details of the exile period, right down to finding an ancient receipt for goods provided to the family of Judah's king Jehoiachin in Babylon (where he was kept in exile). The Bible had precisely indicated that Jehoiachin was given a daily ration (2 Kings 25:27-30).[3]

Four Hundred Years of History Prophesied

As amazing as these prophetic findings were, I had only begun. In reading Daniel chapter 8, I came across an interesting prophecy that is intricate in detail and covers many events over a long period of time.

In about 550 B.C., while in captivity in Babylon, Daniel made an extraordinarily detailed prophecy. In fact, as I confirmed in my research, he accurately prophesied the next 400 years of history that involved Israel. The prophecy used the image of a ram with two horns—one horn being longer—raging east and west and defeating everyone. Then a goat with a single large horn suddenly appeared, furiously attacking the ram and breaking off his two horns and trampling him (Daniel 8:1-14). The images continue with the goat's large horn breaking off at the height of its power and then being replaced with four smaller horns. A small horn came from one of these horns, and it grew in power to the south and east toward the "beautiful land," where it would take over the daily sacrifice from the "Prince of the host" and take over the sanctuary.

If the prophecy had stopped there, it would have been of little value to a skeptic like me, since its imagery is vague and nondescript. However, as I read further, the angel Gabriel precisely interpreted the vision for Daniel. All this was written down in the time of Daniel, long before the events took place.

As I studied the evidence, I found that virtually 400 years of history were precisely foretold.

- The Babylonian Empire was in power in the region at the time (Daniel was in exile in Babylon when this prophecy was made).

- The ram with two horns was the kings of Media and Persia, with the longer horn being the ruler of Persia

(Cyrus) who grew in prominence. *Fulfillment:* History indicates that the Medo-Persian Empire overthrew the Babylonian Empire. Cyrus became the dominant king.

- The goat with one large horn represented the Greek Empire, with the large horn representing its first ruler, Alexander the Great. This is particularly amazing, because at the time of the prophecy, 200 years before Alexander, Greece was a very weak country. No one would have thought it would become a world power.

    The goat's "crossing the whole earth without touching the ground" (8:5) indicates great speed of conquest. The speed with which Alexander conquered that portion of the world had never been seen before. *Fulfillment:* Starting in 326 B.C., it took Alexander only three years to establish the Greek Empire's control over much of the civilized world.

- At the height of its power, the large horn would be broken off. *Fulfillment:* Alexander the Great died suddenly at age 33, in 323 B.C.

- The four horns represented four kingdoms that would arise from the Greek nation, but would "not have the same power" (verse 22). *Fulfillment:* After his death, Alexander's conquests were divided between four of his generals, none of whom would attain the same power. The empire was split into the areas of Macedonia and Greece; Thrace, Bithynia, and most of Asia Minor; Syria and the territory east of Syria (including Babylon); and Egypt and Palestine.

- The small horn was described by Daniel as growing in power to the east and south toward the "beautiful land" (Israel) and eventually setting itself up to be as great as the "Prince of the host"; taking away daily sacrifice and "bringing low" the sanctuary (verses 9-11).

    Later in the chapter Daniel identifies the small horn as a "stern-faced king" who would take power in the latter part of the reign of "wicked rebels" in the land. This king would consider himself superior and would set himself up against the "Prince of princes" (that is, a heavenly authority—verses 11,25). He was described as destroying "the mighty men and the holy people." In the end, this king would "be destroyed, but not by human power" (verse 25).

Fulfillment: In history, these specific events were fulfilled precisely as well. The Seleucids (from the north) took control of Palestine. A particularly wicked king emerged, Antiochus IV Epiphanes (the "small horn" of verse 9), who put an end to Jewish worship and daily sacrifice. Jews were put to death for possessing the Scriptures.

Antiochus killed thousands of Jews who attempted to maintain their worship of God in spite of his decrees (destroying "the mighty men and the holy people"). He considered himself superior to all others, as reflected in the name "Epiphanes," which means "God manifest", and eventually rededicated the Jewish Temple to the Greek god Zeus and sacrificed a pig on the altar (detestable to the Jewish people)—thus fulfilling Daniel's prophecy about the "sanctuary."

This enraged the population and was the catalyst for the Maccabean revolt that ended up in defeat of that hated ruler, and the erection of a new altar and rededication on the 25th of Kislev, 164 B.C., exactly three years later. The success of the ensuing Maccabean revolt against the superior power of Antiochus could be viewed as "not by human power"(verse 25).

All the points of Daniel's prophecy have been confirmed by history—ancient writings and archaeology. All together, they have a probability of coming about randomly of *vastly* less than 1 in 100.

Again I was astounded by the precision of this prophecy. I began to expect to find many, many more such prophecies. Though most of those I allowed to pass my standards had evidence outside the Bible to support their fulfillment, in my research I was also learning to respect the historical accuracy of the Jewish Bible itself.

Prophecies About Cities, Nations, and Peoples

I found scores of prophecies about cities, nations, and peoples. Almost all gave surprising detail about the future. Here are two prophecies about foreign cities, prophecies that especially impressed me. (See appendix B for summaries of many others.)

- *The defeat of Assyria and Nineveh, its capital* (Isaiah 10:5-34). Isaiah made this prophecy in about 735 B.C.

- The King of Assyria would be punished for "willful pride" (verse 12). *Fulfillment:* The historical fall to Babylon in 612 B.C.

- Although destruction of the ten northern tribes of Israel by Assyria had been assured (Isaiah 7:18-25), Jerusalem was to be spared (10:32-34). Even Assyria's route to the intended conquest of Jerusalem was predicted (verses 28-32). *Fulfillment:* History, exactly as prophesied. Despite the odds, Jerusalem was spared destruction at the hands of the Assyrians.

- A remnant of Israel (the ten northern tribes) would return (verse 21). *Fulfillment:* History. A remnant of Jews returned from captivity following the destruction of Nineveh.

- Destruction decreed upon the whole land of the Assyrians (verse 23). *Fulfillment:* History. The Babylonians entirely destroyed the Assyrian kingdom.

The future of the city of Tyre (Ezekiel 26). Tyre was among the mightiest Mediterranean trading ports of Ezekiel's day (his prophecy was made about 586 B.C.). It was a New York or Hong Kong of its time. Tyre rejoiced in the destruction of Judah, with the notion that perhaps further business would come to them (verses 1-2). Many details of Tyre's destruction were predicted—the destruction of both its mainland stronghold and the island portion of the city.

- Nebuchadnezzar of Babylon would be brought from the north to lay siege to Tyre and destroy it (verses 7-9). *Fulfillment:* History. The mainland city was conquered by Babylonian siege, but not the island city.

- Many nations would attack Tyre (verse 3). *Fulfillment:* History.

- Its walls and towers would be destroyed, and the rubble would be scraped away, making it a "bare rock" (verse 4). *Fulfillment:* History. The rubble of the mainland city was scraped away into the sea—by the Greeks under Alexander the Great in order to make a causeway to lay siege to the previously unreachable island portion of the city.

- Fishermen would spread their nets where there was commerce before (verse 5). *Fulfillment:* History. The island part of the city is beneath the sea.

- Tyre would "never be rebuilt" (verses 7-14). *Fulfillment:* History. There is a city named Tyre, but much smaller and in a different location. The great island city itself is under water.

- Nearby rulers would surrender without a fight (verse 16). *Fulfillment:* After the amazing conquest of the island portion of Tyre by Alexander the Great, nearby rulers surrendered.

I was stunned at the number of prophecies I'd tested that were 100-percent accurate, most with additional historical support outside the Bible. Just the ones I'd already listed made me eager to start to estimate probabilities of their all coming true.

And if those didn't provide enough statistical evidence, I also found 80 more prophecies that met my standards! (I've listed these in appendix B.)

I believed I had discovered something of great importance that could literally prove the existence of God—by detecting his influence in the Jewish Bible. Being a skeptic, though, I wanted to at least place some probability parameters of odds around these prophecies so that I could feel justified in doing further study.

16

Does Perfect Prophecy Prove That the Jewish God Is Real?

The Old Testament appeared to pass the test of perfect prophecy. But how would it stack up to the human standard set by scientists—that the random occurrence of anything with a probability of less than 1 chance in 10^{50} is essentially impossible? I wanted to estimate the odds of all these prophecies coming true as conservatively as I could.

To answer the statistical question, I needed to estimate how likely it would be to have each of these individual prophecies come true randomly. Then I could estimate the multiple probability of their all coming true simply by using statistical conventions.

It was not easy to determine the odds of specific events happening since opinions could vary widely. In the beginning I was quite concerned about this. But soon I realized that the number of correct prophecies in the Old Testament was so large that I could assign just about any probability to any specific one. For example, if someone wanted to estimate that the odds of the exiled Jews surviving as an ethnic group and returning to Israel was 1 in 10 rather than 1 in 10,000,000, that would be okay. Or say that the odds that the name of Cyrus would be prophesied years before he was born was also 1 in 10 rather than 1 in 1,000,000, that would be okay too. In other words, there were *so many correct prophecies* that it made little difference what odds were assigned to a particular prophecy. (So feel free to throw out any prophecies you don't like or change the probabilities.)

To keep it simple and conservative, I assumed that each prophesied event had a chance of only 1 in 10 of occurring randomly. This was extremely conservative. After all, what were the real odds of the Jews surviving as a people after their exile, then returning to their homeland 2000 years later? The odds of this alone had to be one out of millions. Or Daniel's prophecy of 400 years of history, the predictions of the exact timing of the first exile, or the naming of Cyrus. The odds of any of these prophesies coming true were extremely remote. Just the sheer quantity of fulfilled historical prophecies was far beyond random chance. And I had counted 118 specific, historical prophecies in the Jewish Bible that fit my acceptability criteria!

Mathematically, the probability of all 118 of these prophecies coming true randomly, if we assign the probability of only 1 in 10 to each, is

$$\frac{1}{10^{118}}$$

In other words, 1/10 x 1/10 x 1/10, and so on, 118 times. How large is this number? Here are some comparisons.

1. It would be like winning 17 state lotteries in a row with a single ticket for each.

2. It would be like dividing all time since the beginning of the universe (an estimated 15 billion years) into seconds, randomly "marking" 7 of those seconds, then correctly guessing by chance every one of the 7 designated seconds.

3. It would be like being struck by lightning 24 times in one year.

From my highly conservative model, I could already see that the prophetic phenomenon of the Jewish Bible would be regarded as impossible by science because the odds of its random occurrence were far, far less than 1 chance in 10^{50}. Therefore, I reasoned, a supernatural God must have inspired the prophets and original writings. My logical extension of this was that the God who provided the information in the Old Testament must be the real God.

As the "ultimate skeptic," I went one step further. I selected only the prophecies whose fulfillment occurred centuries later and which were confirmed by history outside the Bible, assigned reasonable odds, and calculated the probabilities.

Prophecy	My Guesstimate of Odds
1. Isaiah's naming of Cyrus nearly two centuries in advance (Isaiah 44:28–45:3).	$1/10,000$
2. Daniel's 400 years of precisely predicted history (Daniel 8).	$1/1,000,000$
3. Prophecies by five prophets of the total destruction of Ammon, Edom, and Moab.	$1/10,000,000$
4. The detailed prophecy of the destruction of Tyre, hundreds of years in advance (Ezekiel 26).	$1/100,000$
5. The prophecy of the destruction of Nineveh more than 100 years in advance (Isaiah 10:5-34).	$1/1,000,000$
6. The destruction of the Amalekites predicted 450 years in advance (Exodus 17:14).	$1/10,000$
7. Jerusalem to be rebuilt from the "Tower of Hananel to the Corner Gate" (Jeremiah 31:38-40).	$1/1000$
8. Detailed prophecies of the first Jewish exile by seven prophets— some more than a century in advance.	$1/100,000$
9. The ultimate Jews' survival of their dispersion and their return to their homeland in 1948 (Isaiah 11:12; Ezekiel 37:21-22).	$1/100,000$
10. Israel's survival since 1948 despite being heavily outnumbered during many conflicts (Amos 9:14-15).	$1/10,000,000$

The cumulative probability of just the prophecies above all coming true randomly is 1 chance in 10^{53}. Again, this falls outside of what is regarded as possible by scientists.

This was another defining point for me. My conclusions were:

• • •

1. *God definitely exists—proven statistically by the 100-percent fulfilled prophecy in the Jewish Bible (the Tanakh).*

2. *The Jewish Bible was inspired by God.*

• • •

17

Was There Other Ancient Prophecy That Was Valid?

At this point I wondered whether the Jews had been right all along. Was the God of Judaism the one true God? Or had God revealed himself through perfect prophecy in other religions?

———•———

His skin was very dark and his shaggy beard was coal black. His eyes were deep brown. But his most distinctive feature, by far, was the reddish-purple turban he wore. I was fascinated by the intricate care with which it seemed woven around his head. I wondered why many Eastern people wore turbans.

"Do you know what this turban is for?" asked my new acquaintance Arun, as he noticed my stare.

"No," I responded.

"Our family is of the Sikh religion," he said. "Men are not permitted to cut their hair, and therefore we wrap it up in special turbans."

I was having dinner with Arun and his wife, Vinita. They were highly Americanized Sikhs who had done quite well in the business world as entrepreneurs in the health care industry. I was discussing the prospect of adding a travel division to their enterprise. They were among the most friendly people I had ever met, and I was very curious to learn about their religion, which they called Sikhism.

"Exactly what is Sikhism?" I asked.

"It is a derivation of Hinduism," Arun said. "However, we also recognize other religions as well, in particular Islam. Since Islam ties into Judaism and Christianity, naturally there's a tie there too."

"But what do you believe?" I asked. "If there a God? If so, who is he?"

"Of course we believe there is a God," Arun stated matter-of-factly. "We believe in one God, just like the Muslims, Christians, and Jews." (I later learned that this is a point where Sikhism differs from classical Hinduism—many Hindu sects believe in a multiplicity of gods.)

"Then describe God," I asked as I leaned forward, very interested in Arun's answers.

"We view God as life—essentially in everything," he said. "By the way, many Hindus believe that as well."

His wife Vinita, eagerly entering the conversation, said, "Doesn't that make sense, that God would be in everything? Why would a God of the universe be simply a God of one religious group?"

"I don't know," I said. "I do know that wars are fought over the definition of God all the time. Religion seems to be one of the biggest reasons for war throughout the ages, so I guess most of the world thinks its own 'God' is pretty special."

"Sikhs are very peace-loving and tolerant of other religions," Arun continued. "We respect all the world religions."

"What do you base your religion on?" I asked. "Is there some person or holy book?"

Vinita answered. "We were originally founded by Guru Nanak about the year A.D. 1500. Nanak became a teacher of Hindu priests and eventually redefined Hinduism according to Sikhism. A line of gurus continued this teaching. Our holy scripture is the Granth Sahib, which in English means the 'Lord's Book.' And similar to the Muslims, we have daily prayer. As a matter of fact, in our home we have a separate prayer room that you're welcome to see when we return home, if you want."

"Yes, I would like to see it," I quickly said, afraid she would retract the offer. "Tell me—is your guru a prophet? Or were any of the past gurus prophets?"

"Of course," Arun broke in. "They are all prophets."

"How do you know?" I asked.

"Well, through the centuries they have given us wisdom to guide our lives. It has provided much peace and meaning to Sikhs," Arun said.

"Yes, I suppose I can understand that," I responded. "But I mean, what proof do you have? What historical prophecies have they made that precisely and accurately foretold the future?"

Vinita jumped in and said, "Our definition of a prophet is not a fortune-teller. A prophet is a wise man who counsels and guides the Sikhs."

Arun added, "Our prophets do talk about the future and what happens after death, though."

"What does happen at death?" I queried.

Vinita answered, "We believe you obtain salvation by submitting to God. Once salvation is achieved, your soul is absorbed into God and you essentially become one."

"Do you believe in reincarnation?" I asked.

"Yes," Vinita answered.

"How about your holy books—do they contain any history-based prophecy, or what you referred to earlier as 'fortune-telling'?" I asked.

"First, understand that, although we are Hindu-based and most of our religion agrees with the Hindu Upanishads and the Bhagavad Gita, our special holy book is the Granth Sahib, which we believe is divinely inspired," Arun said. "I don't know if it has the kind of fortune-telling prophecy you refer to. But we don't think that what you are calling prophecy has anything to do with something being from God."

"Why don't you know if it has prophecy or not?" I asked, puzzled.

"For one thing," Arun explained, "it was originally written in six different languages. So there are very few people in the world that can even read the original scripture."

Vinita quickly added, "The writings were actually gathered together by the fifth guru after Nanak, Arjan, so we are very certain it was inspired by God. To us it is very holy."

I decided to change the subject to business. We continued our meal as I wondered how such a religion could justify its claim to be from "God." It sounded like prophecy wasn't part of the religion. Then again, I thought that perhaps this religion—and maybe all religions—are really based more on family heritage and on "faith" without really having any evidence. *If so, how do we know what's right?* I wondered. *Or maybe the Hindus and Sikhs are right that "God" is in all religions.*

After dinner, I drove them home. Upon our arrival, Vinita said excitedly, "Do you want to come inside for a while and see the prayer room we told you about?"

"Certainly!" I responded.

A spacious mansion was in front of me. Inside, it was decorated with ornate features, including cut glass and rich Eastern-style art. In a word—it was beautiful.

"We built it ourselves," Arun stated proudly.

"Incredible job," I commented.

After a tour, we ended up at the prayer room. It was sunken down a step and centered on what appeared to be an altar. Above the altar was a picture of a guru. I assumed it was the guru who had put together the Sikh holy book.

"Our prayer life is very important to us," Arun said. "I pray several times a day. We have prescribed prayers that involve a lot of repetition of the name of God."

I was a bit in awe. I thought, *How many houses in the United States have a prayer room? Very few, I would guess.*

After more discussion and some hot tea, I bid my friends goodbye and thanked them for their hospitality. They were certainly right about Sikhs being friendly, at least based on my experience with them. But I couldn't help but wonder how the religion could support its claim of God's involvement.

———•———

The conversation with Arun and Vinita had piqued my interest in Eastern religions, so I decided to look into them, hoping to find historically provable prophecy. I did some research and found out that the Hindu religion was started about the same time as the Jewish religion (the time of Abraham). The Sikhs, as well as various sects of Buddhism, all have roots in Hinduism, as do the Hare Krishnas, and many of them were formed centuries before the time of Jesus.

I also discovered that these religions are essentially philosophy-based. Historical events, along with prophecy connected with those events, do not form their foundations. Traditions, rituals, and sheer faith seemed to be the primary components of the Eastern religions. There was absolutely nothing I could find that could provide me any confidence in their various beliefs.

18

Testable Prophecy in the New Testament

I had enormous doubts about the viability of any "mystical" philosophy-based religion. But the God of the Old Testament was certainly real. I had proven it to myself from history—with hard, statistical analysis. I was fully aware that God had emphatically stated in the law of Moses that he was the one God, a jealous God, and that no other gods should be placed before him. So a lot of questions started flowing through my mind when I started to consider going further in the Bible—for instance, why did the Christians add the New Testament? Where did it stand in prophecy?

The New Testament deals primarily with Jesus Christ—whom Christians believe is the Messiah, the "Anointed One" and Savior promised in the Old Testament. But why would the Jews reject Jesus if he was their promised Messiah? I thought back to my long-ago conversation with Rob Blaine about having "death insurance" just by believing in Jesus. It reminded me of a very well-known verse, John 3:16:

> God so loved the world that he gave his one and only Son, that whoever *believes* in him shall not perish but have eternal life.

Why was simply "believing" in Jesus so upsetting to the Jews? As I studied the New Testament carefully, the answer quickly became apparent. Jesus was claiming to be God!

Jesus' claim to be God was throughout the New Testament, which reported the Jewish religious leaders as very upset by it. I found some examples.

- "I and the Father are one" (Jesus, in John 10:30).

- "Anyone who has seen me has seen the Father. How can you say, 'Show us the Father'? Don't you believe that I am in the Father, and that the Father is in me?" (Jesus, in John 14:9-10).

- "I tell you the truth," Jesus answered, "before Abraham was born, I am" (John 8:58). The statement "I am" was tantamount to a claim to be God (see Exodus 3:14).

- Jesus acknowledged several times that he was the Messiah (Mark 14:61-63; John 4:25-26; Luke 9:20). Mark 14:61-63 implied that a claim to deity was included in Jesus' claim to be the Christ (the Messiah).

- Jesus referred to himself as the Son of God and, more often, Son of Man, both of which spoke of his deity—something the Jewish leaders would have clearly understood from a prophecy by Daniel:

    In my vision at night I looked, and there before me was one like a *son of man*, coming with the clouds of heaven. He approached the Ancient of Days and was led into his presence. He was given authority, glory and sovereign power; all peoples, nations and men of every language *worshiped him*. His dominion is an everlasting dominion that will not pass away, and his kingdom is one that will never be destroyed (Daniel 7:13-14).

At a critical point in Jesus' trial, before his crucifixion, he was asked a question he was required to answer by law:

    The high priest said to him, "I charge you under oath by the living God: Tell us if you are the Christ, the Son of God."

"Yes, it is as you say," Jesus replied. "But I say to all
of you: In the future you will see the Son of Man sitting
at the right hand of the Mighty One and coming on the
clouds of heaven."

Then the high priest tore his clothes and said, "He
has spoken blasphemy! Why do we need any more witnesses? Look, now you have heard the blasphemy"
(Matthew 26:63-65).

Not only did the high priest officially declare that Jesus had
blasphemed, but his tearing of his clothes was a sign of mourning
and revulsion over blasphemy.

———————•———————

I could see a real challenge on my hands. I had just proven the
God of the Old Testament, who commanded that only he be worshiped. Now I realized that, in the New Testament, Jesus is
claiming to be God too. But the Christians said they believed in
the God of the Old Testament. This seemed to me to be a contradiction. *Are there two Gods?* I thought half-seriously, half-jokingly.

But after all those hours of church and Sunday school, I had
some sort of idea of God's having a triune nature in my head,
though I'd never understood it.

"In the name of the Father, the Son, and the Holy Ghost..." I
remembered how those words had confused me as a 14-year-old.
I'd heard all the talk—that a single God was somehow mixed up
into three "persons." But how was I supposed to understand that?
Are they three, or are they one? Three can't also be one, can it? To
say the least, I was puzzled. At a minimum, I would have to reconcile this with Jesus' claim to be God in addition to the "heavenly
God." Then there was the issue of the Holy Spirit.

It all seemed confusing. Why did the early church change—so
it seemed—from the clear, singular God in a singular form to the
concept of three persons in a singular God? It was not surprising
that even the Christians I talked to had great difficulty trying to
explain it. But before getting too bogged down by the concept of
God being three in one, I decided to test Jesus' claim to be the
Messiah.

Beginning My Research
on Prophecies About Jesus

Using the same methods I had already used on the Old Testament, I started looking in it for prophecies relating to Jesus. Again I was stunned. *The entire Old Testament (yes, the Jewish Bible) was filled with prophecies that seemed to match Jesus*—details about his life, death, and resurrection. Whole chapters of books contained considerable numbers of prophecies that seemed to be about Jesus.

But could these prophecies pass my standards? Could I trust that the prophecies were actually recorded before the time of Jesus? Or did the Christians somehow go back and put them into the Jewish Bible? I wanted to have some assurance of their trustworthiness before going too deeply into studying them.

My Basic Assumptions

I realized that my test of prophecies about Jesus relied on two important questions:

1. Was there adequate time distance between the recording of the prophecies in the Old Testament and the record of the fulfillment in the New Testament?

2. Were the New Testament accounts of Jesus accepted as accurate and as fulfillment of prophecy by the early Jews who were close to the events?

I discovered several things that helped establish credibility of the prophetic records. As a foundation, I found that there was a 400-year period between the final prophecies of the coming of a Messiah (recorded in the Jewish Scriptures) and their apparent fulfillment through Jesus. During this time several important things happened.

- The *Tanakh* (Jewish Scripture) canon was popularly recognized.

- The *"Dead Sea scrolls"* were written, including copies of every book in the Tanakh except the book of Esther.

- The *Septuagint* (the Greek translation of the Tanakh) was made.

- *Other translations* of the Tanakh were made.

These events of the 400-year period were important for the following reasons:

- The *Tanakh canon* (those books recognized as divinely inspired Scripture) had been popularly established by about 167 B.C. So by the time Jesus was teaching, there was widespread knowledge among his thousands of hearers of what was meant by "Scripture." There were no doubts about which books were and were not included. In A.D. 70 exactly the same books of Scripture used by Jesus and others were recognized as the official canon by the Jewish religious authorities—the same books in use today by both Jews and Christians.

- The *Dead Sea scrolls* consist of some 900 manuscripts and include all books of the Tanakh except Esther (with multiple copies of most books). A substantial portion of the Tanakh copies were written more than 200 years before Jesus—as indicated by both radiometric dating and paleography (the study of ancient writing). The scrolls were stored in a cave by a Jewish religious sect, the Essenes, just prior to the Roman conquest in A.D. 70 and remained untouched until about 1947, when the first ones were discovered, in Qumran by the Dead Sea (not far from Jerusalem). Hence, they were like a "time capsule."

  The scrolls have been compared to the modern copies and have been found to agree, virtually letter-for-letter. (Most of the differences are in the spelling of names.) The point is, the Dead Sea scrolls essentially "froze in time" the prophecies about Jesus—long before he was born.

- The *Septuagint* is a translation from Hebrew into Greek of the Tanakh made by an appointed team of some 70 scholars ("Septuagint" comes from the word for "seventy"). Since many Jews of the time (about 280 B.C.) spoke

Greek, this official translation was intended to enable everyone to read holy Scripture. (The earliest manuscript portions now in existence are parts of the Torah, copied before 200 B.C.)

The Septuagint is especially important in verifying prophecy, because some scholars contend in retrospect that translations of the original Hebrew made after Jesus' time may have not clearly reflected the original meaning. However, the Septuagint clearly demonstrates the Jewish understanding of the Scriptures at a time *well* before Jesus arrived! It was translated by 70 of the best scholars of the time—scholars who were placing their best understanding of the Hebrew meaning into Greek and who used ancient Hebrew on a daily basis. Furthermore, the Hebrew texts from which they worked were much closer to the originals than the ones we have today.

- *Other translations* of the Tanakh—into several different languages—were made before Jesus' time. All of these also help to document the detailed prophecies of a coming Messiah.

The Septuagint Helps Us Understand the Hebrew Texts

Much is often made of the word for "virgin" in Isaiah 7:14 ("The Lord himself will give you a sign: The virgin will be with child and will give birth to a son"). Some have contended that the Hebrew word translated "virgin"—*almah*—simply means "young woman." This indeed is one of the possible meanings of the Hebrew. However, in the Septuagint the word clearly indicates the Jewish scholarly opinion before the time of Jesus. The Greek word is *parthenos* (also used in Matthew 1:23), which very specifically means "virgin."

Seventy esteemed scholars understood what the ancient Hebrew meant, and they translated this meaning into Greek. Naturally they would have no incentive to invent prophecy about Jesus more than 200 years before he was born. Hence when key words are in question, the Septuagint often clarifies the precise meanings of the ancient Hebrew far better than the critics of today.

I could see that there was a substantial body of evidence that any prophecies in the Tanakh about a coming Messiah and other future events were reliably recorded. They were clearly written before the fact, before Jesus of Nazareth was born. Scholars could see, touch, and study these documents. For me, the credibility of the prophetic record had been firmly established.

My Investigation of Prophecies About Jesus

The prophecies about Jesus that I had heard since childhood seemed pretty outlandish and meaningless. For example, who could ever prove that Jesus was born of a virgin? Nobody. As I had done with the Old Testament, I decided to ignore what I thought were unprovable prophecies, including this one. My goal was simply to see if there was any substantial evidence that Jesus was somehow "part" of God.

The Jewish Bible had already convinced me that the Jewish God was real. I was already convinced that the Jewish Bible contained a reliable record of the prophecies of the Messiah. Did Christianity really add anything with its ideas about Jesus? Was the Christians' claim that Jesus was part of a "Trinity-God" correct? Or was the New Testament a made-up "addendum" to support an unreal faith? Were Christians simply hanging onto a false belief about a "God–man"? I reminded myself again—"Test everything. Hold onto the good" (1 Thessalonians 5:21).

The Prophecies with Substance

Early on in my research of various Christian books, I wondered if Christians tried to stretch the words of the Old Testament prophecies to fit Jesus. One example they cited was Genesis 3:15:

> I will put enmity between you and the woman, and between your offspring and hers; he will crush your head, and you will strike his heel.

Christians said that this was a prophecy about Jesus. The serpent (Satan) strikes at the heel of the woman (through Jesus' crucifixion), and her offspring (Jesus) crushes Satan's head. Although this interpretation was possible, to me as a skeptic, the words from Genesis revealed nothing that was specific or provable. Frankly, it seemed like a really big stretch. There was nothing specific that identified Jesus with the offspring of Eve. The claim that striking at the heel was a symbol of crucifixion and crushing the head was Satan's final defeat by Jesus seemed very ambiguous. The only real tie seemed to be the relationship of a snake to Satan. Were all Christian claims like this? It made me wonder if Christians would interpret Scripture in any way possible to support their faith.

I continued to examine the prophecies about a coming Messiah. After looking at the details, I found many that seemed to be specific to Jesus.

In the Bible's oldest book, Job (from about 2000 B.C.) I found the first prophecy written about a "redeemer" who lives eternally (at both the time of Job and at the "end"). This redeemer was apparently identified as God, who would come to earth.

> I know that my *Redeemer* lives, and that in the end *he will stand upon the earth.* And after my skin has been destroyed, yet in my flesh *I will see God;* I myself will see him with my own eyes—I, and not another. How my heart yearns within me! (Job 19:25-27).

These words weren't definitely specific to Jesus. Yet they were specific to a Redeemer—one like Jesus as described in the New Testament. This prophecy piqued my interest in going further.

Upon continuing my investigation, I found what seemed to be a perfectly descriptive set of prophecies in Isaiah 53. As I worked with the text, I numbered the points that I judged to correspond with the words of the New Testament.

> Who has believed our message and to whom has the arm of the LORD been revealed? He grew up before him like a tender shoot, and like a root out of dry ground. He had no beauty or majesty to attract us to him, nothing in his appearance

that we should desire him ①. He was despised and rejected by men ②, a man of sorrows, and familiar with suffering ③. Like one from whom men hide their faces he was despised, and we esteemed him not ④.

Surely he took up our infirmities and carried our sorrows ⑤, yet we considered him stricken by God, smitten by him, and afflicted ⑥. But he was pierced for our transgressions ⑦, he was crushed for our iniquities; the punishment that brought us peace was upon him, and by his wounds we are healed ⑧. We all, like sheep, have gone astray, each of us has turned to his own way; and the LORD has laid on him the iniquity of us all ⑨.

He was oppressed and afflicted, yet he did not open his mouth ⑩; he was led like a lamb to the slaughter ⑪, and as a sheep before her shearers is silent, so he did not open his mouth ⑫. By oppression and judgment he was taken away ⑬. And who can speak of his descendants? For he was cut off from the land of the living; for the transgression of my people he was stricken ⑭. He was assigned a grave with the wicked ⑮, and with the rich in his death ⑯, though he had done no violence, nor was any deceit in his mouth ⑰.

Yet it was the LORD's will to crush him and cause him to suffer, and though the LORD makes his life a guilt offering ⑱, he will see his offspring and prolong his days, and the will of the LORD will prosper in his hand ⑲. After the suffering of his soul, he will see the light [of life] and be satisfied ⑳; by his knowledge my righteous servant will justify many, and he will bear their iniquities ㉑. Therefore I will give him a portion among the great ㉒, and he will divide the spoils with the strong ㉓, because he poured out his life unto death, and was numbered with the transgressors ㉔. For he bore the sin of many, and made intercession for the transgressors ㉕ (brackets in original).

Now this grabbed my attention! It seemed so descriptive of Jesus. I listed out the New Testament descriptions that corresponded to the points I'd found in Isaiah 53:

1. Jesus came to human beings in a fashion that would seem unattractive—as a baby. He worked as an ordinary carpenter.

2. He was despised and rejected.

3. He knew much suffering.

4. He was not esteemed.

5. He carried mankind's sorrows (sins).

6. People considered him "stricken by God," or afflicted.

7. He was "pierced" for man's transgressions.

8. He spoke of himself as giving his life for the "sheep." All human sin was borne by him.

9. His injuries brought healing.

10. When he was oppressed at his trial, he would not open his mouth except as legally required.

11. He was led to his crucifixion like a lamb to slaughter.

12. "As a sheep before her shearers is silent," Jesus did not defend himself at his trial.

13. He was taken away "by oppression and judgement."

14. He was "stricken" for the transgression (sin) of many.

15. He was crucified with two criminals and was supposed to have been buried with them.

16. A rich man, Joseph of Arimathea, asked for Jesus' body and placed it in his (Joseph's) tomb.

17. Jesus neither resisted by force, nor did he lie in his testimony before the Roman governor Pilate.

18. God the Father accepted Jesus' life as a "guilt offering."

19. God's will "prospered" through Jesus.

20. After suffering, Jesus again saw the light—upon his resurrection.

21. Jesus justified "many" and bore their sins.

22. God exalted him to greatness.

23. He divided the "spoils" with the "strong" (believers would prosper eternally).

24. He poured himself out to the point of death and was considered a sinful man (transgressor).

25. He carried the sins of the many and interceded with God for transgressors (sinners).

My conclusion was that Isaiah 53 matched the New Testament account of Jesus—in 25 specific points.

Isaiah 53

I later discovered that some Jewish groups have actually cut Isaiah 53 out of their Bibles because it so closely matches Jesus. Yet anyone visiting the Shrine of the Book in Jerusalem—the home of the Dead Sea scrolls—can clearly see this passage precisely as it was originally written.

19

A Description of the Messiah from Old Testament Prophecy

Okay, I thought to myself, *Isaiah 53 was pretty impressive. But if I were a God of the universe capable of revealing myself so clearly in biochemistry and the writings of the Old Testament, then what would I do to reveal my exact nature?* The Bible had already proven itself in regard to God's existence, but in order for me to believe that Jesus was somehow part of God, I expected there to be similar hard evidence that

- Jesus had fulfilled a plan preconceived by God
- Jesus had prophetic proof of his claims to be God

Regarding the first point, I decided to look at the prophecy information within the Old Testament as if I were writing a newspaper article. I'd look for prophecies about the "who, what, when, and where" of the Messiah and see what kind of a story I could put together.

Who

According to the Scriptures, the Messiah would come from the line of descent running through

- Shem (Genesis 9–10)
- Abraham (Genesis 22:18)

- Isaac (Genesis 26:4)
- Jacob (Genesis 28:14)
- Judah (Genesis 49:10)
- Jesse (Isaiah 11:1-5)
- King David (2 Samuel 7:11-16)

I investigated the New Testament fulfillment of these prophecies as reported in the accounts of Matthew (Matthew 1) and Luke (Luke 3:23-28). Luke investigated history by talking to eyewitnesses and by reviewing other accounts of Jesus (Luke 1:1). Matthew investigated the legal claim of Jesus to the kingship of Israel, which would have been of paramount importance to the Jews. The kingship of Jesus came from David through the line of Joseph, his stepfather (as recorded in Matthew), while his physical descent from David came through the line of Mary (as recorded in Luke). The difference in their perspectives was not surprising, since Matthew was a tax collector and had to be very aware of legal affairs, whereas Luke was a doctor.

I was fascinated to see how Jesus' dual descent tied in with another prophecy I had discovered. At the time of the Babylonian captivity (586 B.C.), God said that the king of Judah, Jehoiachin, would be cursed:

> This is what the LORD says: "Record this man as if childless, a man who will not prosper in his lifetime, for *none of his offspring will prosper, none will sit on the throne of David or rule anymore in Judah*" (Jeremiah 22:30).

This clearly states that none of Jehoiachin's *offspring* (the seed of his body) would inherit the throne of David, in apparent contradiction to the prophecy that the Messiah would come from the line of David (2 Samuel 7:11-13). I found that the Gospels' accounts of Jesus satisfy both of these prophecies and also the prophecy of a "virgin birth." Matthew reports that the line of kingship was passed on to Jesus, who was the legal heir of Joseph (who was identified as "the husband of Mary"), but not his physical "offspring." (Joseph didn't inseminate Mary—the Holy Spirit had "overshadowed" her—Luke 1:35.)

On the other hand, Jesus' physical descent through Mary, as recorded by Luke, still qualified him as the "son of David." Both accounts are consistent with prophecy. Both are consistent with both the divine nature and human nature of Jesus.

Isaiah 7:14

The Messiah would be called *Immanuel*—meaning "God with us." *Fulfillment:* This is precisely how Jesus was described by Matthew at the time of his birth (Matthew 1:23). And if Jesus' statements in the Gospel accounts were accurate, he was indeed "God with us."

The circumvention of the curse on Jehoiachin through an (alleged) virgin birth was fascinating to me, along with the accuracy of the other prophecies. It all had manuscript support. I was highly intrigued, and felt encouraged to press on with the study of other prophecy.

What

The Messiah's Life Was Vividly Described

Apart from Isaiah 53, I found many other prophetic references to the Messiah's activities, including

- teaching in parables (Psalm 78:2)
- riding into Jerusalem as a king, but on a donkey (Zechariah 9:9)
- being betrayed by a friend (Psalm 41:9)
- earning 30 pieces of silver that were then thrown in the Temple to a potter (Zechariah 11:12-13)
- being rejected by Israel (Isaiah 8:14)
- being mocked with lots cast for his clothing (Psalm 22:18)

- having his hands and feet pierced (Psalm 22)

- being given gall and wine (Psalm 69:21)

- being pierced (Zechariah 12:10)

- being buried in a rich man's grave (Isaiah 53:9)

- being raised from the grave (Psalm 16:10)

The Christian Gospels report these events and assert that Jesus fulfilled these prophecies.

Detailed evidence of Jesus being someone "special" (just as I previously had learned the God of the Bible was special) was accumulating rapidly. I was starting to realize that, statistically, I might be able to prove that all this was directed by God. I went further, gathering more details.

The Messiah Would Perform Certain Miracles

Ancient Israel believed that some miracles could be done *only by God,* including these prophesied by Isaiah:

> Say to those with fearful hearts, "Be strong, do not fear; your God will come, he will come with vengeance; with divine retribution *he will come to save you."* Then will the eyes of the *blind* be opened and the ears of the *deaf* unstopped. Then will the *lame* leap like a deer, and the *mute* tongue shout for joy (Isaiah 35:4-6).

The Gospel accounts, when I examined them, reported that the blind, deaf, lame, and mute were healed by Jesus (Matthew 9:27-30; 11:5; 15:30-31; 21:14; Mark 7:32-37; 10:51-52; Luke 7:22; John 5:3-15; 9:13-25). The verses of the prophecy that indicated God would "come to *save* you" also seemed to tie into the evidence about Jesus and the claims made by Christians—that Jesus' death on the cross was to somehow save us. And then, Jesus actually asked some disciples to report the miracles they had seen.

> Jesus replied, "Go back and report to John what you hear and see: The blind receive sight, the lame walk, those who have leprosy are cured, the deaf hear, the

dead are raised, and the good news is preached to the poor" (Matthew 11:4-5).

Again, one of the Gospels reported miracles that matched the prophecy in Isaiah. (I also encountered some secular writings that acknowledged them as well—including writings in the Jewish Talmud that called Jesus a "sorcerer.")

As a skeptic, I believed that miracles were by definition absurd. On the other hand, in my attempt to be an objective investigator, I had to remember that I had already acknowledged the trustworthiness of the Jewish Scriptures. And the Messiah's miracles were predicted in them. (At some point, however, I knew I would have to investigate the trustworthiness of the Gospel accounts also.)

The Role of the Messiah Was Explained

As I continued asking the "what?" question, I listed more prophecies that identified what the Messiah's role was to be (I had already gotten some indications from Job and Isaiah). He was to be

- a redeemer—one who would save people from their sins

- a prophet and a teacher

As a skeptic, these prophecies meant nothing to me regarding the "proof" that Jesus was God. In fact, maybe they even indicated an "agenda" on the part of the church to deify Jesus. On the other hand, I had to acknowledge that the Old Testament was very precise, indicating that

- a *blood sacrifice* was needed because of mankind's sin: "Sacrifice a bull each day as a sin offering to make atonement" (Exodus 29:36-37).

- *perfection* was required in the sacrifice: "When anyone brings from the herd or flock a fellowship offering to the LORD to fulfill a special vow or as a freewill offering, it must be without defect or blemish to be acceptable" (Leviticus 22:21).

- *God himself* would provide the sacrifice: "Abraham answered [Isaac], *'God himself will provide the lamb* for the burnt offering, my son.' And the two of them went on together" (Genesis 22:8).

I realized immediately that the near-sacrifice of Isaac by Abraham seemed to be a model of the Christian claim about God providing Jesus as the perfect sacrificial "lamb." Despite my skepticism, it seemed strange that God would be so specific in something so hard to comprehend, and then carry it out exactly as he had indicated. It made me think that perhaps my rational, logical mind did not know all the answers.

The Death of the Messiah

Psalm 22 was written about 600 years before crucifixion was even invented. Nonetheless, it struck me as a vivid portrayal of a death by crucifixion, and it seemed to match the events of Jesus' death on the cross.

As I had done with Isaiah 53, I numbered the points in the text.

My God, my God, why have you forsaken me? ① Why are you so far from saving me, so far from the words of my groaning? O my God, I cry out by day, but you do not answer, by night, and am not silent.

Yet you are enthroned as the Holy One ②; you are the praise of Israel. In you our fathers put their trust ③; they trusted and you delivered them. They cried to you and were saved; in you they trusted and were not disappointed.

But I am a worm and not a man, scorned by men and despised by the people ④. All who see me mock me; they hurl insults, shaking their heads: "He trusts in the Lord; let the Lord rescue him ⑤. Let him deliver him, since he delights in him."

Yet you brought me out of the womb; you made me trust in you even at my mother's breast. From birth I was cast upon you; from my mother's womb you have been my God ⑥. Do not be far from me, for trouble is near and there is no one to help ⑦. Many bulls surround me; strong bulls of Bashan encircle me. Roaring lions tearing their prey open their mouths wide against me ⑧. I am poured out like water, and all my bones are out of joint ⑨. My heart has turned to wax; it has melted away within me. My strength is dried up like a potsherd, and my tongue sticks to the roof of my mouth ⑩; you lay me in the dust of death ⑪. Dogs have surrounded me; a band of evil men has encircled me ⑫, they have pierced my hands and my feet ⑬. I can count all my bones ⑭; people stare and gloat over me ⑮. They divide my garments among them and cast lots for my clothing ⑯.

But you, O LORD, be not far off; O my Strength, come quickly to help me. Deliver my life from the sword, my precious life from the power of the dogs. Rescue me from the mouth of the lions; save me from the horns of the wild oxen.

I will declare your name to my brothers; in the congregation I will praise you. You who fear the LORD, praise him! All you descendants of Jacob, honor him ⑰! Revere him, all you descendants of Israel! For he has not despised or disdained the suffering of the afflicted one; he has not hidden his face from him but has listened to his cry for help.

From you comes the theme of my praise in the great assembly; before those who fear you will I fulfill my vows ⑱. The poor will eat and be satisfied; they who seek the LORD will praise him—may your hearts live forever ⑲! All the ends of the earth will remember and turn to the LORD, and he rules over the nations ⑳.

All the rich of the earth will feast and worship; all who go down to the dust will kneel before him—those who cannot keep themselves alive ㉑. Posterity will serve him; future generations will be told about the Lord. They will proclaim his righteousness to a people yet unborn ㉒—for he has done it ㉓.

Though written by David some 1000 years prior to Jesus' time, this one psalm (often called the "crucifixion psalm" by Christians) still seemed to provide many details about the death of Jesus as recorded by the Gospel authors. These authors had even pointed out what they regarded as Jesus' fulfillments of Psalm 22. I noted 23 prophetic details that corresponded with the New Testament accounts.

1. In the first words he spoke on the cross—"My God, my God, why have you forsaken me?"—Jesus called the onlookers' attention to this prophetic psalm. It was an indication that prophecy in God's Word was going to be fulfilled.

2. Jesus acknowledged that God was the One enthroned.

3. Jesus acknowledged that God was the God of the Jewish forefathers.

4. Jesus was scorned and despised.

5. Jesus was mocked (Matthew 27:41-43).

6. Jesus was steadfastly committed to God.

7. Jesus relied on God as always near even when others ran away (Matthew 26:56).

8. His enemies encircled him—both when he was mocked with a crown of thorns on his head and at the foot of the cross (Matthew 27:29,41-43).

9. Bones coming out of joint is typical of crucifixion.

10. Jesus was thirsty during the crucifixion (John 19:28).

11. Jesus died physically.

12. Evil men encircled Jesus.

13. Jesus' hands and feet were nailed to the cross. (The Psalm 22 prophecy was made 600 years before crucifixion was invented.)

14. Crucifixion causes extreme dehydration and wasting of the body.

15. The onlookers gloated over Jesus' death (Matthew 27:29,41-43).

16. The Roman soldiers gambled for Jesus' clothing (John 19:23-24).

17. Jesus gave honor and praise to God.

18. Jesus gave continued praise and reverence to God.

19. Jesus declared that those who sought and found God would live forever.

20. At the end of the earth, all peoples will bow down to God.

21. Everyone will ultimately bow down and worship God.

22.   Future generations will hear of Jesus and God.

23.   "It is finished," Jesus' final words on the cross, convey essentially the same message as the close of the crucifixion psalm, "For he has done it."

Just a coincidence? How likely was it that Psalm 22 in its entirety should describe the crucifixion of Jesus—from the first verse to the last? If it were just a verse or two, it might seem to be open to challenge. But as far as I could see, the psalm as a whole clearly seemed to be consistent with the details of the crucifixion.

When

The Coming of the Messiah to Jerusalem

> From the issuing of the decree to restore and rebuild Jerusalem until the Anointed One, the ruler, comes, there will be seven "sevens," and sixty-two "sevens." It will be rebuilt with streets and a trench, but in times of trouble. After the sixty-two "sevens," the Anointed One will be cut off and will have nothing. The people of the ruler who will come will destroy the city and the sanctuary (Daniel 9:25-26).

This prophecy was very puzzling to me at first. But after I had read it carefully, and had gotten some insight into the Jewish culture, I found it was worth the time to understand it. And when I realized how precisely it predicted when the Messiah would appear to Jerusalem as king, I was amazed.

As I familiarized myself with some key points of Jewish culture, the prophecy became clearer to me. "Anointed One" is the literal translation of the word "Messiah"—the one anointed by God. "Seven 'sevens' " plus "sixty-two 'sevens'"of course equals 69 "sevens." To the Jews, "seven" could be any period of seven—days, months, or years. Assuming 69 periods of seven years, and multiplying those 483 years by the Jewish standard year of 360 days, I could obtain the result of 173,880 days.

This relationship was most famously recognized by Sir Robert Anderson, in his book *The Coming Prince*. I also consulted the work of another scholar, Harold Hoehner. In his book *Chronological Aspects of the Life of Christ*, he came up with exactly the same number of days as Anderson. Within a time period of 173,880 days from the decree by Artaxerxes to rebuild Jerusalem and the Temple, the Messiah would arrive at Jerusalem as "the ruler."[1]

The amazing thing turned out to be the precise relationship of those 173,880 days to the entry of Jesus into Jerusalem on Palm Sunday (the tenth of Nisan by the Jewish calendar), which both scholars recognized. Daniel's prophecy exactly identifies Jesus as the perfect lamb of the Jewish Passover, which was always selected on the tenth of Nisan as prescribed in the Tanakh (Exodus 12:3).

Hoehner explains the precision of the prophecy thus:

> Multiplying the sixty-nine weeks by seven years for each week by 360 days gives a total of 173,880 days. The difference between 444 B.C. and A.D. 33 then is 476 solar years. By multiplying the 476 by 365.24219879 or by 365 days, 5 hours, 48 minutes, 45.975 seconds [there are 365 1/4 days in a year], one comes to 173,855 days, 6 hours, 52 minutes, 44 seconds, or 173,855 days. This leaves only 25 days to be accounted for between 444 B.C. and A.D. 33. By adding the 25 days to March 5 (of 444 B.C.), one comes to March 30 (of A.D. 33) which was Nisan 10 in A.D. 33. This was the triumphal entry of Jesus into Jerusalem.[2]

A few points that further helped me understand Daniel's prophecy were:

- An actual solar year has 365.24219879 days. (This is the exact length of time required for the earth to make one circuit around the sun.) Understanding the prophecy required adjusting the Hebrew year to an exact solar year (and wouldn't the God of the universe know the solar year?).

- Although several "decrees" were made by Persian kings about Jerusalem, the only decree that completely fits with Daniel's words is the decree by Artaxerxes in 444 B.C. ("in the twentieth year of King Artaxerxes"—Nehemiah

2:1-8) that was made for a complete restoration of the city. (Other decrees were focused on the Temple or fell short in restoration of the city.)

The timing of Jesus' entry into Jerusalem on Palm Sunday—the first time he allowed himself to be called "King of Israel"—was precisely predicted by Daniel, to the day. That this could happen by random chance was unimaginable to me. And the prophecy continued on to describe the destruction of the city and the Temple, which happened in A.D. 70 under the Romans. This amazing prophecy, combined with others I had found, totally changed my thinking about the Bible. I began to be convinced that there could be a supernatural connection between the Jewish Bible and the New Testament.

Where

The "Ruler's" Place of Birth Was Prophesied

> But you, *Bethlehem Ephrathah*, though you are small among the clans of Judah, out of you will come for me one who will be ruler over Israel, whose *origins are from of old, from ancient times* (Micah 5:2).

At first I was simply impressed that a prophecy would indicate a small town, out of which a ruler "from ancient times" would come, which I figured was referring to something supernatural. Later, I realized that the *precise* town was indicated—Bethlehem Ephrathah, in Judea, not the Bethlehem closer to Joseph and Mary.

But the "origins" of the ruler over Israel were to be "from of old, from ancient times." This indicated a more significant claim. The Messiah would need to preexist his birth in a supernatural way. I found this claim made of Jesus by the apostle John (John 1, especially verses 1-2 and 14; Revelation 1:8). The apostle Paul also declared that Jesus had been in existence since before the beginning of time (2 Timothy 1:9).

With the prophecy in Micah 5:2, I completed my search in the Old Testament for the "who, what, when, and where" of the coming Messiah.

My Summary of Prophecy About the Messiah

Now that I had gathered so much prophecy evidence about the Messiah, I put all the information together and came up with my "newspaper article."

The Messiah to Come

The Messiah will descend from Shem,[1] through Abraham,[2] Isaac,[3] Jacob,[4] Judah,[5] Jesse[6] and King David.[7] He will be born in the city of Bethlehem in the region of Ephrathah[8] when a bright star appears.[9] It will be a miraculous, virgin birth.[10]

The Messiah will be unique, having preexisted his birth.[8] He will perform many miracles: calming the sea,[11] causing the blind to see, the deaf to hear, the lame to walk, and the mute to talk.[12] He will be referred to in many ways, including God with us,[10] Wonderful Counselor, Mighty God, Everlasting Father, and Prince of Peace.[13] He will be a great teacher and will use parables.[14] One day he will rule over everything…all nations will bow down to him.[15,22]

But the Messiah will come to save mankind.[16] He will become the offering for man's sin[16]; he will present himself to Jerusalem as both the anointed king[18] and the Passover Lamb.[16] This will occur exactly 173,880 days after the decree by Artaxerxes to rebuild Jerusalem.[17] So four days before Passover, the Messiah will present himself to a rejoicing Jerusalem riding on a donkey.[18] But then he will suffer greatly.[16] He will be rejected by many, including his friends.[16] He will be betrayed by a friend[19] for 30 pieces of silver.[20] Later that money will be thrown down in the temple[20] and will eventually go to a potter.[20] At his trial he will not defend himself. He will say nothing[16] except as required by law. Israel will reject him.[21]

The Messiah will be taken to a mountaintop identified by Abraham as "the Lord will provide."[22] There he will be put to death with his hands and feet pierced.[23] His enemies will encircle him,[24] mocking him, and will cast lots for his clothing.[25] He will call out to God, asking why he was "forsaken."[26] He will be given gall and wine.[27] He will die with criminals.[28] But none of his bones will be broken.[29] He will be pierced.[30] He will be buried in a rich man's grave.[31] But he will not remain in the grave.[32]

Prophecy About the Messiah	Location	Fulfillment
[1] Shem an ancestor	Genesis 9,10	Luke 3:23-37
[2] Abraham an ancestor	Genesis 22:18	Luke 3:23-37
[3] Isaac an ancestor	Genesis 26:4	Luke 3:23-37
[4] Jacob an ancestor	Genesis 28:14	Luke 3:23-37
[5] Judah an ancestor	Genesis 49:10	Luke 3:23-37
[6] Jesse an ancestor	Isaiah 11:1-5	Luke 3:23-37
[7] King David an ancestor	2 Samuel 7:11-16	Luke 3:23-37
[8] Bethlehem Ephrathah as birthplace	Micah 5:2	Matthew 2:1; Luke 2:4; John 7:42
[9] Star connected with birth	Numbers 24:17	Matthew 2:2
[10] Called "God with us"	Isaiah 7:14	Matthew 1:23
[11] Calming the sea	Psalm 107:29	Matthew 8:23-27
[12] "Special" miracles	Isaiah 35:4-6	Matthew 9:27-30; 11:5; 15:30-31; 21:14; Mark 7:32-37; 10:51-52; Luke 7:22; John 5:3-15; 9:13-25
[13] Names given	Isaiah 9:6	Names applied to Jesus today
[14] Use of parables	Psalm 78:2	Matthew 13:10-13
[15] Ultimate king over all	Isaiah 45:23	Historical context
[16] Sin offering and Passover lamb	Isaiah 53:3-7	John 1:29
[17] Timing of entry into Jerusalem	Daniel 9:20-27	Matthew 21:1-11
[18] Entering Jerusalem as a king on a donkey	Zechariah 9:9	Matthew 21:1-11
[19] Betrayed by a friend	Psalm 41:9	John 13:18; 18:2-3
[20] 30 pieces of silver	Zechariah 11:12-13	Matthew 26:15
[21] Israel will reject him	Isaiah 8:14	History—the Jews have rejected Jesus
[22] Identifying the place of crucifixion	Genesis 22	Mark 15:15-24
[23] Hands and feet pierced	Psalm 22:16	All Gospel accounts
[24] Encircled by enemies	Psalm 22:11-13	Matthew 27:41-43

[25] Lots cast for clothing	Psalm 22:18	Mark 15:24; John 19:24
[26] Forsaken by God	Psalm 22	The crucifixion accounts of the Gospels
[27] Will be given gall and wine	Psalm 69:21	Matthew 27:34
[28] Will die with "wicked men"	Isaiah 53:9	Matthew 27:38
[29] No bones broken	Psalm 34:20	John 19:36
[30] Will be "pierced"	Zechariah 12:10	John 19:34
[31] Will be buried with a rich man	Isaiah 53:9	Matthew 27:57-60
[32] Would not remain in grave	Psalm 16:10	John 20

The prophecies in my "newspaper article" were only a partial listing of the many messianic prophecies that seemed to be about Jesus. I found that some scholars had counted 322 prophecies that were apparently fulfilled by Jesus.[3]

20

The Critical Question

What about Jesus? There seemed to be firm evidence that he must be someone special—maybe a "part" of God. What kind of results would I get if I used statistical analysis on the prophecies I'd gathered, just as I had done earlier with the prophecies within the Jewish Bible? I took 30 prophecies that passed my acceptability standards and estimated the odds.

Messianic Prophecy	My Guesstimate of Odds
1. Shem an ancestor	1/3
2. Abraham an ancestor	1/1000
3. Isaac an ancestor	1/10,000
4. Jacob an ancestor	1/100,000
5. Judah an ancestor	1/1,000,000
6. Jesse an ancestor	1/10,000,000
7. King David an ancestor	1/100,000,000
8. Bethlehem Ephrathah as birthplace	1/100,000
9. Star connected with birth	1/100,000
10. Called "God with us"	1/100,000
11. Calming the sea	1/10,000,000
12. "Special" miracles	1/100,000,000
13. Names given	1/10,000
14. Use of parables	1/10
15. Ultimate king over all	1/10

16. Sin offering and Passover lamb	1/100
17. Will die with "wicked men"	1/10
18. Will be buried with a rich man	1/10
19. Timing of entry into Jerusalem	1/10,000,000
20. Entering Jerusalem as a king on a donkey	1/100
21. Betrayed by a friend—for 30 pieces of silver	1/1000
22. Rejection by Israel; will say nothing at his trial	1/10,000
23. Hands and feet pierced	1/10,000
24. Identifying the place of crucifixion	1/1,000,000
25. Will thirst while being put to death	1/10
26. No bones broken	1/10
27. Identification of words at the beginning and end of execution	1/1000
28. Lots cast for clothing	1/1000
29. Will be given gall and wine	1/10
30. Will be "pierced"	1/100

The cumulative probability of all these prophecies randomly coming true in one person would be 1 chance in 10^{110}. Even if I were to substantially reduce some of my estimates, I would still get a result that was "impossible"—unless there had been divine involvement.

If I could trust the New Testament, my logical conclusion was this—

———————————— • • • ————————————

Jesus was the Messiah, as planned by a supernatural God and predicted in the Bible.

———————————— • • • ————————————

Prophecies Made by Jesus Himself

Now reasonably convinced that Jesus was the Messiah, I turned to the next issue: Jesus' claim that he was God. To convince me that

Jesus' claims about his deity were true, I would have to find something that proved he was an accurate prophet—an *exceptional* prophet—who could prophesy and fulfill his own prophecy with the accuracy of God himself. Though many prophecies of Jesus were recorded, the one that most struck me was that he would be betrayed, crucified, and on the third day would *rise from the dead*. One major example is,

> Now as Jesus was going up to Jerusalem, he took the twelve disciples aside and said to them, "We are going up to Jerusalem, and the Son of Man will be betrayed to the chief priests and the teachers of the law. They will condemn him to death and will turn him over to the Gentiles to be mocked and flogged and crucified. On the third day he will be raised to life!" (Matthew 20:17-19).

Many Examples

Jesus prophesied his death and resurrection numerous times, in all four Gospels:

- Matthew 12:40; 16:21; 17:22-23; 20:17-19; 26:61; 27:40; 27:63

- Mark 8:31; 9:30-32; 10:32-34; 14:58; 15:29-30

- Luke 9:21-22,44-45; 18:31-34

- John 2:13-22; 3:14-16; 12:32-34

If there was ever an unusual and amazing prophecy, it would be one with the specific details of the prophesier's death, and far more, that he would rise from the dead in three days! Out of all kinds of prophecy, this one struck me as phenomenal!

So central was this prophecy to Jesus' life that he stated it many times; it was recorded in the Gospel accounts in 18 places! It is a prediction that only an all-knowing God could make and fulfill. And in addition to this, Jesus also prophesied specifically about other things as well:

- One of his disciples would betray him (Matthew 26:21; Mark 14:17-21; Luke 22:21-22).
- His disciples would desert him (Matthew 26:30-31; Mark 14:26-27).
- Peter would disown him three times (Matthew 26:33-34; Mark 14:29-30; Luke 22:31-34).
- He would meet the disciples in Galilee after he had risen (Mark 14:28).

Did Other People Believe That Jesus Was God?

With all this prophetic evidence, I had to ask myself: Did the Jews of the day, who certainly would be aware of the prophecies in the Tanakh, think that Jesus was God? After all, I knew that most Jews today do not accept Jesus. What about them?

I discovered that the Jews in Jerusalem were very rapidly accepting Jesus as Messiah in the months after his death. The Bible reported that the number who immediately believed in the resurrection (presumably the eyewitnesses) was only about 120 (Acts 1:15) before the Feast of Pentecost—which was 50 days after the resurrection. When Peter spoke on the Day of Pentecost, immediately 3000 men were added to the group of believers (2:41). Why was Peter's message so compelling? Because it was based on the prophecies the Jews knew and the events they had witnessed or had heard about. The Bible further reports that the number increased daily (2:47).

I continued examining the biblical record. When Peter and John were speaking before the people and the Sanhedrin (the ruling religious council) could not figure out why to punish them, the number of followers had already grown to 5000 men. Adding in women and children, the count could easily have approached 20,000 people—in a city of a little over 100,000 at the time. Within days, believers in Jesus had become nearly 20 percent of the local population. No wonder the religious leaders were extremely concerned! And of course the great persecution of Jesus' followers was soon underway.

I found other evidence from biblical writings that the early Jews believed Jesus was God. First, I considered the Gospel writers in further analyzing the deity of Jesus. After all, they not only were with Jesus and knew him well, but they also took the time to write the accounts while the eyewitnesses to the events were still alive. All of them faced persecution and risked death, based on the truth of what they had written in the Gospel accounts.

One of the most striking indications of the early belief that Jesus was God is in the Gospel of John. John himself was an eyewitness to all the events of Jesus' life, and his account was both written and circulated during the lifetime of other eyewitnesses:

> *In the beginning was the Word,* and the Word was with God, and *the Word was God. He was with God in the beginning.*
>
> Through him all things were made; without him nothing was made that has been made. In him was life, and that life was the light of men. The light shines in the darkness, but the darkness has not understood it.
>
> There came a man who was sent from God; his name was John. [This is speaking of John the Baptist.] He came as a witness to testify concerning that light, so that through him all men might believe. He himself was not the light; he came only as a witness to the light. The true light that gives light to every man was coming into the world.
>
> He was in the world, and though the world was made through him, the world did not recognize him. He came to that which was his own, but his own did not receive him. Yet to all who received him, to those who believed in his name, he gave the right to become children of God—children born not of natural descent, nor of human decision or a husband's will, but born of God.
>
> *The Word became flesh and made his dwelling among us.* We have seen his glory, the glory of the One and Only, who came from the Father, full of grace and truth (John 1:1-14).

John's words clearly showed that he believed that Jesus was God. And others who were close to him also believed that he was God.

- Peter worshiped him (Luke 5:8). A Jew would worship no one other than God.

- Likewise, Thomas worshiped him (John 20:28).

- Peter, James, and John witnessed and reported the "transfiguration" (Matthew 17), a visible demonstration that Jesus possessed the same glory as God the Father.

- Elizabeth, Jesus' relative, believed that he was God (Luke 1:41-55).

- Simeon, a devout Jewish prophet, believed that Jesus was God (Luke 2:25-35).

- Anna, a prophetess, believed he was God (Luke 2:36-38).

- Even Jesus' half brothers James and Jude eventually believed that Jesus was God (see the books of James and Jude).

- A Roman centurion and others who were at the crucifixion believed Jesus to be God:

> At that moment the curtain of the temple was torn in two from top to bottom. The earth shook and the rocks split. The tombs broke open and the bodies of many holy people who had died were raised to life. They came out of the tombs, and after Jesus' resurrection they went into the holy city and appeared to many people.
>   When the centurion and those with him who were guarding Jesus saw the earthquake and all that had happened, they were terrified, and exclaimed, "Surely he was the Son of God!" (Matthew 27:51-54).

Part V

Legal Proof
of God

21

A Response from an Atheist

His face was drawn down and seemed weathered; his eyes were sunk deep into his head. Though not an angry man—far from it—his demeanor was always somber, as if no hope had ever existed. His name was Gene, and he seemed to be a full-blown atheist. Since I had formerly shared his viewpoint of atheism, we sometimes talked about the concept of God. And how Gene loved to philosophize!

After I had discovered the prophecy evidence within the Bible, I decided to call Gene to set up a meeting to talk to him, just in case I had overlooked something. We decided to meet at his home later that week.

"Gene, I know you're not going to believe this," I began, "but I've found something in the Bible that you won't believe. I couldn't believe it myself, but it's right there, and anyone can check it out," I said, eager to show my new information to a fellow skeptic. "Get this, I've discovered there are lots and lots of ancient prophecies buried in the books of the Old Testament, written thousands of years ago, that have all been perfectly fulfilled."

"Right," he muttered. "'Tall, dark, handsome strangers'?"

"No!" I excitedly replied. "I'm talking about incredibly specific things. Names of people, specific places and events, even dates! I even created my own system to weed out all the 'junk prophecies' that Christians sometimes claim."

"Does this have anything to do with Jesus?" he asked scornfully.

"Actually, many prophecies do," I replied. "Some of the strongest prophecies I found predicted specific events regarding Jesus. There are many details foretold hundreds of years ahead of time about his life, his death, and his role. The odds are far, far beyond statistical probability!"

Gene raised an eyebrow.

"I'm not kidding," I said. "Just the historical Old Testament prophecies that we can verify as having come true, not even concerning Jesus—just those coming true randomly would be like winning many lotteries in a row. And when you take only the prophecies about Jesus, the probability of their being fulfilled by chance would be like winning another sixteen or so lotteries in a row, with a single ticket for each!" I really thought Gene would be amazed at this.

"Right," Gene said sarcastically. "How do you know Jesus wasn't some kind of strange guy who set out to fulfill the prophecies?"

I had to think about that. Gene had a way of coming up with good points. "Well," I admitted, "there are several prophecies that Jesus could have planned to fulfill if he wanted to, such as riding into Jerusalem as a 'king' on a donkey. But there are dozens of others he couldn't possibly have controlled. For example, he couldn't control his ancestors, nor his birthplace, nor how he would be executed, nor what people would do after his execution. Those prophecies alone coming true would be impossible without some supernatural influence.

"And Jesus himself even gave many perfect prophecies," I added. "In fact, he made the most incredible prophecy of all—that he would come back from the dead in exactly three days.

"So, Gene, here's how I'm reasoning: 1) Prophecy is a test of something from God. 2) Jesus claimed to be God. 3) Assuming Jesus' incredible prophecies were true, and they seem to be…then maybe we should consider his claim to be God. See the logic?"

"Not so fast, my atheist friend—"

"Former atheist," I corrected.

"Whatever," said Gene, exasperated. "How do you know that the record of Jesus is true? After all, didn't the Roman Catholic Church control the Bible for years? How do you know they didn't create a 'story' of Jesus to fit the prophecies?"

Gene had a way of bringing me back to basics. I didn't tell him that I had started investigating the historical evidence already. I wasn't prepared—my ducks weren't in a row yet. So at this point I simply acknowledged his comment. "Gene, you're right. Something as important as who or what God is, absolutely must be very tight with historical accuracy. It should be comparable to the history we learn in school."

With my conversation with Gene in mind, I started putting together the research I had been collecting regarding the trustworthiness of the Bible as it related to history, archaeology, and manuscript reliability, and I started searching for more information. I had to discover the truth.

But by now, I was fully absorbed by the possibility that Jesus might really be what he claimed—God incarnate! This was another defining point for me as I concluded that—

Jesus was the prophesied Son of God if legal evidence could prove the Bible's account trustworthy.

22

Blood Evidence

The next day I caught Gene in the hall at work and asked him to join me for lunch. We went to a local spot where we could sit alone in the corner. I wanted to tell him what I was learning and thinking.

"Okay," I said to Gene, "I realize that a claim as unbelievable as 'God on earth' should require substantial evidence to back it up. You make a good point—we must know that the records of the prophecies themselves and their fulfillment are trustworthy."

Not surprisingly, he said, "Okay, so how can you prove they were accurate?"

"Gene, as you know, we discussed that we could conclude the Bible was inspired by God if, and only if, its prophecies are correct. The real unresolved issue is, do history and the original manuscripts truly support the prophecies and their fulfillment? But before getting to the manuscripts themselves, I decided it would be better to 'think backward' in history.

"After all, there is an enormous Christian church today, all based on a single event in history. How did this church come about if it was based on a lie? To ignore this factor would be like acknowledging the existence of the earth and life and somehow denying that it could come to be.

"So I went backward from today, through the Renaissance, the Crusades, the Byzantine period (the 400s to the 1100s or so), back through the unofficial canonization of the Bible by everyday Christians before the early 200s—back through the widespread persecution of Christians ever since Christ. Gene, it's become obvious to me that we have an unbroken historical timeline of people who truly believed in the factualness of the life, death, and resurrection of Jesus. There are no gaps."

"Well?" said Gene.

I continued. "It seems I need to approach this pursuit of evidence almost as if I were about to present a case in a court of law. First, research the earliest Christians—those nearest to the time of Jesus' death. Second, address the manuscript evidence for both the Old and New Testaments to see if flawed documentation was responsible for false beliefs. And third, seek out circumstantial evidence.

"Gene, I don't know exactly how to prove it to you yet. But it seems to me that to have centuries of people and a third of the world today believing in *historical events* indicates that there must be some factual basis for their beliefs. I have a lot of research to do before I can commit with confidence to the accuracy of the documentation of the accounts about Jesus. I want to also verify the accounts in the Old Testament, especially regarding the prophecies about Jesus. Give me a few months and I'll see what I can find."

"Good luck," Gene said, seeming somewhat interested. "But don't expect to find anything. If it existed, I would expect Christians to be shouting it from the streets, not just burying it in books."

Investigating the Early Christians

In my investigation I looked first at the very first Christians—many of whom became martyrs. They would certainly have known whether Jesus had actually performed miracles, whether he had actually claimed to be God, and most importantly, whether he had actually fulfilled his own prophecy by rising from the dead.

I became convinced that the early Christian church was founded on real, historical beliefs. From the evidence of the first and second centuries, the early church founders strongly believed in the historicity of the death and resurrection of Jesus Christ.

First the apostles who knew Jesus closely, and who would definitely know whether Jesus actually lived, died, and rose from the dead, all willingly faced horrible persecution and death to tell the gospel message.

Historical tradition tells us that one by one, all the apostles except John were executed over a period of years—simply for spreading a historical message, the gospel. Records of tradition tell us that

- Peter was crucified upside down

- James the half brother of Jesus was stoned (he did not believe until after the resurrection)

- Matthew was killed by the sword

- James son of Alphaeus was crucified

- James son of Zebedee was killed by the sword

- Thaddaeus was killed by being shot with arrows

- Bartholomew was crucified

- Andrew was crucified

- Philip was crucified

- Simon the Zealot was crucified

- Thomas was killed with the spear

- Paul was beheaded (he also did not believe until after the resurrection)

Why would all of these men, who certainly would have known the truth about the events, die for something that was false? Would they die for a lie? Or did they know that Jesus was God? They all died one by one—over a period of years. No mass execution, no mass suicide. Each of them knew what might be coming, and yet they boldly proclaimed the gospel message anyway.

The Death of Peter

Clement of Alexandria, one of the early church fathers, records an example of calm assurance in the resurrection of Jesus and hope after death. He tells of the apostle Peter's last words to his wife as they both were being led off to execution at the instigation of the emperor Nero. In a calm and encouraging voice, Peter called to his wife by name and said, "O thou, remember the Lord."[1]

Second, I found substantial evidence that many other early Christians firmly believed in the death and resurrection of Jesus. Tens of thousands of people who had contact with the early eyewitnesses or who later received the gospel message died horrible martyr deaths for their beliefs. Archaeological evidence bears this out. The catacombs in Rome contain some seven million graves—in about 900 miles of multilayered caves under the streets of Rome. The catacombs served as a hiding place for Christians during the period of intense persecution that started with Nero in about the year 64 and did not end until Constantine made Christianity the official religion of the Roman Empire in the year 324. After that time, the catacombs were gradually forgotten. Eventually they were rediscovered by accident, in 1578.

Like the apostles, many of the Christians who took refuge in the catacombs willingly gave their lives rather than renounce Christianity. Some had to fight to the death in the arena. Others were thrown in lions' dens to be eaten. Some were even impaled on wooden stakes, then burned to provide light for Roman orgies. Yet ancient historical records (even non-Christian ones) recount the amazing joy of early Christians even when they were going to such horrible deaths.

My Visit to Rome

As a young man, I visited the catacombs with my family. I will never forget the awe-inspiring atmosphere of that place. As we walked down narrow pathways hewn out of rock, there were countless niches lining both walls, where the bodies of Christians were placed. Occasionally we would enter a larger chamber where the early Christians worshiped secretly. Ancient markings and writing on the walls attested to their strong faith in Jesus as Savior.

After a few weeks of research, I went out to lunch with Gene again.

"Gene," I exclaimed, "did you know that many thousands of Christians, including Jesus' disciples died horrible deaths as martyrs because they believed in the Gospel record?"

"Big deal," Gene retorted. "Virtually every religion has martyrs. Think about it—the Japanese in World War II or the Islamic people that blow themselves to pieces to attack Israel. What does that prove? It seems to me Christian martyrs are just as stupid as everyone else."

I began to feel stronger in the discussion because I recognized a crucial factor he didn't know yet. "Well, Gene, there's one big difference that I've learned in studying these religions and the Christian martyrs," I said firmly.

"What's that?" he asked me with a puzzled look on his face.

"The Christian martyrs' deaths were all because of a single *historical* event that either happened or didn't happen. They had to believe in something historical, or their martyrdom was empty. All other martyrs, including those you mentioned, died for some *philosophical* belief—a belief that they would get to some eternal paradise or a belief in a metaphysical cause. But in the case of the Christians, if there had been no crucifixion and resurrection verifying the prophecies that Jesus was God, there would be no reason for martyrdom. There would be no Christianity in the form we know today. Who would ever die for a fake Messiah who just 'claimed' to be God, whose prophecy of his own resurrection was false? *History is the difference* here, Gene. Even the Islamic martyrs don't die because 'Muhammad rose from the dead,' or because 'Muhammad claimed to be a god—which was proven by prophecy.' No! They just die based on the idea that in a 'holy war' their martyrdom will guarantee them a place in heaven. They have no basis in historical events for their belief. But Jesus taught his disciples simply to *spread history*—not to commit suicide."

"You still haven't answered my initial question," Gene responded somewhat belligerently. "How do you know this 'Bible' is accurate? Maybe it's just some holy book trying to convince people of its own agenda. How do you know it wasn't corrupted or changed in the past?"

"Good point, Gene." I was a bit embarrassed because I had violated my own research principles. I still needed to investigate the sources—especially those that the early martyrs based their beliefs upon.

"That's my next step—to investigate the documentation itself," I said. "I'll try to find corroboration for the New Testament's claims about the fulfillment of the Old Testament prophecies."

23

Could I Trust the Bible Texts?

The Old Testament

I briefly reviewed my research regarding the Old Testament (the Tanakh) and summarized my points. The following considerations had led me to believe that the Jewish Bible was a reliable copy of the original scrolls.

● ● ●

- Miraculously, the Jews exist today as a people, exactly promised by God in the book of Genesis, even through 2000 years of separation from their homeland.

- The Jewish nation was a theocracy—governed by God—and therefore placed a special emphasis on holy Scripture from prophets of God such as Moses and others.

- The copying of holy Scripture was regarded as of the highest importance. Exhaustive procedures were followed to ensure accuracy (see pages 139–140).

- The Jews were avid memorizers of Scripture. This provided another cross-check of the accuracy of the written Scripture.

- The Scripture was so highly esteemed that any degree of corruption would have been taken very seriously. Further, to deliberately corrupt the Scripture would have required changing all the many copies throughout the entire nation.

- The Dead Sea scrolls demonstrate that the Old Testament has suffered almost no corruption in the past 2000 years. The prophecies about the Messiah were "frozen in time" hundreds of years before Jesus' time. (See pages 168–170 for a full explanation.)

- The Septuagint—the translation of the Hebrew Scriptures into Greek, made in 280 B.C.—provides another cross-check for the accuracy of the prophecies about the Messiah. It was widely used at the time of Christ, and it became the "authorized version" of the Old Testament in the early Christian church.

Ancient Documents That Talk

I was convinced of the reliability of the Old Testament. But what kind of evidence was in existence today for the New Testament? What might convince skeptics like Gene or me? Was there anything like the Dead Sea scrolls? Or did a "legend" of Jesus just develop as time passed and memories faded?

The first thing I discovered was that there are lots of ancient New Testament manuscripts in existence today, ones that we can see in museums throughout the world. And they are consistent in their accounts of Jesus—with each other and with today's Greek New Testament. I discovered that there are nearly 25,000 New Testament documents, written in 15 languages, from within only a few hundred years of the death of Jesus. At least 5600 Greek manuscripts and fragments still exist, dating to within a few decades of Jesus' death. Many scholars recognized the abundance of evidence that supports the accounts of Jesus, such as the renowned archaeologist W.F. Albright:

> No other work from Graeco-Roman antiquity is so well attested by manuscript tradition as the New Testament. There are many more early manuscripts of the New Testament than there are of any classical author, and the oldest extensive remains of it date only about two centuries after their original composition.[1]

Sir Frederic Kenyon, a director of the British Museum and a foremost manuscript authority, wrote,

> Besides number, the manuscripts of the New Testament differ from those of the classical authors….In no other case is the interval of time between the composition of the book and the date of the earliest extant manuscripts so short as in that of the New Testament.[2]

He concludes that "both the authenticity and the general integrity of the books of the New Testament may be regarded as finally established."[3]

What About the Discrepancies?

I had been impressed by the precise copying techniques used by the scribes of the Old Testament. However, under persecution, *many* Christians not trained as scribes had made copies of the New Testament accounts. I expected to find major problems but (miraculously?) many of the differences between copies were in spelling and what would be considered "typos" today. Regarding the larger inconsistencies, I found that scholars had investigated that issue. For instance, Dockery, Mathews, and Sloan have stated in their research,

> Although there are certainly differences in many of the New Testament manuscripts, not one fundamental doctrine of the Christian faith rests on a disputed reading.[4]

F.J.A. Hort, another researcher, adds this:

> In the variety and fullness of the evidence on which it rests, the text of the New Testament stands absolutely and unapproachably alone among ancient prose writings.[5]

I found many other researchers with similar opinions regarding the vast quantity and the great consistency of the manuscripts, and their remarkable proximity to the events of Jesus' life.

It became apparent to me that the vast number of the copies of the New Testament—in a day when all copies were made by hand—demonstrated a clear belief in the truth of the accounts about Jesus. Certainly this huge number also gave critics an opportunity to question the variations between copies. Yet I was still overwhelmed by the consistency of the manuscript evidence.

Looking at the big picture, I concluded that the vast quantities of the accounts about Jesus and his teaching, translated into numerous languages at an early date, indicated vast belief in a historical event. It seemed that it all had to be real.

Other Ancient Writings

I compared the quantity of early biblical manuscripts with the quantity of manuscripts for some other ancient writings we commonly regard as history.

- *The Gallic Wars* by Julius Caesar. Every Roman history book and good encyclopedia recount the conquest of Gaul (modern-day France) by Julius Caesar in the first century B.C. The primary resource for this information is 10 copies of the original writings. The oldest of these copies we have today dates to 1000 years after the autograph by Caesar.

- *The History of Rome* by Livy (lived from about 59 B.C. to A.D. 17). This commonly accepted work forms a basis for modern accounts of Roman history. Currently we have one partial copy made 400 years after the original. The earliest complete copy was made about 1000 years after the autograph.

- The *Annals* of Tacitus. A historian, Tacitus wrote his *Annals* of Roman history about A.D. 100. Today we base our knowledge of his original writings on only 20 copies that were made 1000 years later.

- *Natural History* by Pliny the Elder (lived from about A.D. 23 to A.D. 79). We base our knowledge of Pliny's writings on this work, yet the earliest of the seven copies now in existence was made about the year 850, nearly 750 years after the fact.

Edward Glenny best summed up my thinking:

> No one questions the authenticity of the historical books of antiquity because we do not possess the original copies. Yet we have far fewer manuscripts of these works than we possess of the NT.[6]

The Importance of the Eyewitnesses

The New Testament accounts were widely circulated at the time of eyewitnesses to the events. I became convinced of that because

- *Directly*, we have fragments from five different New Testament books that apparently date to within 35 years of Jesus' death (from among the Dead Sea scrolls).[7]

- *Indirectly*, we have the evidence of the book of Acts, the history of the early church written by the historian Luke. In it, Luke doesn't mention the persecution under Nero, which began in the year 64. The persecution is attested to by many non-Christian documents and by archaeological evidence, including that found in the catacombs. Therefore, Luke's Gospel, written earlier, and the book of Acts were both being circulated by A.D. 64.

I tried to put this evidence in today's perspective. Suppose a tabloid newspaper reported that Elvis Presley had returned from the dead. Would anyone take it seriously? Would the story turn into a bestseller for centuries? Of course not—because all the eyewitnesses would deny that such a thing had ever happened!

In our world today, a few bizarre people might die for a belief that Elvis had come back from the dead. But would the people who absolutely knew the truth willingly face an excruciating death just to tell the story? Would tens of thousands of others "jump on the bandwagon" and die to defend its historicity? Never!

The point I emphasized to myself was that the death and resurrection of Jesus were said to be historical events. The writings about these events were circulated during the time of many eyewitnesses. And many of these eyewitnesses would have been in a position to actually know the truth for certain. Their acceptance of the accounts was very strong evidence for their validity.

Survival of the New Testament Manuscripts

As I moved later in history with my studying, I found that during the intense persecution of Christians from the time of Jesus' death until the time of Constantine (about A.D. 33 to 324), not only were great numbers of Christians killed, but vast numbers of New Testament manuscripts were destroyed. This destruction reached a peak in the year 303, when the Roman Emperor Diocletian decreed that anyone found with a Bible would be executed.

What other holy book has ever had a mandate to be destroyed by a world empire? I could not find any evidence of one. So I asked myself these questions: What sets the Bible apart? Why do people want to get rid of it so much? Could it be because it really is from God, as the statistics were indicating?

More importantly, was there some divine strength in the Bible so that it could survive such intense attempts to eradicate it? And not just survive, but be preserved in far greater numbers and with far more credibility than any other ancient manuscript?

Apart from the 5600-plus ancient manuscripts still in existence in Greek, there are more than 10,000 in Latin and more than 2000 in Ethiopic, 4000 in early Slavic, 2500 in Armenian, and more than 350 in Syriac, in addition to smaller numbers of manuscripts in nearly a dozen other languages. Many of these copies were made within a few hundred years after Jesus' time. It almost seemed to me as if God wanted to ensure that the Bible would survive for everyone, not just a few people.[8]

The Bible's Popularity

Voltaire, the great French writer and philosopher of the 1700s, once said that within a hundred years, Christianity and the Bible would disappear (implying that his works would last much longer). Today, few people know much about Voltaire's writings, but the Bible has constantly grown in popularity—remaining by far the bestselling book every year since the beginning of printing. Ironically, Voltaire's house and printing press are now used by the Geneva Bible Society to print Bibles.

The Consistency of the Bible

I discovered that the Bible is also unique in its consistency. Even though it contains many controversial points, written centuries apart by very different authors, yet it is in complete agreement with itself.

For example, just consider the many authors who at many different times and in many different locations recorded the words of the Bible.

- *Moses* (wrote about 1450 B.C.). A political leader, he recorded in the wilderness the part of the Bible the Jews honor most highly, the Torah (the first five books).

- *Joshua* (wrote about 1400 B.C.). A military general, he wrote his book in Canaan (modern-day Palestine) during a period of war.

- *Samuel* (wrote about 1000 B.C.). A prophet, he wrote his books during a time of internal strife within the nation of Israel.

- *David* (wrote about 1000 B.C.). A king, he wrote most of the Psalms, at various times—some in times of despair; some in times of rejoicing.

- *Solomon* (wrote about 970 B.C.). A king, he wrote Proverbs, Ecclesiastes, and the Song of Songs in a period of peace and prosperity.

- *Amos* (wrote about 750 B.C.). A herdsman, he wrote his book of prophecy before the first Jewish exile, while in the fields.

- *Jeremiah* (wrote about 600 B.C.). A prophet, he did much of his writing in a dungeon during a period of depression.

- *Daniel* (wrote about 535 B.C.). A prime minister while in exile, he wrote his remarkable prophecies while on a hillside and in a palace.

- *Nehemiah* (wrote about 440 B.C.). A cupbearer to the King of Persia, he wrote his book after his return to Jerusalem, while rebuilding the walls of the city.

- *Mark* (wrote between A.D. 35 and 60). A scribe for Peter, it is thought he wrote one of the four Gospels in Jerusalem during the earliest time of Christianity, during the first persecution.

- *Matthew* (wrote between A.D. 40 and 60). A tax collector, Matthew was originally a hated member of the Jewish aristocracy. After converting to Christianity, he wrote one of the four Gospels in Jerusalem during persecution.

- *Luke* (wrote between A.D. 40 and 64). A physician and noted historian, Luke wrote mostly in Rome during the early Christian era. He wrote one of the four Gospels, and his book of Acts became the Bible's major historical work about the early church.

- *John* (wrote between A.D. 60 and 95). Originally a fisherman, John wrote one of the four Gospels while in Asia Minor. He also wrote three New Testament letters (books) and the book of Revelation. (John was the only apostle who was not martyred for proclaiming the gospel of Jesus.)

- *Paul* (wrote between A.D. 45 and 65). Originally a rabbi and esteemed leader of the Jewish religion, Paul zealously persecuted the early Christians. Once he had met the risen Jesus, his life was totally changed, and instead of persecuting Christians, he began starting churches. Paul wrote more books of the New Testament than anyone else.

• *Peter* (wrote between A.D. 60 and 64). A fisherman, Peter was known as a very impulsive person, with little tact and with little education. Yet he later was one of the leaders of the early church and wrote two books of the New Testament.

The complete Bible was written by at least 40 authors over a span of 1500, perhaps 2000, years (scholars are not certain who the authors are in the case of a few books). As I had found out, these authors had come from many backgrounds, many time periods, and many different circumstances. Yet, as I read it and studied it again and again, I saw that it was still consistent on many controversial subjects (such as adultery and homosexuality, for example).

And those were but two examples of controversial issues in which the Bible was consistent over hundreds of years. When I looked at others, such as drug abuse, stress management, the benefits of love and forgiveness—the list goes on and on—I continued to find amazing consistency in the Bible despite the centuries over which it was recorded. This was especially surprising to me when I considered the different types of people involved with it—from different cultures, from different circumstances. Was this just by chance?

Even today it would be extremely difficult to get 40 authors together in one room to discuss such controversial and relevant issues and have them agree—even if they were all from the same city, the same social status, and the same background. The authorship and content of the Bible were seeming more and more miraculous to me.

24

I Find More Support for the Bible

Non-Christian Writings

Gene had challenged me about the accuracy of the Bible texts. And this raised another question for me: Are the only records of Jesus those that are in the New Testament? I discovered that this was not true—there were numerous first- and second-century references from non-Christian sources. Further research showed me that the number of references was surprising, considering the general rarity of any document at all from that time. I also kept in mind that Jesus had confined his activities to a small, mostly rural area—not a city like Rome—for only three years, and had been generally unknown then except to the people of Palestine. I found some fascinating comments about Jesus and early Christians in ancient works.

- *Pliny the Younger* was a governor of Bithynia in Asia Minor. At the time of the document (about A.D. 112), Christians were ruining the business of making idols, a major part of the provincial economy.

  In a letter (which still exists) written to the Emperor Trajan in Rome, Pliny discussed the worship practices of the Christians, indicating that they worshiped Jesus as "God incarnate." (This was an affront to the Roman

217

religion, which declared the emperors themselves to be gods.)

Trajan ordered the governor to test those accused and punish them if they were found guilty of being Christians. The required proof of not being a Christian was to demonstrate adoration of "our gods"—the accused had to 1) renounce his faith, 2) curse Jesus, and 3) bow down to worship the statue of the emperor Trajan.

- *Hadrian,* emperor of Rome from A.D. 117 to 138, also wrote concerning the punishment of Christians. In a letter written through his court official Suetonius, he matter-of-factly referred to the resurrection as a "superstition."

- *Thallus,* in a historical work that was referenced by Julius Africanus, had mistakenly claimed there was a solar eclipse at the time of Jesus' death, trying to explain the darkness that fell during the crucifixion. Africanus points out in this letter that no such eclipse occurred. The death of Jesus was stated as a matter of fact. (It was interesting to me that non-Christian writers seemed to be trying to explain the miraculous events at Jesus' crucifixion.)

- *Josephus,* the well-known Jewish historian (active about A.D. 64 to 93) wrote the following in his book *Antiquities of the Jews:*

  > Now, there was about this time, Jesus, a wise man, if it be lawful to call him a man, for he was a doer of wonderful works—a teacher of such men as receive the truth with pleasure. He drew over to him both many of the Jews, and many of the Gentiles. He was Christ; and when Pilate, at the suggestion of the principal men amongst us, had condemned him to the cross, those that loved him at the first did not forsake him, for he appeared to them alive again the third day, as divine prophets had foretold these and ten thousand other wonderful things concerning him; and the tribe of Christians, so named from him, are not extinct at this day.[1]

To me, this quote seemed too close to the Gospel record to be written by a non-Christian (a "hostile witness"). Though I found that some have suggested it was corrupted by early Christians, most scholars believe much of it is accurate. What virtually all scholars agree upon regarding this passage is the basic content: that Jesus existed, was crucified, and performed many wondrous things. The only questionable words are those that seem to "glorify" Jesus. Josephus also mentioned Jesus' brother James and his martyrdom by stoning:

> He [Ananus] assembled the sanhedrim of the judges, and brought before them the brother of Jesus, who was called the Christ, whose name was James, and some others [or some of his companions]; and when he had formed an accusation against them as breakers of the law, he delivered them to be stoned.[2]

- *Cornelius Tacitus* (A.D. 64–116), a historian, wrote about the atrocities that Nero committed on the Christians who were blamed for the fire of Rome:

> He falsely charged with the guilt, and punished with the most exquisite tortures, the persons commonly called Christians, who were hated for their enormities. Christus, the founder of the name, was put to death by Pontius Pilate, procurator of Judea in the reign of Tiberius: but the pernicious superstition, repressed for a time, broke out again, not only through Judea, where the mischief originated, but through the city of Rome also.[3]

I was struck by the words "pernicious superstition," which obviously referred to the resurrection. Since Tacitus used the word "pernicious" ("causing great harm"), it was clear that the talk about the resurrection was taken seriously.

- *Lucian of Samosata,* a second-century author, wrote contemptuously of the beliefs of Christianity; yet his words still reflect the fact that very strong Christian beliefs existed. In one place he stated,

> The Christians, you know, worship a man to this day—the distinguished personage who introduced their novel rites, and was crucified on that account....You see, these misguided creatures start with the general conviction that they are immortal for all time, which explains the contempt of death and voluntary self-devotion which are so common among them; and then it was impressed on them by their original lawgiver that they are all brothers, from the moment they are converted, and deny the gods of Greece, and worship the crucified sage, and live after his laws.[4]

- *The Jewish Talmud* from the period of A.D. 70 to 200 referred to Jesus, though later Christian persecution of the Jews destroyed much of this evidence. For example, the Babylonian Talmud states,

> On the eve of Passover Yeshu was hanged. For forty days before the execution took place, a herald went forth and cried, "He is going forth to be stoned because he has practiced sorcery and enticed Israel to apostasy. Any one who can say anything in his favour let him come forward and plead on his behalf." But since nothing was brought forward in his favour he was hanged on the eve of Passover![5]

This was a very revealing passage to me. The Jewish leaders actually admitted Jesus' existence, his crucifixion ("hanged" on a tree), the motive for wanting him "stoned" (having "enticed Israel to apostasy"—his claim to be God), and his miracle-working ("sorcery").

Another Conversation About the Evidence

Several months had gone by. By now my mind was racing with facts. I was pretty certain that the Bible was true in its entirety.

What a switch—from total atheist to a believer in the entire Bible…almost. Forever the skeptic, I decided to give Gene one last shot at killing the evidence I had gathered. I called him and scheduled another meeting at his home.

———————•———————

"Come in!" Gene yelled after I rang the bell.

I entered and looked back toward his office, where he was leaning back in his chair, hands clasped behind his head, staring at the ceiling.

"Gene, it's Ralph," I said.

"Yep, I figured so," he replied. Slowly he spun his chair around. I took the guest seat.

"Hard day at work?" I asked.

"You know it," he sighed. "Another day and no sales."

"Well, you know it can only get better," I said, hoping to cheer him up.

"Right. Thanks for your thought, anyway," Gene responded, rolling his eyes in frustration. "Anyway, you can talk all you want about religious philosophy and the Bible today—it can only improve my mood."

I was thinking to myself that Gene's mood was always sour anyway, so a bad day at work might be really bad. On the other hand, maybe our talk would take his mind off things.

"Gene, I've done some pretty exhaustive research about the point you made when we had lunch—you know, the reliability of the manuscripts of the prophecies and Jesus' fulfillment of them."

"Oh yeah," Gene muttered. "What happened this time? Did Jesus appear to you in bed and tell you that you're going to burn in hell if you don't accept every single word of the Bible? Whoops— I'm sorry, I didn't mean to be so sarcastic."

I was pleased to see Gene sit up a bit in his chair. Maybe a little sarcasm was what he needed.

"First," I said, "let's go back over where we've come from. I know you didn't want to get into all that 'scientific stuff' that caused me to believe in some God to begin with. But we've been talking about 100-percent perfect prophecy—perfect beyond human reason—all contained in the Bible.

"Second, you brought up a very valid point. How do we know that the original Old Testament prophecies were accurately recorded? You emphasized this regarding the prophecies about Jesus Christ. You suggested a possible 'agenda' of the Christian church—Christians may have gone back and altered the prophecies.

"Third, you brought up another very valid point. How do we know that the New Testament accounts of Jesus were accurately recorded? You brought up a potential agenda on Jesus' part—that perhaps he'd been deliberately trying to fulfill the Scripture. And again you mentioned the possible agenda on the church's part, so that perhaps they changed the early record of Jesus.

"But bottom line, we both agreed that if historical, legal evidence supported the vast number of precise prophecies and their fulfillment in Jesus, statistical proof would indicate that Jesus was who he claimed to be. And Jesus claimed to be God."

"Yeah," Gene said, "that pretty much sums it up."

"Well, let me tell you what I've discovered," I said. "Let's deal with the Old Testament prophecies before we move on to their fulfillment through Jesus."

"Okay," Gene replied. His interest seemed to be growing.

"Already we have discussed the importance of holy Scripture in the theocracy that Israel was. Scripture would have a role in the Jewish nation comparable to, even exceeding, the importance of a combination of the United States Constitution and statutes together with any religious books. Scripture was such that it shouldn't, wouldn't, and essentially couldn't be tampered with. There were strict copy rules, and the highest reverence was given to the vast numbers of copies. In addition, virtually everyone memorized large quantities of Scripture. So any attempt to change it was essentially impossible. Not only would great numbers of scrolls need to be changed simultaneously, but also the minds of all the people who had memorized them."

"I can buy that for back then," Gene said. "But what about then to now? The Jews were scattered over the face of the earth, and, to my knowledge, once they had left Palestine, such a theocracy and such practices ceased."

"That's where archaeology comes in," I said. "There are several key finds of Old Testament scrolls that have been verified as written before the time of Jesus. The most famous one, the Dead Sea scrolls, contains all the books of the Old Testament except Esther. Many scrolls were written before 200 B.C. and they lay buried, like a time capsule, until 1947, when they were discovered. Most importantly, when the scrolls were compared to the current Hebrew texts, they were virtually identical, indicating that the content of the Old Testament remained unchanged for 2000 years. That means the prophecies were clearly made before Jesus."

"No kidding!" Gene said. "I've heard of the Dead Sea scrolls, but had no idea they matched today's Bible. That's pretty interesting."

"There are translations of the Old Testament that we have today that were also written before Jesus. They confirm the prophecies as well, but we don't need to go into all that," I said.

"To me, the most exciting part of my research was to find out how well-documented the New Testament is," I continued eagerly. "Do you know that we have vastly more ancient manuscripts supporting the account of the New Testament than any other ancient work? And Gene, I'm talking about documents that you can go to museums to see!"

"What's so surprising about that?" Gene asked. "You get a bunch of monks together with nothing else to do, and they sit around copying the Bible!"

"I'm not done, Gene," I said a little impatiently. "I'm not referring only to documents made after Christianity was 'allowed,' I'm also referring to ancient copies made during the time of the persecutions, when people literally risked their lives for even having a Bible, let alone copying it. Some ancient portions exist that are believed to have been written during the time of the eyewitnesses to the events of Jesus' life, so we know that the accounts were in circulation that early.

"In fact," I continued, "there are such vast quantities of these early documents, so far in excess of other ancient writings we currently deem history, that many renowned scholars have indicated that the textual accuracy of the New Testament far exceeds that of any other ancient work ever created!

"To me the especially amazing things are these: First, millions of people died to defend this book. They believed in it as history. Second, the book survived despite the many attempts to eradicate it. Did you know that in the year 303 an edict came from Rome that anyone caught with a Bible would be executed?"

"No," Gene replied flatly.

"Don't you see, Gene! There's something special, something supernatural, something amazing, about this book!" I said excitedly. "You're talking to the skeptic of all skeptics, but I'm really starting to believe in my heart of hearts that this Bible is really and truly inspired by God."

"Mmmm." Gene was thinking now.

There was a long silence; pondering out loud, he went on:

"The non-Christian credibility...the manuscript reliability...the prophecy odds...it all makes sense. But I've done so many bad things for so long. How could I ever believe in a God who allows such suffering, and could any such God ever forgive me for all the trash in my life?" Gene turned away so I wouldn't see the tear in his eye.

"Gene, I know how you feel. I'm still sorting things out for myself. You're a 'bud' and just as big an atheist as I was. But I wanted you to know this stuff. Both you and I know that a real God might be able to determine our eternity. And the Bible says that trusting in Jesus is key!

"Think of it—we all need to know why we believe what we believe. To put our potential eternity in the hands of 'blind faith'—it's as ridiculous as sitting on the front porch with our eyes closed, knowing a tornado is coming down the street. With the tornado, we'd *probably* face a bad outcome, but death is *certain* for you and me. It would be foolish not to prepare for it."

I spent the next hour talking philosophy with Gene. I told him that with spirituality, it was not just a "tornado" that hits, it was an eternal issue that would affect us forever. It must at least be investigated. After all, if the Bible was wrong, I reasoned, I was just wasting some time. Maybe not even that—I had run onto some studies showing that if I followed the Bible's guidelines anyway—about forgiveness, getting rid of resentment, love, not participating in immorality, and so on—I would have a better, more carefree life anyway. So what would I lose? On the other hand, if the Bible was right, I now understood that if I didn't follow it I might lose forever. Eternal paradise versus eternal torment? To me it seemed like an easy choice.

Gene didn't like hearing what I was saying about death. He would have preferred to believe that he could somehow earn his chance for heaven—if it existed. In essence he was burying his head in the sand. I had done the same thing earlier, when I didn't want to hear about "heaven and hell"—I just wanted to believe that everything would be okay if I was a "good guy."

———————•———————

I looked at Gene closely. His face hardened—and he stared at me and said, "Well, I just don't know what to think about all this. Maybe it's just not right for me." With that he turned his chair around. Glancing back at me over his shoulder, he said, "Thanks for coming by. I know you mean well, but I've got to get back to work."

Heading toward the door, I looked back. Gene seemed deep in thought. "Well, just think about what we've discovered," I said. "Sorry for taking so much time, but I just had to see what you'd say about my research. See ya, Bud—I've gotta run too. I'll talk to you later."

I had known Gene only a short time, through a job I was doing some part-time work on. I haven't seen him since. But I'll never forget the hardened look on his face. And I hoped he'd remember our conversation.

25

The Final Barriers

I continued my search to confirm the actual historical account of the Bible by using sources from outside the Bible. By now I had read it in chronological order several times and was very familiar with the history it presented. I turned next to the resources I could find in archaeology.

"Smoking-Gun" Archaeology

It now became easy for me to compare biblical history to world history. For example, when I started to study the tower of Babel, which was constructed after the flood of Noah, I discovered that several similar towers still exist in that portion of the world (now Iraq). While the exact identification of the tower is debated, regarding the general structure and intent of the tower, the biblical account is consistent with modern findings. The Bible states that the purpose of the builders was to construct a tower that "reaches to the heavens, so that we may make a name for ourselves" (Genesis 11:4). The towers found in Iraq, known as ziggurats,[1] had temples at the top, apparently for the worship of gods. Certainly these would have been abhorrent to God.

Misconceptions Corrected by Archaeology

Soon after I began my research in archaeology, I learned about "higher criticism of the Bible." This system of thought flourished in the late 1800s and led to many errors that were later corrected by modern archaeology. I was fascinated by what I discovered.

227

- "Higher critics" believed the Hittite culture of the time of Abraham could not possibly have existed as reported in the Bible (Genesis 10:15; 15:20; 23:7-20; 25:10; 49:32). Now, archaeology has uncovered numerous artifacts of the early Hittites. So numerous are these artifacts that they fill an entire museum in Israel.[2]

- The Bible speaks of Tubal-Cain (a descendent of Cain, Adam and Eve's son) as forging "all kinds of tools out of bronze and iron" (Genesis 4:22). However, science has dated the beginning of the Iron Age at about 1200 B.C., much later than the estimated time of Tubal-Cain. Yet an iron blade has been found just northwest of Baghdad—not far from the probable site of the Garden of Eden—that dates back to no later than 2700 B.C., long before the previous estimate.[3]

- It was believed that domesticated camels did not exist at the time of Abraham (as indicated in Genesis 12:16). Then archaeologists discovered paintings of domesticated camels on the walls of the temple of Hatshepsut (near the city of Thebes, Egypt), which date back to that period.[4]

- It was once argued that the account of the strong, bolted doors of Lot's house (Genesis 19:9-10) was illogical because at that time cities were in a state of decline. Then archaeologists discovered the biblical city of Kiriath Sepher in the same area, with evidence of walls and strong doors. The construction dates from 2200 to 1600 B.C., the time of Lot.[5]

- It was insisted that the laws of the Old Testament (the Torah, the first five books written by Moses) could not possibly have been written as far back as 1450 B.C. No culture was thought to be that advanced. Then in 1902, archaeologists found an artifact from Babylon with similar laws—the code of Hammurabi, which dated before the time of Moses.[6]

- The existence of the Philistines was once doubted. The Bible reports them as active enemies of Israel during the time of the judges. Now, many Philistine cities are just beginning to be uncovered. To date, more than 28 sites and 5 major centers have been uncovered in Palestine. Even the burning of the city of Gibeah, as indicated in Judges 20:8-40, has been confirmed.[7]

- It was thought that David could not have been a musician since the instruments the Bible says he played were not developed until later. Then, archaeologists discovered the types of instruments used by David in the city of Ur (Abraham's hometown)—including lyres, flutes, harps, and even a double oboe, dating back to 2500 B.C. Additional discoveries of musical instruments were made in Egypt (dating back to 1900 B.C.) and in Palestine (dated about 2000 B.C.), both long before the time of David (which was about 1000 B.C.)[8]

Unfortunately, I also found some of the errors of higher criticism still in print—ones that I had believed before and that had led me to believe that the Bible was unsound.

Archaeological Confirmation for the Bible's Accounts

As I continued to pursue the evidence for the historical accuracy of the Bible, I found it time and time again to prove to be solid and scientific. I had to reprogram my mind not to think of archaeology as "old science" just because it deals with old things. Instead, I discovered that it really is a new science. Only in the last 50 years has archaeology approached things in a highly organized, sophisticated way that utilizes many other branches of science. But modern archaeological research is extremely time-consuming and expensive. Hence I discovered that only a minuscule portion of possible sites have been studied, and that progress is slow.

Perhaps most importantly, I learned that the Bible is now a *standard historical text* for archaeologists in the Middle East, Asia Minor, and Macedonia. So it was no surprise that I learned of many, many archaeological finds supporting the Bible. But I found a number that were very convincing of the supernatural accuracy of the Bible.

- *Flood accounts and fossil graveyards.* More than 200 accounts of a great flood have been found in cultures throughout the world. Also, "fossil graveyards" are found throughout the world. These contain vast numbers of plants and creatures that are indigenous to many regions of the earth—all together in single "graves." These graveyards seem to indicate rapid mass burial—as in a major flood—of plants and creatures from different parts of the earth.

- *Sarah's grave.* A cave has been found in Hebron (in southern Israel) that is believed to be the actual grave of Abraham's wife, Sarah. It would then also be the grave of Abraham, Isaac, and Jacob (Genesis 25:9; 49:29-30). Though a Muslim mosque has been built over it (Muslims accept Abraham and parts of the Old Testament) and entry into the cave has generally been denied, at least twice non-Muslims have entered the cave and have reported what seem to be tombs.[9]

- *Hebrew slaves building cities in Egypt.* Archaeologists have discovered illustrations of Hebrews making bricks for the cities of Pithom and Rameses (Exodus 1:11; 5:13-18). Some ancient sites contain bricks made without straw, which possibly may corroborate the biblical account that the Pharaoh would not provide straw for brickmaking (Exodus 5:7).[10]

- *The existence of David.* Some scholars argued that King David was a myth, until in 1993 a stone monument was discovered at Tel Dan, near the border of Syria and Israel. It mentioned a victory over King David and the house of David, just as indicated in 1 Kings 15:20.[11]

- *Solomon's Empire.* Several interesting archaeological finds support the existence of King Solomon as indicated in the Bible. First, there are indications of trade with Hiram, king of the Phoenician city of Tyre (1 Kings 5:1). A sarcophagus (stone coffin) found in Syria shows the name of Hiram, and the Cyprus Museum possesses inscriptions referring to Solomon's relations with the Phoenicians.

Second, the Bible tells of Solomon rebuilding three cities: Gezer, Megiddo, and Hazor (1 Kings 9:15). All of these cities have buildings and pottery dating back to Solomon's reign.

Finally, Solomon's "city of horses" (1 Kings 9:19; 2 Chronicles 8:6) has been located in Megiddo (north of Jerusalem). It contains large compounds with stables.[12]

- *Nebuchadnezzar.* The king of Babylonia, he destroyed Jerusalem and the Temple and took the Jews into exile. He actually wrote a chapter of the Bible (Daniel 4). In Babylon, archaeology has uncovered enormous building projects—some 20 temples and docks—by Nebuchadnezzar. Many bricks found in those structures are stamped with an inscription that reads, "The fortifications of Esagila and Babylon I strengthened and established the name of my reign forever." A similar boast by Nebuchadnezzar was recorded in the Bible (Daniel 4:30).

- *The birthplace of Jesus.* The events surrounding the birth of Jesus were very unusual and were no secret. The shepherds talked to many people (Luke 2:17-18) about the angels; Simeon and Anna's proclamations in the Temple would have been heard by many others (Luke 2:25-38); the visit by the Magi (who would have been accompanied by a small army) was hardly unnoticeable (Matthew 2:3); and the murder of the children of Bethlehem by Herod was not forgotten (Matthew 2:16). There were *many witnesses* to these events.

Logically, the events (and the location of Jesus' birth) would be remembered. And in fact, even the very early generations of Christians venerated the place of Jesus' birth. Though during persecution the Romans tried to obscure it, people still knew where it was and passed on their knowledge. Finally, when the persecution was ended, Emperor Constantine's mother sought the site out and honored the location by building a church over it. Archaeologists have not seriously challenged the identification of this site as the actual place of Jesus' birth.[13]

- *The house of Joseph,* the legal father of Jesus. If Jesus really was a miracle worker and was acknowledged by some as a king and Messiah, people in his hometown would certainly have made note of where he lived. And likely, ensuing generations would have passed this knowledge down, attaching reverence to the location.

  Archaeology has discovered what has been considered to be the house of Joseph, just 100 meters from where Mary lived in Nazareth. A Crusader church was found on the site, built on top of a Byzantine church dating to about the 500s, which in turn was on top of two vaults identifying the house of Joseph. These vaults contained writings of the first-century church and also Roman artifacts.[14]

- *Peter's house in Capernaum.* The Gospel accounts indicate that Jesus had a place to stay in Capernaum, perhaps at Peter's house. It was likely that Jesus performed miracles there, perhaps even the healing of the paralyzed man (Mark 2:1-5).

  Archaeology has found a house that has been revered for centuries as Peter's house and was located close to the synagogue. Several churches have been built on top of it, indicating that it was believed by earlier Christians to be a holy site. Inside was found substantial Christian graffiti (writings) dating to the early second century, writings demonstrating that at that time the house was truly believed to be Peter's. Early writings by Christian fathers also indicated that such a house existed.[15]

- *The synagogue in Capernaum.* Jesus often stayed in Capernaum, taught in its synagogue (Matthew 4:13; 8:5;

17:24; Mark 1:21; 2:1; 9:33; Luke 4:23; 7:1; John 2:12; 6:17,24,59). Archaeologists have located the synagogue in Capernaum that is almost certainly the place where Jesus taught.[16]

- *Pontius Pilate, the Roman governor.* In the excavation of the Roman theater in Caesarea, a stone was found in the landing of a flight of steps bearing the inscription "To the people of Caesarea Tiberium Pontius Pilate Prefect of Judea." Another line uses the word "dedication," indicating the commemorating event of the theater's construction.[17]

- *The tomb of Lazarus.* In one of the most remarkable stories in the Gospels, Jesus raised Lazarus from the dead (John 11), which caused the Jewish leaders to want to kill Jesus. Amid a "honeycomb" of tombs in the area of Bethany, where Lazarus lived, is one that has been venerated since early Christian times. Archaeological findings—artifacts dating back to the time and early Christian graffiti—make it probable that it was the actual tomb of Lazarus.[18]

- *The sites of Jesus' death and resurrection.* Most archaeologists agree that the Church of the Holy Sepulchre in Jerusalem marks the original sites of Jesus' crucifixion and resurrection (they are at different ends of the church).

    The reason is logical. So important was this site to early Christians that the Emperor Hadrian erected a statue of the pagan god Venus on Golgotha (the crucifixion site) and a statue of the pagan god Jupiter on the site of the resurrection. He hoped this would obscure the significance of the locations. Instead, the statues preserved the memory of the sites for a couple hundred years, until Constantine made Christianity the religion of the empire. Then the sites were readily marked. Many early writers and modern archaeologists refer to them as authentic.[19]

Indications of Authenticity

Sir William Ramsey, one of the greatest archaeologists of all time, spent 30 years of his life trying to disprove the New Testament, especially Luke's writings. After much intensive research, with many expecting a thorough refutation of Christianity, Ramsey concluded that Luke was one of the greatest historians of all time and became a Christian based on his archaeological findings.

Were the Right Books in the Bible?

The final question I had regarding the legal proof of the Bible was, were the right books selected? After all, I had heard stories that only a few men in a room had decided what the Bible would be. However, I found that nothing could be further from the truth.

First, I had to understand what "regulations" were required for determining what the Bible would consist of. The word *canon* came up frequently. The word, I discovered, really means "standardized," but in a biblical sense it means "inspired by God."

Then I discovered that there were three distinct canons in the Bible: the Torah—the five books of the law of Moses; the rest of the Tanakh, or Old Testament; and the New Testament, accepted only by Christians (who also believe that the Old Testament is the foundation for the New Testament). What were the criteria?

1. The *Torah* canon was essentially accepted at the time of Moses (about 1450 B.C.). After all, the Hebrews at the time had observed firsthand the miracles and presence of God and the relationship of Moses to God. However, formally, this canon was not recognized—by decree of the religious leaders—until after the first exile (about 500 B.C.).

2. The entire *Tanakh* (Old Testament) canon had essentially been accepted by the Jewish people by 167 B.C. (around the time of the Maccabean revolt). It was the canon at the time of Jesus.

Again, however, it was not formally recognized by the religious leaders until later—in A.D. 70 at the time of the second Jewish exile.

3. The *New Testament* canon was accepted by the people during the early development of the church, probably within a century of Jesus' resurrection. In the early 200s, Origen (an early church leader) listed all the accepted books of the New Testament—a list that matches today's canon (even at that time only six books were in question). The Council of Carthage in the year 397 gave formal recognition to today's New Testament canon.

The point I discovered was, none of the canons was simply devised by a few men in a room. Rather, in each case they had much earlier, broadscale approval by the people. Recognition by councils was a mere formality. Hence the books that were declared to be from God had already been trusted as such for hundreds of years.

Further investigating the New Testament canon, I discovered that certain principles had been used in recognizing which books were considered as "from God." Those principles were:

- Were the books authoritative, that is, divinely inspired?

- Were they prophetic (100-percent correct)?

- Were they authentic? (Were the documents known to be valid?)

- Were they dynamic? (Did they contain life-transforming guidance?)

- Were they acceptable? (Did they conform consistently to the rest of the Bible?)

Also, all New Testament authors were to have either personally known Jesus or have been in close association with someone who did.

Legal Proof that Jesus Was God

I summarized the evidence that I had been gathering over the last months, as if I were going to present my case in a court of law. Could I give evidence that was convincing beyond a reasonable doubt that God exists and that Jesus is God, as indicated in the Old and New Testaments? I came up with 15 points.

● ● ●

1. The Old Testament prophecies of the Messiah are historically accurate. They predate Jesus by as much as 200 years, as verified by the Dead Sea scrolls, the Septuagint, and other translations.

2. The Old Testament was accurately transcribed over centuries of meticulous work by scribes who were professionally trained.

3. Changing any Old Testament prophecies would have involved an impossible task of changing many scrolls and the memories of tens of thousands of the Hebrew people.

4. The odds of any one person fulfilling the Messianic prophecies in the Old Testament are beyond statistical possibility without divine intervention.

5. The accounts of Jesus in the New Testament are verified by thousands of existing manuscripts—far more than for any other accepted historical document.

6. The copies of the accounts of Jesus date far closer to the actual events than do the copies of any other ancient document.

7. The accounts of Jesus were circulated at the time of the eyewitnesses to the events of Jesus' life. They would have been rejected if they had been incorrect or fictional.

8. People willingly gave their lives to attest to the historical events that they believed had changed their lives.

9. Non-Christian writers attested to many events concerning Jesus.

10. Hostile witnesses attested to events concerning Jesus.

11. The disciples who knew Jesus well were changed—suddenly inspired with boldness to tell the Gospel account in spite of the risk of painful execution.

12. Despite radical attempts to erase history and make the Gospel account disappear, it survived.

13. Despite radical attempts—through horrible persecution—to erase belief in the history of the death and resurrection of Jesus, Christianity continued to spread rapidly.

14. Christianity has become the predominant religion in the world today—based on the *historical event* of the death and resurrection of Jesus.

15. The development of canons of Scripture indicated that the people in the best position to know the facts, especially the eyewitnesses, widely accepted the Bible's books as Scripture long before they were formally recognized as such.

━━━━━━━━━━━━━━ ● ● ● ━━━━━━━━━━━━━━

Though I had discovered other convincing points such as the details of the trial of Jesus, the witnesses, and the corroboration of the documents, just the points above gave me substantial reason to reach a conclusion.

━━━━━━━━━━━━━━ ● ● ● ━━━━━━━━━━━━━━

Legal evidence proved that Jesus is the prophesied Son of God.

━━━━━━━━━━━━━━ ● ● ● ━━━━━━━━━━━━━━

26

Will the Real Jesus Please Stand Up?

It didn't take me long to realize that many different types of churches were proclaiming Jesus in various ways. I discovered many groups that agreed with the fundamental points I had learned from the Bible—that Jesus was crucified and buried, and was physically resurrected from the dead on the third day and seen by many people.

So I wondered about the other religions I heard about that seemed to go beyond the foundational points I had already researched. Several "Christian" organizations claimed to have additional insight, often through additional holy books. I decided to investigate some to see if there was any statistical or legal proof that would add to or supersede the New Testament. Again, the fundamental test I would apply would be, could I find provable, verifiable prophecy whose fulfillment would be impossible without God?

The Mormons (Church of Jesus Christ of Latter-Day Saints)

The name certainly sounded appealing. I liked the idea that some modern theme ("Latter-Day Saints") could be included in the Bible. The doctrines sounded appealing. But "appealing" wasn't what I was seeking. I wanted truth. Did the Mormons' holy books add any truth that would help me define who God is? Were the books valid? Did they contain prophecy and provable legal evidence?

The Mormons proclaim there are three holy books that supersede the Bible: *The Book of Mormon, The Pearl of Great Price,* and the book of *Doctrine and Covenants.* I found the following:

- *The Book of Mormon* incorrectly predicted that Jesus would be born in Jerusalem (Alma 7:9-10) rather than in Bethlehem.

- *The Book of Mormon* failed legal historical proof. It portrays two civilizations, including some 38 cities, with substantial detail. Despite substantial attempts, no supporting evidence has been found. Archaeologists and anthropologists flatly reject the book's historical claims.

- *Doctrine and Covenants* contains Joseph Smith's prophecy that the Mormon temple would be built in western Missouri at a specified site *within his generation* (D & C 84:1-5). As of this day it has still not been built.

- *The Pearl of Great Price* contains the "Book of Abraham," which Joseph Smith, the founder of Mormonism, claimed to have divinely translated from the original Egyptian hieroglyphic writings. Yet in the mid-1900s, some decades after the Rosetta Stone had been deciphered and the key to hieroglyphics had been found, one of the Mormons' own Egyptologists translated the original documents.[1] He discovered that the "book of Abraham" was a hoax. (The original document was actually a remnant of a funerary text.)[2]

I quickly concluded that Mormonism did not provide anything that would supersede the Bible. And within their books I found no evidence of the God whose influence I had been able to prove to be in the Bible.

The Jehovah's Witnesses

I soon discovered that the Jehovah's Witnesses had a foundational belief that Jesus was not God. This troubled me after all the research I had already done regarding the veracity of the Bible, in which I had found Jesus' claim to be God supported by statistical and legal proof.

I immediately began to research the Jehovah's Witnesses' additional sources of information so I could examine them for fulfilled prophecy. What could the new revelations of the Jehovah's Witnesses add to the Bible?

It didn't take long for me to answer that question. I discovered that the religion (founded in the late 1800s by Charles Russell) had made many prophetic claims about the "end times." The Watchtower (their official name) had prophesied the end of time in 1914. Then it prophesied the end of the world in 1918. It was prophesied again in 1925, and at later times. Applying the test of perfect prophecy, the Jehovah's Witnesses failed miserably. I decided not to trust their claims or their definition of God.

Christian Science

At first I loved the words. "Christian" and "science." To me they seemed to fit together perfectly since I had accepted the Bible. However, when I read Christian Science's key text for interpreting the Bible—*Science and Health*—I found that it rejected the Bible's concept of sin and blood atonement by Jesus for sin. This hardly made it Christian.

Later in my studies of *Science and Health*, I found that matter (material things) were regarded as mere illusion. This hardly made it scientific.

Nor could I find any testable historical prophecies in the book. That, combined with a lack of any legal evidence supporting its claims, caused me to steer completely clear of this concept of "God."

Part VI

Proving God Three Ways

27

The Verdict

"Okay," I sighed as I sank back in my chair and let out a deep breath, overwhelmed by several years of intense research about God. "I'm done."

I had been determined to disprove God. It didn't work, no matter how I looked at it. I was beaten by an advertising promotions person whose name I'd long since forgotten. He was right. God *did* exist. And further, I had learned exactly who that God was—it was the God whose existence was revealed in the Bible.

Though I had to swallow my pride in defeat, a smile slowly came over my face, and I felt a warmth within me like I never had before. Instead of defeat, I thought about what I had to gain. Now I had both a reason to live and a reason to die. What an amazing story to tell others!

Incredible—the most important life-changing news anyone could hope for, and it lies buried in a bunch of books that hardly anyone reads. This was not just any news. This was news that would change people's lives for eternity. *It should be on the front page in huge type,* I thought.

In my mind, I reviewed the facts—

- I had *analytical evidence.* First, life could not possibly have come about by random chance (naturalism). Since the only choices for the origin of life are random chance and creation, therefore God must exist. And by definition, God = Creator.

  Second, a planet so precisely suited to man could not have come into existence by random

chance. Therefore God must exist, and by extension, he must be all-powerful.

- I had *statistical evidence.* If any holy book has many
  significant prophecies that are 100-percent correct—with a statistical probability of their coming
  true randomly of less than the scientific standard of
  1 chance in 10^{50}—that book must be supernatural,
  which essentially proves the existence of God.
  Valid prophecy in the Old Testament (the Jewish
  Bible) far exceeded that standard. This indicated
  that God is real.

  Furthermore, the many valid prophecies of the
  Messiah that Jesus had fulfilled were verified in the
  New Testament. This also had a statistical probability that far exceeded the standard—which indicated Jesus' deity.

- I had *legal evidence.* The prophecies I had evaluated statistically were precisely copied and accurately transmitted. The New Testament was
  reliable, based on the manuscript evidence. And as
  important, the people who definitely knew the
  facts willingly died based on the historicity of
  Jesus' death and resurrection.

———•———

By now, I had gained considerable insight into the Bible and
was wise enough to know what to do, but stupid enough not to do
it quickly. As I sat in my office at home, I thought again about the
words in Matthew's Gospel:

> "Not everyone who says to me, 'Lord, Lord,' will enter
> the kingdom of heaven, but only he who does the will
> of my Father who is in heaven. Many will say to me on
> that day, 'Lord, Lord, did we not prophesy in your
> name, and in your name drive out demons and perform
> many miracles?' Then I will tell them plainly, *'I never*

knew you. Away from me, you evildoers!' " (Jesus, in Matthew 7:21-23).

The word for "know" in Greek—*ginosko*—I had discovered, had a broader meaning than to simply intellectually "know about." The broader application included "feel," "be resolved to," "be sure of."[1] In other words, it implies a closer knowledge of the true Jesus than the simple knowledge that he existed.

I also recalled my study of the word "believe" in the well-known verse John 3:16:

> God so loved the world that he gave his one and only Son, that whoever *believes* in him shall not perish but have eternal life (John 3:16).

I had discovered that the Greek word for "believe," *pisteuo,* had a deeper meaning than to simply intellectually acknowledge a fact. It carried the sense of "to put one's trust in."[2]

So here I was. Knowing the truth and yet not acting. *I needed to have a close relationship with Jesus. I needed to place my trust completely in him.* What was holding me back?

I thought about all the questions I still had. The ones from my childhood about the 900-year-old men, the parting of the Red Sea, and Noah's ark. I thought about my questions from later on, such as when I realized Steve Conoman couldn't count to 1.4 million in a day—let alone name that many animals. Questions, questions, and more questions. Should I wait to answer them all?

My mind turned to my discussion with Gene. I thought about the analogy of the advancing tornado and how stupid it would be to just sit in its path, knowing it was coming. I knew of one tornado that was coming for certain—death. And I knew it would strike me, just not when, where, or how. Why wasn't I moving out of its way? Pride? Fear of being a "Jesus freak"?

It struck me that I had really started to love God and Jesus in the process of my research. I realized that I really enjoyed reading the Bible and enjoyed the thrill of discovery that a supernatural God would actually display himself to us in the heavens, in the human cell, and in the Bible so we could find him. It thrilled me to know that Christianity was not like any other religion. It was a religion based on facts—lots of facts and evidence that could be verified. It was not based on blind faith. And the God of the universe actually wanted us to use our minds to put it to the test alongside every other idea of "God."

When Jesus was asked what the greatest commandment was, he replied,

> "Love the Lord your God with all your heart and with all your soul and with all your mind and with all your strength" (Mark 12:30-31).

God must have included loving him with all our *mind* for a reason.

Thinking over the last few years of research, I was almost sad that it seemed to be coming to an end. A sense inside me told me I had to really commit to Jesus and decide to make him Lord of my life no matter what the consequences—Jesus freak or not. I could always continue my search for answers to the many questions that still troubled me. But there was no doubt about the fundamentals anymore. God was God. Jesus was God. I accepted what the Bible said about the Holy Spirit.

Since the Bible—with its hundreds of imbedded prophecies—could be trusted, I was willing to bet that the parts I didn't understand yet could be trusted as well. I decided to put off any research on the other questions until later. I slowly leaned forward in my chair, stood up, and walked out of my office.

Getting Washed Clean

There was no lightning bolt from heaven. There was no apparition of Jesus. There was no passionate clinging to a cross at church. In my case, once I was firmly convinced that God really did exist in the way he was described in the Bible, and that Jesus was God—I calmly left my home office, walked into the bathroom, and started to take a shower.

Then it hit me. As water was flooding over my hair and eyes, I lowered my head and started to cry. Tears were streaming down my face intermingled with the flow of water. Then I sat down and held my head in my hands—and started praying. I remember thanking God for his patience and for revealing the truth to me. As the warm water flowed down over my back, I asked for forgiveness for all the doubt I had for all those years. Forgiveness for years of games of trying to draw people away from God. I asked Jesus to help me fix my life—to draw me to a life of love instead of a life motivated by money and power. I asked him to truly direct my life and said I would follow. I gave myself to him and committed all I had to give to him. And I asked him for daily guidance.

Somehow I knew my life had changed forever.

But looking down, all I saw right then was my bare feet and a lot of soapy water.

———•———

As I went out and encountered the people I had known for years, they wondered why my prior arrogance and pride seemed to be melting away. It didn't happen overnight. But within a short period of time I began to truly care about people, not just things.

Along with Jan, my wife, and our three boys (ages 6 to 11), I was now attending Saddleback Church on a fairly frequent basis. Within about a year-and-a-half, the previously unthinkable happened—Jan asked me if I thought we should "join" the church. To me this was a very big step. I thought back to the "horror" of church in my youth. But I had a new commitment and relationship with Jesus now, and it was time to grow up. We agreed to go through introductory classes as a family (there were special classes for children). On January 8, 1989, my family was baptized together at Saddleback Church.

Epilogue

The New Path of a Former Skeptic

It seemed that everything in my search for God had gone in slow motion. But I realized that, just as it had taken me years to become an atheist, so it had taken me years to climb out of it. It had taken me 1456 hours to learn to detest church and Sunday school, so it would take time for me to become "involved." And it had taken time for me to develop a phobia about becoming a Jesus freak—something I still had to overcome.

What I didn't count on was a passion that was building within me to share what I had learned with others. Having led a skeptical life myself, I realized that most people try to ignore the "tornado of death" that will certainly strike them. I realized that most people don't examine the evidence for the existence of God. Nor do they prepare for the future. This bothered me when I considered that all the evidence we need to know God with certainty is *right before our eyes.* We don't have to accept a blind faith, and God doesn't expect us to.

I increased my research in the Bible to a breakneck pace. I still had lots of questions left. But I had no idea what God had in store for me in the future.

In 1991, I founded a volunteer ministry (Strong Basis to Believe) at Saddleback Church that taught skeptics and Christians the information I had learned through my research.

I'll never forget the day my name first appeared in the church bulletin—announcing the class in front of thousands of people. A

251

chill went down my spine. *The cat's out of the bag*, I thought. *If people want to consider me a Jesus freak, it's too late to stop it now.*

It's funny how old ideas can haunt you for so many years.

A New Direction

One day in 1996, I was in my home office during my daily quiet time, the time when I pray and read the Bible. This particular day I was troubled because I was under considerable stress from three major work projects I was involved in. On the other hand, I felt excited about a second small booklet I was writing for my Strong Basis to Believe class that I taught at Saddleback Church. In addition to handing them out in class, I also usually made copies and placed them in the lobby of the church office. This time I was intending to make extra copies to test in our local Christian bookstore, Sonshine. Its owner, Mark Swenson, had become a good friend and was willing to test my homemade books in his store to see if his clientele had an interest in them. He had already tested a few copies of my first booklet, which I had placed in his store just before Easter and had forgotten about. Months later, I had returned, expecting to take the remaining ones to give to my class. Mark informed me they had all sold.

While praying, I started thinking about my enormous workload. Three major consulting projects were reaching final deadlines, which meant many late hours and a lot of pressure to produce work quickly. Normally I would turn a consulting project for a client into a follow-up project. I realized I could not continue to work for everyone. I recall feeling totally overwhelmed. Thinking back to the first time I had asked Jesus to direct my life, I prayed that God would remove all the areas that he didn't want me working in.

Within two weeks, all the consulting projects had vanished—with no follow-up projects. I was shocked. All my income-producing work was gone! The only remaining project was the little booklet I was writing, which provided no income whatsoever. So at that point I prayed, "God, if this is what you want, I need help, and lots of it. I need money, time, and people."

Within a week an advertising agency owner, Vern Hunt of Synergy, Inc., who happened upon the homemade versions of the books I was writing, called me and offered to design all the covers and advertising materials at no cost.

Vern and his partner Ron were the two dedicated employees who had left my firm many years ago, during my arrogant days with Keith Tomkin and Steve Conoman. I'll never forget the first day I saw Vern after all those years. He walked up to me in the hall outside his advertising offices, gave me a big smile, and shook my hand.

After several minutes of conversation, Vern said, "I just can't believe how you've changed!" Vern saw a new, more humble attitude that had left materialism behind in favor of more lasting "treasure" involving people and the teaching I was doing.

Later Ron Scheibel, Vern's partner, came in. He and Vern designed the covers for my first self-published books, along with lots of advertising materials. Step one in God's plan to have me spread the research knowledge I had gained was underway, through an answer to prayer.

Other things started to fall into place as well. A distributor relationship, production, sales, displays, marketing, warehousing, billing and collection—all starting from scratch and still providing enough funds for our family to scrape by. God was clearly working in our lives.

With God's help, a new ministry had blossomed. At first I had to do everything from writing the books to collecting the payments—everything. It seemed that whenever something was needed, God provided it. Volunteers, sales, and even contributions on occasion. By the time I started working with Harvest House Publishers, I had written nine books and personally sold about 200,000 copies.

———◆———

As of today, only a few years later, God has provided in so many ways: I've written more than 18 books, developed an Examine the Evidence teaching course, written and helped produce a major videotape, conducted seminars, and had many speaking engagements at churches and organizations. I've also spoken on national TV dozens of times, radio hundreds of times, and created a major Web site: www.evidenceofgod.com. Who would have thought a former corporate executive—*an atheist*—would be transformed into someone who is championing God?

Today, I do exactly what my challenger, "Bob," did. Apart from the efforts above, I often personally challenge others to investigate the Bible. I point out the importance of discovering God, tell them about my own journey, and help them find the information they need to make a knowledgeable decision. I've learned that when people discover things for themselves it seems much more meaningful than when someone simply tells them what to believe.

And opportunities come up at all kinds of times and in all kinds of places to talk to others. Almost always when I'm traveling, God places people in my path who are looking for him...

———•———

"You'll have to go to that counter," the immigration official said. He pointed me to a long hall with many windows, but only two had people behind them. I went to one with a dark-skinned young man of about 30.

"Why are you coming to Canada?" he asked.

"I'm an author of books and will be on television promoting them," I responded.

"Will you be selling any books while here in Canada?"

"No," I replied. "My publisher simply set up a media tour here."

"Oh," he said as he started to become more friendly, perhaps stepping out of his official role a little. "What kind of books do you write?"

"Books about the reality of God, Jesus, and the Bible. Would you like to see some?"

"Yes," he said. I fumbled through my briefcase and brought out a half-dozen of the books I'd written. The official saw two of the titles: *How Do We Know Jesus Is God?* and *What Is the Proof for the Resurrection?* Then we started talking about Jesus, not about my entry into Canada. I explained my former skepticism, my exploration, and the evidence for him today.

Soon into the conversation, the agent told me he was a Muslim, and while they too believe in Jesus, they don't believe he was God. The discussion went on for at least half an hour—certainly unusual for an immigration official. I offered to give him some books, but he refused to take any, saying that it would appear to be a bribe and would be unacceptable. Perhaps God set this up to "plant some seeds."

———————●———————

I'm a football fanatic. Once—also in Canada—I was determined to see the playoffs, which weren't on my hotel room TV. The only place to go was the sports bar in the hotel lobby. While I was watching the game by myself at a table, a person alone at the next table started asking which team I liked and why. After we'd discussed that for a while, he asked me why I was in Canada. Naturally, this led into the discussion of why I was writing books about Jesus Christ.

It turned out he was a Hindu. Before I knew it, he had joined me at my table and was asking lots and lots of questions. Again I realized how thirsty people are to know the truth...the facts. I didn't see much of the playoff game I had come down to watch, because of the very involved conversation. Later, I gave the man some of my books, which he had requested. While he didn't come to know Christ that day, his eyes were opened to at least examining the evidence.

———————●———————

"What are you reading?" asked the woman sitting next to me, as we awaited the announcement of a flight from Chicago to Dallas.

"Oh, just a book I wrote. I'm preparing for an interview."

"On what topic?" she said, obviously eyeing the Bible beside me.

"I write about the Bible, Jesus...things like that," I replied—somewhat abruptly because I had to call my wife to tell her I might not make it into Dallas because of the weather. We continued the discussion for a few minutes, when I finally had to excuse myself to call Jan.

A while later, the plane actually boarded. Upon arriving at my seat, I noticed the only seat left on the plane was the one next to me. The next thing I knew, the woman I had spoken to was heading down the aisle—of course to the seat next to me. I had hoped to rest, but God didn't plan it that way. We spent the next three hours in intensive discussion about the reliability of the Bible (which she doubted), the reality of Jesus (which she also doubted), and what to do to go to heaven. I thought she had enough information by the end of the flight to be convinced, but perhaps was embarrassed to accept Jesus right then. She had a serious illness that she confided to me about, and I encouraged her to take some of the books I had written and study them so she could know how to give herself to Jesus and enter the kingdom of heaven by the grace of God.

———•———

I often think back to that day I "took the challenge" to research the Bible. I ended up finding God. How different my life would have been had I not examined the evidence. I would probably still be arrogantly climbing the corporate ladder for all I was worth, trampling over anyone, anytime, to get to the top. Instead, knowing God, my perspectives have completely changed. I have peace of mind in the present. I'm forgiven of the past. And most importantly, I look forward to the future—to the day I will be with God.

My prayers for everyone are—

- that anyone reading this book will be challenged, like I was, to *truly seek God.*

- that in seeking God, no one will simply follow the crowd, but that everyone will do an honest investigation and *examine the evidence.*

- that churches and church leaders will take the Information Age seriously and realize that many people (like me) demand answers. ("Answers" are taught in school, but often not in church—certainly not to the satisfaction of intelligent youth. Recognize the power of the Internet and use it to inform people.)

- that families who are Christian would teach their children at home and prepare them to face a world filled with misinformation. Arm yourselves with facts.

- that Christians would learn about the many resources available to help them know the facts. (Evidence of God Ministries, Inc., already has lots of free information on the Internet at www.evidenceofgod.com.

- that all Christians would tell others about their own experience of seeking God.

If God can change a problem person (like me) from a hard-core atheist into a champion for Jesus—an idea I once detested—he can change anyone. I encourage everyone to follow what the Bible says:

> "Seek first his kingdom and his righteousness, *and all these [other worldly] things will be given to you as well*" (Matthew 6:3).

And remember that it is impossible to please God without faith. He wants you to *believe* that he exists and that he will *reward* those who *earnestly seek him* (see Hebrews 11:6).

Earnestly seek God. You will be rewarded. Seeking leads to believing, and believing leads to real, convinced faith. As a former hard-core skeptic, I can say that truly seeking God was the best decision of my life. And I want everyone who reads this book to share that reward of eternal joy that I am looking forward to.

———————●———————

"Whew!" I exclaimed as I leaned back in my booth at the Shanghai Palace. I had just finished my final review of this book's manuscript while eating my favorite lunch, "vegetable

shrimp." As I paid the check, I pondered my long search for God, my countless hours of research, and my new labor of love—telling other skeptics what I've learned. I got my change back and left my usual tip. Just before leaving, I broke open my fortune cookie for fun. And the message inside read,

Skepticism is the first step toward truth.

How to Know God

If you would like to have a relationship with the God of the universe, a relationship ensuring eternal life, all you need to do is the following:

1. Believe that God exists and that he came to earth in the human form of Jesus Christ (John 3:16; Romans 10:9).

2. Accept God's free forgiveness of sins and gift of new life through the death and resurrection of Jesus Christ (Ephesians 2:8-10; 1:7-8).

3. Switch to God's plan for your life (1 Peter 1:21-23; Ephesians 2:1-7).

4. Expressly make Jesus Christ the director of your life (Matthew 7:21-27; 1 John 4:15).

Prayer for Eternal Life with God

"Dear God, I believe you sent your Son, Jesus, to die for my sins so I can be forgiven. I'm sorry for my sins, and I want to live the rest of my life the way you want me to. Please put your spirit in my life to direct me. Amen."

Then What?

- Find a Bible-based church you like and attend regularly.

- Set aside some time each day to pray and read the Bible.

- Locate other Christians to spend time with on a regular basis.

Appendix A

Some Evidences That a Planet Was Designed to Support Life

Parameter	Estimated probability of galaxy, star, planet, or moon falling in required range for support of life
local abundance and distribution of dark matter	.1
galaxy cluster size	.1
galaxy cluster location	.1
galaxy size	.1
galaxy type	.1
galaxy location	.1
variability of local dwarf galaxy absorption rate	.1
star location relative to galactic center	.2
star distance from corotation circle of galaxy	.005
star distance from closest spiral arm	.1
z-axis extremes of star's orbit	.02
proximity of solar nebula to a supernova eruption	.01
timing of solar nebula formation relative to supernova eruption	.01
number of stars in system	.7
number and timing of close encounters by nearby stars	.01
proximity of close stellar encounters	.1
masses of close stellar encounters	.1
star birth date	.2
star age	.4
star metallicity	.05
star orbital eccentricity	.1

star mass	.001
star luminosity change relative to speciation types and rates	.00001
star color	.4
star carbon-to-oxygen ratio	.01
star space velocity relative to local standard of rest	.05
star short-term luminosity variability	.05
star long-term luminosity variability	.05
number and timing of solar system encounters with interstellar gas clouds	.1
H_3+ production	.1
supernovae rates and locations	.01
white dwarf binary types, rates, and locations	.01
planetary distance from star	.001
inclination of planetary orbit	.5
axis tilt of planet	.3
rate of change of axis tilt	.01
period and size of axis tilt variation	.1
planetary rotation period	.1
rate of change in planetary rotation period	.05
planetary orbit eccentricity	.3
rate of change of planetary orbit eccentricity	.1
rate of change of planetary inclination	.5
period and size of eccentricity variation	.1
period and size of inclination variation	.1
number of moons	.2
mass and distance of moon	.01
surface gravity (escape velocity)	.001
tidal force from sun and moon	.1
magnetic field	.01
rate of change and character of change in magnetic field	.1
albedo (planet reflectivity)	.1
density	.1
thickness of crust	.01
oceans-to-continents ratio	.2
rate of change in oceans-to-continents ratio	.1
global distribution of continents	.3
frequency, timing, and extent of ice ages	.1
frequency, timing, and extent of global snowball events	.1
asteroidal and cometary collision rate	.1
change in asteroidal and cometary collision rates	.1
rate in change in asteroidal and cometary collision rates	.1
mass of body colliding with primordial earth	.002
timing of body colliding with primordial earth	.05

location of body's collision with primordial earth	.05
position and mass of Jupiter relative to earth	.01
major planet eccentricities	.1
major planet orbital instabilities	.05
drift and rate of drift in major planetary distances	.05
number and distribution of planets	.01
atmospheric transparency	.01
atmospheric pressure	.01
atmospheric viscosity	.1
atmospheric electrical discharge rate	.01
atmospheric temperature gradient	.01
carbon dioxide level in atmosphere	.01
rate of change in carbon dioxide level in atmosphere	.1
rate of change in water vapor level in atmosphere	.01
rate of change in methane level in early atmosphere	.01
oxygen quantity in atmosphere	.01
chlorine quantity in atmosphere	.1
cobalt quantity in crust	.1
arsenic quantity in crust	.1
copper quantity in crust	.1
boron quantity in crust	.1
fluorine quantity in crust	.1
iodine quantity in crust	.1
manganese quantity in crust	.1
nickel quantity in crust	.1
phosphorus quantity in crust	.1
tin quantity in crust	.1
zinc quantity in crust	.1
molybdenum quantity in crust	.05
vanadium quantity in crust	.1
chromium quantity in crust	.1
selenium quantity in crust	.1
iron quantity in oceans	.1
tropospheric ozone quantity	.01
stratospheric ozone quantity	.01
mesospheric ozone quantity	.01
water vapor level in atmosphere	.01
oxygen-to-nitrogen ratio in atmosphere	.1
quantity of greenhouse gases in atmosphere	.01
rate of change of greenhouse gases in atmosphere	.01
quantity of forest and grass fires	.01

quantity of sea salt aerosols	.1
soil mineralization	.1
quantity of anaerobic bacteria in the oceans	.01
quantity of aerobic bacteria in the oceans	.01
quantity of decomposer bacteria in soil	.01
quantity of mycorrhizal fungi in soil	.01
quantity of nitrifying microbes in soil	.01
quantity and timing of vascular plant introductions	.01
quantity, timing, and placement of carbonate-producing animals	.00001
quantity, timing, and placement of methanogens	.00001
quantity of soil sulfur	.1
quantity of sulfur in planet core	.1
quantity of silicon in planet core	.1
quantity of water at subduction zones in the crust	.01
hydration rate of subducted minerals	.1
tectonic activity	.05
rate of decline in tectonic activity	.1
volcanic activity	.1
rate of decline in volcanic activity	.1
viscosity at planet core boundaries	.01
viscosity of lithosphere	.2
biomass to comet infall ratio	.01
regularity of comet infall	.1
number, intensity, and location of hurricanes	.02
dependency factors estimate	1,000,000,000,000,000,000.
longevity requirements estimate	.0000001
probability for occurrence of all 128 parameters	$\approx 10^{-166}$
maximum possible number of planets in universe	$\approx 10^{22}$

Summary

For all of these factors to come together in a single planet is less than one chance in 10^{144}. Earth was clearly designed for human beings, and the odds of the existence of another such planet are nil, now that we have a defined boundary for and an estimated number of potential planets in the universe.

For more information on this and other scientific facts supporting the existence of a God of the universe, contact Reasons to Believe, PO Box 5978, Pasadena, CA 91117, or call (626) 335-1480. See also their Web site: www.reasons.org.

Appendix B

Analyzed Prophecies of the Old Testament

In addition to the prophecies discussed on pages 139–158, I also used the following ones in my statistical analysis of prophecy fulfillment in the Old Testament.

1. Abraham's son Ishmael would be father of a great nation (Genesis 17:20).
    Fulfillment: Ishmael is considered the father of the Arab nations.

2. The Amalekites would be destroyed (Moses, c. 1450 B.C., Exodus 17:14).
    Fulfillment: About 1000 B.C., 1 Chronicles 4:43).

3. Assyria would fall and be destroyed (Isaiah, c. 735 B.C., Isaiah 14:24-27).
    Fulfillment: Completed with the destruction of Nineveh in 612 B.C.

4. Destruction of Damascus predicted (Isaiah, c. 735 B.C. Isaiah 17:1-4).
    Fulfillment: Destruction by Assyria (history).

5. Prophecy against Egypt (Isaiah, c. 740 B.C., Isaiah 19:1-17).
    Fulfillment: Invasion by Assyria and Babylon along with internal fighting (history).

6. Prophecy against Babylon (Isaiah, c. 740 B.C., Isaiah 21:1-10).
    Fulfillment: Conquest by Medes and Persians in 539 B.C.

7. Prophesies against Edom and Petra (Isaiah, c. 745 B.C., Isaiah 34:5-15; Jeremiah, c. 600 B.C., Jeremiah 49:17-18; Ezekiel 25, 35).
    Fulfillment: History. "Unpopulated," conquered by heathen (500s B.C.), conquered by Israel (Ezekiel 25:14); desolate to Teman (Ezekiel 25:13); void of trade (Isaiah 34:10; Jeremiah 49:17); inhabited by wild animals (Isaiah 34:11-15; Ezekiel 35:7). All of these prophetic elements have transpired.

8. Prophecy of Jerusalem being destroyed, yet with blessings to follow (Isaiah 29:1-24).
    Fulfillment: 2 Chronicles 36:15-21.

9. Israel would not be helped by Egypt after their alliance with them (Isaiah 30:1–31:9).
    Fulfillment: History.

10. Jerusalem would be destroyed along with other Judean towns (Jeremiah, c. 620 B.C., Jeremiah 9:11).
    Fulfillment: History.

11. Children and young would be killed, as well as those in Egypt, Edom, Ammon, and Moab (Jeremiah, c. 620 B.C., Jeremiah 9:17-26).
    Fulfillment: 2 Chronicles 36:15-21.

12. Those living in the land God promised to Abraham would experience God's wrath, and by breaking the covenants of Moses, Israel would experience curses (Jeremiah, c. 600 B.C., Jeremiah 10:17-25; 11:1-8).
    Fulfillment: 2 Chronicles 36:15-21.

13. Israel would have drought, famine, and wars. Their prophets would die (Jeremiah, c. 620 B.C., Jeremiah 14:1-16).
    Fulfillment: 2 Chronicles 36:15-21.

14. Jeremiah would be saved, but Jerusalem would fall and be plundered (Jeremiah, c. 600 B.C., Jeremiah 15:5-21).
    Fulfillment: History—exile to Babylon.

15. Israel would be hunted—to exile its people into captivity (Jeremiah, c. 620 B.C., Jeremiah 16:16-18).
    Fulfillment: 2 Chronicles 36:15-21.

16. Judah's wealth would be taken, its people would be enslaved, and they would lose their inheritance (Jeremiah, c. 620 B.C., Jeremiah 17:1-14).
    Fulfillment: History.

17. Israel would be destroyed and its treasure would be taken to Babylon (Jeremiah, c. 620 B.C., Jeremiah 20:1-6).
    Fulfillment: 2 Chronicles 36:15-21.

18. Jerusalem would be destroyed unless it surrendered (Jeremiah, c. 620 B.C., Jeremiah 21:8-14).
    Fulfillment: 2 Chronicles 36:15-21.

19. Israel's kings and holy places would be destroyed (Jeremiah, c. 620 B.C., Jeremiah 22:1-23).
    Fulfillment: 2 Chronicles 36:15-21.

20. God would judge lying prophets (Jeremiah, c. 620 B.C., Jeremiah 23:9-40).
    Fulfillment: 2 Chronicles 36:15-21.

21. Babylon would conquer Israel; Israel would surrender (Jeremiah, c. 620 B.C., Jeremiah 27:1-22).
    Fulfillment: 2 Chronicles 36:11-21.

22. Jerusalem would be rebuilt "from the Tower of Hananel to the Corner Gate" (Jeremiah, c. 620 B.C., Jeremiah 31:38-40).
    Fulfillment: History.

23. Jerusalem would be conquered; its houses would be filled with dead (Jeremiah, c. 620 B.C., Jeremiah 33:1-5).
    Fulfillment: 2 Chronicles 36:11-15.

24. Babylon would conquer and burn Jerusalem; King Zedekiah would face punishment (Jeremiah, c. 620 B.C., Jeremiah 34:1-22).
    Fulfillment: 2 Kings 24:18–25:10.

25. The Babylonians would come back after fighting Egypt and attack Jerusalem and destroy it (Jeremiah, c. 620 B.C., Jeremiah 37:1-17).
    Fulfillment: 2 Chronicles 36:11-15.

26. Fall of Jerusalem predicted several times (Jeremiah, c. 620 B.C., Jeremiah 38).
    Fulfillment: 2 Chronicles 36:11-15.

27. Egypt would be defeated by Babylon (Jeremiah, c. 620 B.C., Jeremiah 46:1-26).
    Fulfillment: History, in approximately 605 B.C.

28. The land of the Philistines would be destroyed (Jeremiah, c. 620 B.C., Jeremiah 47:1-7).
    Fulfillment: History, in 609 B.C.

29. Moab would be destroyed as described (Jeremiah, c. 620 B.C., Jeremiah 48:1-47).
    Fulfillment: History, in 585 B.C. by the Babylonians.

30. Ammon would be destroyed (Jeremiah, c. 620 B.C., Jeremiah 49:1-6).
    Fulfillment: History.

31. Edom would be destroyed (Jeremiah, c. 620 B.C., Jeremiah 49:7-22).
    Fulfillment: History, about 550 B.C.

32. Damascus would be destroyed by fire (Jeremiah, c. 620 B.C., Jeremiah 49:23-27).
    Fulfillment: Many times in history.

33. Kedar and Hazor would be destroyed (Jeremiah, c. 620 B.C., Jeremiah 49:28-33).
    Fulfillment: History—the Babylonian invasion.

34. Jerusalem falls and captivity begins (Jeremiah, c. 620 B.C., Jeremiah 52: 1-31).
    Fulfillment: History, 586 B.C.

35. Israel would be destroyed and their property taken from them (c. 590 B.C., Ezekiel 7:1-27).
    Fulfillment: 2 Chronicles 36:11-15.

36. Israel would be restored to its land (c. 590 B.C., Ezekiel 11: 16-25).
    Fulfillment: History, in 537 B.C.

37. Jerusalem portrayed as an "unfaithful wife" who would be subject to judgment (c. 590 B.C., Ezekiel 16:1-63).
    Fulfillment: 2 Chronicles 36:11-15.

38. Jerusalem would be enticed by Egypt, conquered by Babylonians, and ultimately destroyed (c. 590 B.C., Ezekiel 17:1-24).
    Fulfillment: 2 Kings 24:17–25:10; 2 Chronicles 36:11-15.

39. Israel would be judged through a defeat at the hands of Babylon (c. 590 B.C., Ezekiel 21:1-27).
    Fulfillment: 2 Chronicles 36:11-15.

40. Ammon would fall by sin (c. 590 B.C., Ezekiel 21:28-32).
    Fulfillment: History.

41. Samaria and Jerusalem depicted as two "sinful sisters" being judged for sin (c. 590 B.C., Ezekiel 23:1-48).
    Fulfillment: History—conquest by the Assyrians and Babylonians.

42. There would be no time for mourning when many in Israel were killed (c. 590 B.C., Ezekiel 24:15-27).
    Fulfillment: 2 Chronicles 36:11-20.

43. Ammon would be destroyed (c. 590 B.C., Ezekiel 25:1-7).
    Fulfillment: The race disappeared from history.

44. Moab would be destroyed (c. 590 B.C., Ezekiel 25:8-11).
    Fulfillment: The race disappeared from history.

45. Edom would be destroyed (c. 590 B.C., Ezekiel 25:12-14).
    Fulfillment: The race disappeared from history.

46. The Philistines would be judged by God (c. 590 B.C., Ezekiel 25:15-17).
    Fulfillment: The race disappeared from history.

47. Destruction of Egypt (Ezekiel 31:1-18).
    Fulfillment: History—in 663 B.C. and 571 B.C. when Egypt was invaded by the Babylonians.

48. Another prophecy against Edom (c. 590 B.C., Ezekiel 35:1-15).
    Fulfillment: The race disappeared from history.

49. The impending doom of Israel (c. 830 B.C., Joel 2:1-11).
    Fulfillment: Assyria started devastation of the land beginning about 722 B.C.

50. Tyre and Sidon would be judged for selling the children of Israel as slaves to the Greeks; their children in turn would be sold to the people of Judah (c. 830 B.C., Joel 3:4-8).
    Fulfillment: History—Alexander the Great's conquest, 326-323 B.C.

51. Israel would again enjoy abundant food and water (c. 830 B.C., Joel 3:16-21).
    Fulfillment: History, following the first exile; and again, following the second exile—today.

52. Destruction of Damascus, Gaza, Tyre, Edom, Ammon, and Moab (c. 760 B.C., Amos 1:1–2:5).
    Fulfillment: History—under the Assyrians, Babylonians, Medo-Persians, and Greeks.

53. Judgment of Israel for specific sins (c. 760 B.C., Amos 5:1-27).
    Fulfillment: 722 B.C.—Assyrian captivity; and 587–586 B.C.—Babylonian captivity.

54. Judgment of Israel for complacent and luxurious living (c. 760 B.C., Amos 6:1-14).
    Fulfillment: 722 B.C.—Assyrian captivity; and 587–586 B.C.—Babylonian captivity.

55. Judgment of Israel—enemies would "strip the land clean" and Israel's sons and daughters would die by the sword (c. 760 B.C., Amos 7:1-17).
    Fulfillment: 722 B.C.—Assyrian captivity; and 587–586 B.C.—Babylonian captivity.

56. Israel ripe for judgment—like a basket of ripe figs (c. 760 B.C., Amos 8:1-14).
    Fulfillment: 722 B.C.—Assyrian captivity; and 587–586 B.C.—Babylonian captivity.

57. Prophecy that Israel would never be uprooted from its land after returning from exile (Amos 9:14-15).
    Fulfillment: History, since 1948—against all odds, the nation of Israel has survived repeated attacks.

58. Edom would be destroyed (c. 650 B.C., Obadiah 1:1-21).
    Fulfillment: History—by invading Arabs.

59. The city of Nineveh would be destroyed (c. 785 B.C., Jonah 1:1).
    Fulfillment: In 612 B.C. when conquered by the Medes and Scythians.

60. The destruction of Israel (c. 740 B.C., Micah 1:2–3:12).
    Fulfillment: 722 B.C.—Assyrian captivity; and 587–586 B.C.—Babylonian captivity.

61. Israel would be regathered (c. 740 B.C., Micah 2:12).
    Fulfillment: Both in 538–537 B.C. after the first exile and in 1948 after the second exile.

62. Babylonian captivity for Israel (c. 740 B.C., Micah 4:9-13).
    Fulfillment: In 587–586 B.C. under Nebuchadnezzar.

63. Judgment of Nineveh (c. 660 B.C., Nahum 1:1-14).
    Fulfillment: The conquest of Nineveh by the Medes and Scythians in 612 B.C.

64. Nineveh's destruction would be complete (c. 660 B.C., Nahum 3:1-19).
    Fulfillment: The conquest of Nineveh by the Medes and Scythians in 612 B.C. was destructive to the point that the city remained hidden under the sand for centuries until discovered by archaeologists in 1845.

65. Babylon would conquer the land of Israel (c. 610 B.C., Habakkuk 1:1-11).
    Fulfillment: The conquest by Babylon in 605–586 B.C.

66. Judgment of Babylon after the conquest (c. 610 B.C., Habakkuk 2:4-17).
    Fulfillment: Babylon's conquest by the Medo-Persian Empire.

67. The coming judgment upon Judah (c. 625 B.C., Zephaniah 1:2-18).
    Fulfillment: The conquest of Judah by Babylon in 587–586 B.C.

68. The invading nations would later be judged (c. 625 B.C., Zephaniah 2:1-15).
    Fulfillment: The conquest of Babylon by the Medo-Persians.

69. Joshua was promised a chance to enter the Promised Land, with God's blessing (Moses, c. 1450 B.C., Deuteronomy 31:23).
    Fulfillment: c. 1406-1375 B.C., Joshua 21:43-45.

70. A curse would come upon the one who would rebuild Jericho (c. 620 B.C., Joshua 6:26).
    Fulfillment: c. 874 B.C., 1 Kings 16:34.

71. Bodies of the pagan priests of "high places" would be burned on an altar (c. 970 B.C., 1 Kings 13:1-3).
    Fulfillment: c. 640 B.C., 2 Kings 23:15-16.

72. Jezebel would be eaten by dogs (c. 870 B.C., 1 Kings 21:23).
    Fulfillment: c. 840 B.C., 2 Kings 9:30-37.

73. Hezekiah would be delivered from a siege by Sennacherib (c. 735 B.C., Isaiah 37:21-35).
    Fulfillment: c. 700 B.C., 2 Kings 19:35-37.

74. Those who plotted to kill Jeremiah would die (c. 620 B.C., Jeremiah 11:18-23).
    Fulfillment: 2 Chronicles 36:15-21.

75. King Zedekiah would die and others would not receive pity (c. 620 B.C., Jeremiah 21:1-7).
    Fulfillment: 2 Chronicles 36:15-21.

76. King Jehoiachin (also called "Coniah") cursed as "childless" regarding an heir to the throne (c. 620 B.C., Jeremiah 22:24-30).
    Fulfillment: None of Jehoiachin's descendants became king of Israel.
    (Jehoiachin's legal heir, Jesus, was not his physical descendant, since Jesus had been conceived in Mary by the Holy Spirit.)

77. Shemaiah (a false prophet) would be punished (c. 620 B.C., Jeremiah 29:24-32).
    Fulfillment: 2 Chronicles 36:11-15.

78. Jehoiakim's descendants would not have the throne of David (c. 620 B.C., Jeremiah 36:27-31).
    Fulfillment: 2 Chronicles 36:11-21.

79. False prophets would be destroyed (c. 590 B.C., Ezekiel 13:1-23).
    Fulfillment: 2 Chronicles 36:11-15.

80. Idolaters to be judged (c. 590 B.C., Ezekiel 14:1-23).
    Fulfillment: 2 Chronicles 36:11-15.

Appendix C

Other Prophecies in the Old Testament

I excluded the following prophecies from my statistical analysis simply because they were fulfilled close to the time the prophecy was made, and the fulfillment was sometimes recorded within the same writings. (These are the same standards that I would apply to the analysis of any other book. See pages 139–142 for my reasoning in developing the standards.)

1. Prophecy of judgment (for eating forbidden fruit) (Genesis 2:16-17).
   Fulfillment: Genesis 3:6-7.

2. The curse on Cain (Genesis 4:11-15).
   Fulfillment: Genesis 4:17-22.

3. The Flood (Genesis 6:11-21).
   Fulfillment: Genesis 7:10-23.

4. Abraham's own son, not Eliezer of Damascus, would be his heir (Genesis 15:4).
   Fulfillment: Genesis 21:7.

5. Israel would leave Egypt with great wealth (Genesis 15:12-14).
   Fulfillment: Exodus 12:33-36.

6. Promise of the birth of Isaac to Abraham (Genesis 17:15-19).
   Fulfillment: Genesis 21:7.

7. Joseph's brothers would bow down to him (Genesis 37:5-11).
   Fulfillment: Genesis 42:6.

8. Pharaoh's butler would be restored to his position (Genesis 40:12-13).
   Fulfillment: Genesis 40:21.

9. Pharoah's baker would be hanged (Genesis 40:18-19).
   Fulfillment: Genesis 40:22.

10. Joseph's prediction of seven years of plenty followed by seven years of famine (Genesis 41:1-32).
    Fulfillment: Genesis 41:45-47.

11. Jacob would see his son in Egypt (Genesis 46:4).
    Fulfillment: Genesis 46:29.

12. Moses would be a deliverer (Exodus 3:10).
    Fulfillment: Exodus 12:37-51.

13. God promised a sign to Moses of his leadership (Exodus 3:12).
    Fulfillment: Exodus 19.

14. The firstborn of Egypt would die (Exodus 4:22-23).
    Fulfillment: Exodus 12:29.

15. Moses would lead Israel out of Egypt (Exodus 6:1-8).
    Fulfillment: Exodus 12:37-51.

16. Ten plagues would come on Egyptians (Exodus 7:1–12:36).
    Fulfillment: Exodus 7:20–12:30.

17. Israel would be protected when crossing through the Red Sea, and the Egyptians would drown (Exodus 14:13-18).
    Fulfillment: Exodus 14:21-28.

18. Because Israel failed to trust God, the adult generation leaving Egypt would not be permitted to enter the Promised Land, except for Joshua and Caleb (Numbers 14:20-34).
    Fulfillment: Numbers 26:63-65.

19. Promise of land given to Joshua (Joshua 1:1-9).
    Fulfillment: Joshua 21:43-45.

20. Promise of conquering Jericho (Joshua 6:1-5).
    Fulfillment: Joshua 6:6-27.

21. Israel would conquer the city of Ai (Joshua 7:1–8:2).
    Fulfillment: Joshua 8:18-26.

22. Israel would conquer the kings of the Amorites (Joshua 10:7-8).
    Fulfillment: Joshua 10:9-15.

23. The destruction of the northern kings (Joshua 11:1-6).
    Fulfillment: Joshua 11:7-15.

24. Tribe of Judah promised a victory over the Canaanites (Judges 1:1-2).
    Fulfillment: Judges 1:4-20.

25. Deborah and Barak promised victories over Sisera (Judges 4:1-9).
    Fulfillment: Judges 4:12-24.

26. Gideon selected by God and promised victory over Midianites (Judges 6:11-24).
    Fulfillment: Judges 7:1-25.

27. Israel promised oppression (Judges 10:13-14).
    Fulfillment: 11:1-40.

28. Samson promised to be the deliverer from the Philistines (Judges 13:5).
    Fulfillment: Judges 13:4-7; 16:25-30.

29. Hannah promised a son (1 Samuel 1:17).
    Fulfillment: 1 Samuel 1:20.

30. Curse on Eli, Hophni, and Phinehas—they would die on the same day
    (1 Samuel 2:27-36; 3:11-14).
    Fulfillment: 1 Samuel 4:12-18; 1 Kings 2:27,35.

31. The ark of the covenant would go to Beth Shemesh (1 Samuel 6:8-9).
    Fulfillment: 1 Samuel 6:13.

32. Samuel's promise of deliverance (1 Samuel 7:3).
    Fulfillment: 1 Samuel 7:10-13.

33. Saul to be chosen as king (1 Samuel 9:1–10:2).
    Fulfillment: 1 Samuel 10:17–11:15.

34. Saul would be filled with the Spirit (1 Samuel 10:5-6).
    Fulfillment: 1 Samuel 10:10-11.

35. Saul's kingdom would not endure (1 Samuel 13:13-14).
    Fulfillment: 2 Samuel 5:1-4.

36. Destruction of the Amalekites (1 Samuel 15:1-4).
    Fulfillment: 1 Samuel 15:7-9.

37. Again, Saul's kingdom would not endure (1 Samuel 15:26).
    Fulfillment: 2 Samuel 5:1-4.

38. David to be anointed king (1 Samuel 16:1-23).
    Fulfillment: 2 Samuel 5:1-4.

39. David would kill Goliath (1 Samuel 17:45-47).
    Fulfillment: 1 Samuel 17:48-54.

40. David would be victorious over Philistines (1 Samuel 23:1-4).
    Fulfillment: 1 Samuel 23:5.

41. Saul and his sons would die in battle (1 Samuel 28:16-19).
    Fulfillment: 1 Samuel 31:8.

42. David would conquer the Amalekites (1 Samuel 30:7-8).
    Fulfillment: 1 Samuel 30:16-20.

43. David would become king over the 12 tribes (2 Samuel 5:1-2).
    Fulfillment: 2 Samuel 5:3-5.

44. Solomon would build a house for the Lord (2 Samuel 7:13).
    Fulfillment: 1 Kings 6:37-38; 7:1-51; 2 Chronicles 3:1–5:14.

45. Solomon was promised that God would never forsake him, even if he sinned
    (2 Samuel 7:14-15).
    Fulfillment: 1 Kings 11:41.

46. David's sin with Bathsheba would cause their child to die (2 Samuel 12:14).
    Fulfillment: 2 Samuel 12:18-23.

47. David's sin with Bathsheba would cause a close relative or friend of David's to "lie with his wives" in broad daylight (2 Samuel 12:11-12).
    Fulfillment: 2 Samuel 16:22.

48. Three days of plagues predicted for Israel because of David's sin (2 Samuel 24:1-14; 1 Chronicles 21:1-13).
    Fulfillment: 2 Samuel 24:15-25; 1 Chronicles 21:14-30.

49. Solomon promised wisdom, honor, and riches (1 Kings 3:10-15).
    Fulfillment: 1 Kings 10:14-29; 2 Chronicles 9:13-28.

50. Solomon warned that Israel would be taken from the land if he didn't follow the Lord (1 Kings 9:1-9).
    Fulfillment: 2 Chronicles 36:14-21.

51. Solomon promised that his kingdom would not be taken from him during his lifetime (1 Kings 11:9-13,29-39).
    Fulfillment: 1 Kings 12.

52. Jeroboam to be king over ten tribes (1 Kings 11:11-39).
    Fulfillment: 1 Kings 12:20.

53. Disobedient prophets would die (1 Kings 13:20-22).
    Fulfillment: 1 Kings 13:23-26.

54. Disaster predicted for Jeroboam (1 Kings 14:10-12).
    Fulfillment: 1 Kings 14:17-20.

55. The line of King Baasha would be destroyed (1 Kings 16:1-4).
    Fulfillment: 1 Kings 16:11-13.

56. A drought would come upon Israel (1 Kings 17:1).
    Fulfillment: 1 Kings 18:36-45.

57. The flour and oil of the widow would not be exhausted (1 Kings 17:7-14).
    Fulfillment: 1 Kings 17:15-16.

58. Rain would come at Elijah's request (1 Kings 17:1).
    Fulfillment: 1 Kings 18:41-46.

59. Ahab would have a victory over Syria (1 Kings 20:13-14).
    Fulfillment: 1 Kings 20:18-21.

60. Attack by Syria would be renewed (1 Kings 20:22).
    Fulfillment: 1 Kings 20:26-30.

61. A disobedient prophet would die (1 Kings 20:35-36).
    Fulfillment: 1 Kings 20:36.

62. Ahab and his people would suffer because they spared Ben-Hadad (1 Kings 20:42).
    Fulfillment: 1 Kings 22:34-35.

63. Ahab would die in the same place he had killed Naboth (1 Kings 21:17-20; 2 Chronicles 18:33-34).
    Fulfillment: 1 Kings 22:37-38.

64. Ahab to be defeated (1 Kings 22:13-28; 2 Chronicles 18:16-27).
    Fulfillment: 1 Kings 22:34-38.

65. Ahaziah would die because he consulted a false god (2 Kings 1:4).
    Fulfillment: 2 Kings 1:16-17.

66. A double portion of Elijah's power would come to Elisha (2 Kings 2:9-10).
    Fulfillment: 2 Kings 2:13-14.

67. Israel, Judah would conquer Moabites (2 Kings 3:15-20).
    Fulfillment: 2 Kings 3:21-27.

68. The widow's jars would be refilled with oil (2 Kings 4:3-4).
    Fulfillment: 2 Kings 4:5-6.

69. The pot of stew would not be harmful (2 Kings 4:38-40).
    Fulfillment: 2 Kings 4:41-44.

70. Naaman would wash seven times in the Jordan and be cured of leprosy (2 Kings 5:10).
    Fulfillment: 2 Kings 5:14.

71. Gehazi would get leprosy (2 Kings 5:27).
    Fulfillment: 2 Kings 5:27.

72. The Lord's protection would be upon Elisha (2 Kings 6:15-17).
    Fulfillment: 2 Kings 6:17.

73. There would be abundance of food in time of siege (2 Kings 6:24–7:1).
    Fulfillment: 2 Kings 7:5-20.

74. Officer of king would not eat of abundance of food (2 Kings 7:2).
    Fulfillment: 2 Kings 7:17.

75. Seven-year famine would come (2 Kings 8:1).
    Fulfillment: 2 Kings 8:2-3.

76. Ben-Hadad would recover from his illness but would then die (2 Kings 8:7-10).
    Fulfillment: 2 Kings 8:14-15.

77. Hazael would kill many Israelites (2 Kings 8:12).
    Fulfillment: 2 Kings 10:32; 12:17-18; 13:3,22-25.

78. Hazael would become king of Aram (2 Kings 8:13).
    Fulfillment: 2 Kings 8:14-15.

79. Jehu would destroy the house of Ahab (2 Kings 9:7-10).
    Fulfillment: 2 Kings 9:14-28.

80. Jehu's house would occupy the throne for four generations (2 Kings 10:30-31).
    Fulfillment: 2 Kings 15:8,12.

81. Jehoash would conquer Syria three times (2 Kings 13:14-19).
    Fulfillment: 2 Kings 13:25.

82. Jeroboam would possess the land (2 Kings 14:25).
    Fulfillment: 2 Kings 14:25.

83. Hezekiah told that Assyrians would besiege Jerusalem, then leave, then the king of Assyria would be assassinated (2 Kings 19:5-7, 20-34).
    Fulfillment: 2 Kings 19:35-37.

84. Hezekiah would have an additional 15 years of life (2 Kings 20:1-11; 2 Chronicles 32:24-29; Isaiah 38).
    Fulfillment: 2 Kings 20:8-11.

85. Babylonian captivity would not start until after Hezekiah's death (2 Kings 20:16-19).
    Fulfillment: 2 Kings 20:21.

86. Downfall of Manasseh (2 Kings 21:10-15).
    Fulfillment: 2 Chronicles 33:10-13.

87. Disaster to Israel because of sin (2 Kings 22:1-20).
    Fulfillment: 2 Chronicles 35:15-21.

88. Josiah, after humbling himself, would not see Judah's disaster (2 Kings 22:15-20).
    Fulfillment: 2 Chronicles 34:26-28.

89. God would continue to destroy Judah in spite of reform (2 Kings 23:25-27).
    Fulfillment: 2 Kings 25:8-21; 2 Chronicles 36:1-21.

90. The army of Jehoshaphat would see the defeat of the army of Edom without even fighting it (2 Chronicles 20:15-17).
    Fulfillment: 2 Chronicles 20:20-25.

91. Jehoshaphat's venture at shipbuilding would fail (2 Chronicles 20:37).
    Fulfillment: 2 Chronicles 20:37.

92. Jehoram would see God's judgment (2 Chronicles 21:12-15).
    Fulfillment: 2 Chronicles 21:16-20.

93. King Joash would be forsaken by the Lord (2 Chronicles 24:20-22).
    Fulfillment: 2 Chronicles 24:23-24.

94. Amaziah would be destroyed because he had not listened to God (2 Chronicles 25:15-17).
    Fulfillment: 2 Chronicles 25:27.

95. God would allow Nehemiah to rebuild the wall of Jerusalem (Nehemiah 2:20).
    Fulfillment: Nehemiah 6:15-16.

96. Job would ultimately "come forth as gold" after suffering severe tests (Job 23:10-11).
    Fulfillment: Job 42:12-17.

Bibliography

General Reference

Archer, Gleason L. *Encyclopedia of Bible Difficulties.* Grand Rapids, MI: Zondervan Publishing House, 1982.

Elwell, Walter A., ed. *Evangelical Dictionary of Theology.* Grand Rapids, MI: Baker Book House, 1984.

Geisler, Norman L. *Baker Encyclopedia of Christian Apologetics.* Grand Rapids, MI: Baker Books, 1999.

————, and Ron Brooks. *When Skeptics Ask: A Handbook on Christian Evidences.* Grand Rapids, MI: Baker Books, 1990.

Moreland, J. P., and Kai Nielsen. *Does God Exist?: The Debate Between Theists and Atheists.* Amherst, NY: Prometheus Books, 1993.

Smith, F. LaGard, commentator. *The Daily Bible.* Eugene, OR: Harvest House Publishers, 1984.

Strobel, Lee, *The Case for Christ.* Grand Rapids, MI: Zondervan Publishing House, 1998.

Youngblood, Ronald F., Herbert Lockyer Sr., F.F. Bruce, and R.K. Harrison, eds. *Nelson's New Illustrated Bible Dictionary.* Nashville, TN: Thomas Nelson Publishers, 1995.

Zodhiates, Spiros, ed. *The Complete Word Study New Testament. King James Version.* Chattanooga, TN: AMG International, Inc., 1991.

————, and Warren Baker, eds. *The Complete Word Study Old Testament, King James Version.* Chattanooga, TN: AMG International, Inc., 1994.

Analytical Evidence

Alcamo, I. Edward. *Schaum's Outline of Microbiology.* Blacklick, OH: McGraw-Hill, 1998.

Behe, Michael J. *Darwin's Black Box: The Biochemical Challenge to Evolution.* New York, NY: The Free Press, 1996.

Darwin, Charles, *On the Origin of Species.* Cambridge, MA: Harvard University Press, 1964.

Dembski, William A., ed. *Mere Creation.* Downers Grove, IL: InterVarsity Press, 1998.

Denton, Michael. *Evolution: A Theory in Crisis.* Bethesda, MD: Alder & Alder Publishers, Inc., 1985.

Eastman, Mark, and Chuck Missler, *The Creator Beyond Time and Space.* Costa Mesa, CA: Word For Today, 1996.

Hanegraaff, Hank. *The Face That Demonstrates the Farce of Evolution.* Nashville, TN: Word Publishing, 1998.

Heeren, Fred. *Show Me God: What the Message from Space Is Telling Us About God.* Wheeling, IL: Searchlight Publications, 1995.

Hoyle, Fred. *Mathematics of Evolution.* Memphis, TN: Acorn Enterprises LLC, 1999.

Milton, Richard. *Shattering the Myths of Darwinism.* Rochester, VT: Park Street Press, 1997.

Moreland, J.P., ed. *The Creation Hypothesis: Scientific Evidence for an Intelligent Designer.* Downers Grove, IL: InterVarsity Press, 1994.

———, and John Mark Reynolds, eds. *Three Views on Creation and Evolution.* Grand Rapids, MI: Zondervan Publishing House, 1999.

Morris, Henry M., and Gary E. Parker, *What Is Creation Science?* El Cajon, CA: Master Books, 1987.

Ridley, Matt. *Genome: The Autobiography of a Species in 23 Chapters.* New York: Harper-Collins Publishers Inc., 1999.

Ross, Hugh. *The Creator and the Cosmos: How the Greatest Scientific Discoveries of the Century Reveal God.* Colorado Springs, CO: NavPress Publishing Group, 1993.

———. *The Fingerprint of God.* Orange, CA: Promise Publishing Co., 1991.

Schroeder, Gerald L. *The Hidden Face of God: How Science Reveals the Ultimate Truth.* New York: The Free Press, 2001.

———. *The Science of God: The Convergence of Scientific and Biblical Wisdom.* New York: Broadway Books, 1997.

Spetner, Lee. *Not By Chance! Shattering the Modern Theory of Evolution.* Brooklyn, NY: Judaica Press, Inc., 1998.

Stewart, Don. *The Bible and Science: Are They In Conflict?* Spokane, WA: AusAmerica Publishers, 1993.

Wells, Jonathan. *Icons of Evolution: Science Or Myth? Why Much of What We Teach About Evolution is Wrong.* Washington, DC: Regnery Publishing, Inc., 2000.

Statistical Evidence

McDowell, Josh. *The New Evidence That Demands a Verdict.* Nashville, TN: Thomas Nelson Publishers, 1999.

———. *A Ready Defense.* San Bernardino, CA: Here's Life Publishers, Inc., 1990.

Walvoord, John F. *The Prophecy Knowledge Handbook.* Wheaton, IL: Victor Books, 1990.

Major Religions

Ali, Maulana Muhammad. *The Religion of Islam*. Columbus, OH: Ahmadiyya Anjuman Isha'at Islam, 1990.

Campbell, William. *The Qur'an and the Bible in the Light of History and Science*. Lake Forest, CA: L.M. Carter, n. d.

Cowell, E.B., ed. *Buddhist Mahayana Texts*. Mineola, NY: Dover Publications, Inc., 1989.

Dawood, N.J. *The Koran*. London, England: Penguin Group, 1993.

Gethin, Rupert. *The Foundations of Buddhism*. Oxford, England: Oxford University Press, 1998.

Goodall, Dominic, ed. *Hindu Scriptures*. Berkeley and Los Angeles, CA: J.M. Dent, Orion Publishing, 1996.

Halverson, Dean C., ed. *The Compact Guide to World Religions*. Minneapolis, MN: Bethany House Publishers, 1996.

McDowell, Josh, and Don Stewart. *Handbook of Today's Religions*. San Bernardino, CA: Here's Life Publishers, Inc., 1983.

Prabhupada A.C. Bhaktivedanta Swami. *Bhagavad-Gita As It Is*. Los Angeles: Bhaktivedanta Book Trust International, Inc., 1997.

References for the Old Testament

Free, Joseph P., and Howard F. Vos. *Archaeology and Bible History*. Grand Rapids, MI: Zondervan Publishing House, 1992.

Josephus, Flavius. *The Complete Works of Josephus*. Grand Rapids, MI: Kregel Publications, 1981.

Kertzer, Morris N. *What Is a Jew?* rev. by Lawrence A. Hoffman. New York: Touchstone, 1996.

Shanks, Hershel, and Dan P. Cole, eds. *Archaeology and the Bible: The Best of BAR*. Vol. 1, *Early Israel*. Washington, D.C.: Biblical Archaeology Society, 1990.

References for the New Testament

Black, David Alan. *New Testament Textual Criticism: A Concise Guide*. Grand Rapids, MI: Baker Books, 1994.

Finegan, Jack. *The Archeology of the New Testament: The Life of Jesus and the Beginning of the Early Church*, rev. ed. Princeton, NJ: Princeton University Press, 1992.

Green, Michael. *Who Is This Jesus?* Nashville, TN: Thomas Nelson, Inc., 1992.

Habermas, Gary R., and Antony G.N. Flew. *Did Jesus Rise From the Dead? The Resurrection Debate*. San Francisco, CA: Harper & Row, 1987.

McBirnie, William Steuart. *The Search for the Twelve Apostles*. Wheaton, IL: Tyndale House Publishers, Inc., 1973.

McDowell, Josh, and Bill Wilson. *He Walked Among Us*. Nashville, TN: Thomas Nelson Publishers, 1993.

McRay, John. *Archaeology and the New Testament*. Grand Rapids, MI: Baker Book House, 1991.

Shanks, Hershel, and Dan P. Cole, eds. *Archaeology and the Bible: The Best of BAR*. Vol. 2, *Archaeology in the World of Herod, Jesus, and Paul*. Washington, D.C.: Biblical Archaeology Society, 1992.

White, James R. *The Forgotten Trinity*. Minneapolis, MN: Bethany House Publishers, 1998.

Evidence of the Bible's Accuracy

Blomberg, Craig. *The Historical Reliability of the Gospels*. Leicester, England: InterVarsity Press, 1987.

Bruce, F.F. *The Canon of Scripture*. Downers Grove, IL: InterVarsity Press, 1988.

Comfort, Philip Wesley, ed. *The Origin of the Bible*. Wheaton, IL: Tyndale House Publishers, Inc., 1992.

How We Got the Bible. Torrance, CA: Rose Publishing, 1998.

Price, Randall. *Secrets of the Dead Sea Scrolls*. Eugene, OR: Harvest House Publishers, 1996.

Vos, Howard F. *Nelson's Quick Reference: Introduction to Church History*. Nashville, TN: Thomas Nelson Publishers, Inc., 1994.

References for
"Alternative Christian" Religions

Bodine, Jerry and Marian. *Witnessing to the Mormons*. Rancho Santa Margarita, CA: The Christian Research Institute, 1978.

Martin, Walter. *Cults Reference Bible*. Santa Ana, CA: Vision House Publishers, 1981.

———. *The Kingdom of the Cults*. Minneapolis, MN: Bethany House Publishers, 1996.

———. *The Maze of Mormonism*. Ventura, CA: Regal Books, 1978.

McDowell, Josh, and Don Stewart. *The Deceivers*. San Bernardino, CA: Here's Life Publishers, Inc., 1992.

Smith, Joseph. *The Book of Mormon*. Salt Lake City, UT: The Church of Jesus Christ of Latter-Day Saints, 1981.

Watson, William. *A Concise Dictionary of Cults & Religions*. Chicago, IL: Moody Press, 1991.

Notes

Chapter 2—Watering the Seeds of Agnosticism
1. Edythe Draper, *Almanac of the Christian World* (Wheaton, IL: Tyndale House Publishers, 1992), p. 80.

Chapter 4—Atheism at the University
1. Patrick Glynn, *God: the Evidence—The Reconciliation of Faith and Reason in the Postmodern World* (Rocklin, CA: Prima Publishing, 1999).

Chapter 8—What It Takes to Randomly Assemble Life
1. Lee Spetner, *Not By Chance—Shattering the Modern Theory of Evolution* (Brooklyn, NY: Judaica Press, 1998), p. 30.
2. Spetner, p. 39.
3. Gerald L. Schroeder, *The Hidden Face of God: How Science Reveals the Ultimate Truth* (New York: The Free Press, 2001), p. 189.
4. Henry M. Morris and Gary E. Parker, *What Is Creation Science?* (El Cajon, CA: Master Books, 1987), pp. 61-68.
5. Morris and Parker, pp. 52-61.
6. Chuck Missler and Mark Eastman, *The Creator Beyond Time and Space* (Costa Mesa, CA: Word for Today, 1996), p. 52.
7. Hugh Ross, *The Creator and the Cosmos* (Colorado Springs, CO: Navpress, 1993), p. 139.

Chapter 9—The Molecular Anatomy of Life
1. Lee Spetner, *Not By Chance—Shattering the Modern Theory of Evolution* (Brooklyn, NY: Judaica Press,1998), p. 30.
2. Gerald L. Schroeder, *The Hidden Face of God: How Science Reveals the Ultimate Truth* (New York: The Free Press, 2001), p. 189.
3. Spetner, p. 45.
4. Sir Frederick Hoyle, as cited in Chuck Missler, *The Creator Beyond Time and Space* (Costa Mesa, CA: The Word for Today, 1996), p. 60.
5. Sir Frederick Hoyle, *The Mathematics of Evolution* (Memphis, TN: Acorn Enterprises, 1999), pp. 137-138.
6. Hoyle, *Mathematics*, p. 13.
7. Michael Denton, *Evolution: A Theory in Crisis* (Bethesda, MD: Adler & Adler Publishers, Inc., 1986), p. 323.
8. Hugh Ross, *The Creator and the Cosmos* (Colorado Springs, CO: Navpress, 1993), p. 141.
9. Michael H. Hart, "Atmospheric Evolution, the Drake Equation and DNA: Sparse Life in an Infinite Universe," *Physical Cosmology and Philosophy*, as cited in Ross, *The Creator and the Cosmos*, pp. 141-142.
10. Denton, p. 235.

11. Ross, p. 143.

12. Henry M. Morris and Gary E. Parker, *What Is Creation Science?* (El Cajon, CA: Master Books, 1987), p. 270.

13. Ross, p. 141.

14. Hugh Ross, *Facts for Faith* (Colorado Springs, CO: Navpress, 2000).

Chapter 10—Back at the University

1. Michael J. Behe, *Darwin's Black Box—The Biochemical Challenge to Evolution* (New York: The Free Press, 1996).

2. Charles Darwin, *Origin of the Species* (Cambridge, MA: Harvard University Press, 1964), p. 95.

3. Robert Shapiro, "Prebiotic Ribose Synthesis," *A Critical Analysis of the Origin of Life and Evolution of the Biosphere* 18, 1988, pp. 71-85; and Shapiro, "Protomabolism: A Scenario for the Origin of Life," *The American Scientist,* July-August, 1992, p. 387; both as cited by Hugh Ross, *The Creator and the Cosmos* (Colorado Springs, CO: Navpress, 1993), p. 143.

4. Richard Dawkins, *The Blind Watchmaker* (New York: W.W. Norton, 1996), p. 139.

Chapter 11—I Start to Investigate God

1. Lee Spetner, *Not By Chance—Shattering the Modern Theory of Evolution* (Brooklyn, NY: Judaica Press, 1998), p. 64-65.

2. George Wald, "The Origin of Life," *Scientific American*, May 1954, as cited by Chuck Missler and Mark Eastman, *The Creator Beyond Time and Space* (Costa Mesa, CA: Word for Today, 1996), p. 62.

Chapter 13—Could I Develop Statistical Standards for Determining God's Existence?

1. Jeane Dixon, *Parade* magazine, May 13, 1956, as cited by Josh McDowell, *A Ready Defense* (San Bernardino, CA: Here's Life Publishers, 1990), p. 387.

Chapter 15—Testable Prophecies I Found in the Old Testament

1. Joseph P. Free and Howard F. Vos, *Archaeology and Bible History* (Grand Rapids, MI: Zondervan Publishing House, 1992), pp. 203-204.

2. Free and Vos, pp. 149-152.

3. Free and Vos, pp. 189-190.

Chapter 19—A Description of the Messiah from Old Testament Prophecy

1. Anderson calculated the Messiah's year of arrival as A.D. 32, Hoehner as the year 33. Either may be right, since the ancient dates are based on the reigns of kings, which carries a degree of uncertainty in virtually all cases. However, both scholars agree on the exact length of the time period between Artaxerxes' decree and the Messiah's arrival.

2. Harold W. Hoehner, *Chronological Aspects of the Life of Christ* (Grand Rapids, MI: The Zondervan Corporation, 1977), p. 138.

3. Hamilton Cannon Liddon, *The Basis of Christian Faith* (New York: Harper, 1946), p. 156, as cited in Joseph P. Free and Howard F. Vos, *Archaeology and Bible History* (Grand Rapids, MI: Zondervan Publishing House, 1992), p. 241.

Chapter 22—Blood Evidence

1. Clement of Alexandria, *Miscellanies,* as quoted by Eusebius, *Church History,* as cited by William Steuart McBirnie, *The Search for the Twelve Apostles* (Wheaton, IL: Tyndale House Publishers, Inc., 1973), p. 75.

Chapter 23—Could I Trust the Bible Texts?

1. W.F. Albright, as cited by Josh McDowell, *The New Evidence that Demands a Verdict* (Nashville, TN: Thomas Nelson Publishers, 1999), p. 36.

2. Sir Frederic Kenyon, as cited by McDowell, p. 35.

3. Kenyon, as cited by McDowell, p. 35.

4. David Dockery, Kenneth Mathews, and Robert Sloan, as cited by McDowell, p. 35.

5.   F.J.A. Hort, as cited by McDowell, p. 35.

6.   Edward Glenny, as cited by McDowell, p. 36.

7.   Grant Jeffrey, *The Signature of God* (Toronto, Ontario, Canada: Frontier Publications, Inc., 1996), pp. 103-104.

8.   McDowell, p. 34.

Chapter 24—I Find More Support for the Bible

1.   Flavius Josephus, *The Complete Works of Josephus* (Grand Rapids, MI: Kregel, Inc., 1981), p. 79.

2.   Josephus, p. 423.

3.   As cited by Josh McDowell, *A Ready Defense* (San Bernardino, CA: Here's Life Publishers, 1990), p. 198.

4.   As cited by Josh McDowell, *The New Evidence that Demands a Verdict* (Nashville, TN: Thomas Nelson Publishers, 1999), p. 59.

5.   As cited by McDowell, *The New Evidence,* p. 58.

Chapter 25—The Final Barriers

1.   Joseph P. Free and Howard F. Vos, *Archaeology and Bible History* (Grand Rapids, MI: Zondervan Publishing House, 1992), p. 41.

2.   Josh McDowell, *The New Evidence that Demands a Verdict* (Nashville, TN: Thomas Nelson Publishers, 1999), p. 11.

3.   Free and Vos, p. 37.

4.   Free and Vos, pp. 51-52.

5.   Free and Vos, pp. 56-57.

6.   Free and Vos, p. 55.

7.   Free and Vos, pp. 59-60, 121.

8.   Free and Vos, pp. 126-127.

9.   Free and Vos, pp. 61-62.

10. Free and Vos, p. 82.

11. John Noble Wilford, in the *New York Times,* as cited by the *Orange County Register* (Costa Mesa, CA), August 6, 1993, p. 26.

12. Free and Vos, pp. 141-143.

13. Free and Vos, p. 242.

14. John McRay, *Archaeology and the New Testament* (Grand Rapids, MI: Baker Book House, 1991), pp. 157-158.

15. McRay, pp. 80-81, 164-166.

16. Free and Vos, pp. 246-247.

17. Free and Vos, pp. 238-239.

18. McRay, p. 195.

19. Free and Vos, p. 214.

Chapter 26—Will the Real Jesus Please Stand Up?

1.   Walter Martin, *The Kingdom of the Cults* (Minneapolis, MN: Bethany House Publishers, 1996), pp. 183-184.

2.   Jerry and Marian Bodine, *Witnessing to the Mormons* (Rancho Santa Margarita, CA: The Christian Research Institute, 1978), p. 22.

Chapter 27—The Verdict

1.   Spiros Zodhiates, "Greek Dictionary of the New Testament," *The Complete Word Study of the New Testament* (Chattanooga, TN: AMG Publishers, 1991) appendix p. 58.

2.   Zodhiates.

Ralph Muncaster

The Examine the Evidence Series

Tough Questions—Quick, Factual, Convincing Answers

Both believers and skeptics ask hard questions about the Christian faith—and need answers that bring theology into real life. That's exactly what you'll find in the Examine the Evidence series by Ralph Muncaster—concise, compelling, fact-filled presentations that can be read quickly and are enhanced with easy-to-follow charts and graphics that help clarify the vital points of each issue. Each book draws on the facts of God's Word and the latest scientific discoveries to provide practical answers to the tough questions about God, the Bible, and life.

Are There Contradictions in the Bible?

Some people claim the Bible has many contradictions in it. This book demonstrates the Bible's consistency on all major issues and equips skeptics and believers to analyze supposed discrepancies for themselves. It explores the similarities and differences in Gospel accounts; the contrasts between Genesis chapters 1 and 2; and the "divergent" resurrection accounts.

Can Archaeology Prove the New Testament?

Non-Christian sources have long said that outside of the Bible, there is no evidence that Jesus ever lived. Are they right? And what about the evidence found in the Bible—is it trustworthy? An exciting survey of discoveries and proofs that counters skepticism and confirms the Bible.

Can Archaeology Prove the Old Testament?

Has archaeology ever proven the Bible wrong? Careful investigation, even by skeptics, has supported and verified much of the Bible's history down to the smallest detail. Find out how science and archaeology are confirming Old Testament history and facts.

Can We Know for Certain We Are Going to Heaven?

When it comes to guarantees, can we trust what the Bible says about the future? Is our destination secure? Is there something we must do to ensure that we'll be welcomed into God's presence when we die? This careful investigation of the Bible's statements shows that our certainty about heaven rests on who God is and on His ability to bring to completion in us what He begins through Jesus Christ.

Can You Trust the Bible?

Tracing the advancement of writing and materials, this book reveals how the Bible was written, how biblical accuracy was maintained, how the historical and archaeological evidence proves translation integrity, and how the canon was developed.

Creation vs. Evolution: What Do the Latest Scientific Discoveries Reveal?

More than 100 years ago, Darwin hoped fossils would someday provide transitional evidence. Now, millions of fossils later, the data actually suggests *creation,* not evolution. Join the author in this fascinating look at the scholarship that proposed evolution and how belief in pure evolution theory is declining as scientific conclusions increasingly support creationism.

Creation vs. Evolution VIDEO: What Do the Latest Scientific Discoveries Reveal?

This compelling and powerful video presentation illustrates and simplifies science's most recent finds. Moving beyond fossil analysis, Ralph Muncaster reveals stirring discoveries in the fields of microbiology, physics, cosmology, and probability analysis and what they reveal about evolutionary theory. Brought to life by exciting computer animation and vivid graphics, this visual presentation provides sound, authoritative research for the skeptic and scientist, clearly explained for the beginner.

Presented in ten short segments to better facilitate understanding and discussion, each section focuses on a specific area of science. Also included are reasons for and history of the creation/evolution debate and discussions of Bible analysis and Bible prophecy, extraterrestrial life finds, and more.

Does Prayer Really Work?

If there is a God, then we can talk to Him—but will He talk to us? Will He answer our requests, or is He uncaring and impersonal? Can we "change His mind," or is prayer just a noble habit that makes us feel better? This exciting study digs into the Scriptures to help reveal the inspiring truth about communicating with God.

Does the Bible Predict the Future?

When it comes to determining the future, only the Bible can claim 100-percent accuracy. Discover how prophecies proclaimed hundreds and even thousands of years in advance have been fulfilled precisely! A "Prophecies of Christ" chart makes this a valuable reference tool.

How Do We Know Jesus Was God?

Did the biblical Jesus really exist? Were the miracles He performed real? Was He sent by God? Readers will find these questions, and more, carefully addressed and the evidence examined. Includes a chronology of Jesus' miracles.

How Is Jesus Different from Other Religious Leaders?

Buddha, Confucius, Gandhi, Jesus—did they all say the same thing, just in different words? Can they all be our guides on the path to personal enlightenment? Or does Jesus Christ stand alone in who He is and what He said? This concise booklet takes a step-by-step look at the hard evidence in the Bible of the once-for-all uniqueness of Jesus.

How to Talk About Jesus with the Skeptics in Your Life

"I don't know what to say when I try to talk about God—I'm afraid I'll be embarrassed." How many of us feel like this? What can help us more effectively share the truth that reveals Jesus Christ—the truth that affects everyone's eternal future? The author speaks from his own experience as both a skeptic and a Christian, concisely showing point-by-point how we can understand and sympathize with skeptics, and directing us to the Bible as our final basis for confidence when we talk to other people about Jesus.

Is the Bible Really a Message from God?

God has concealed an incredible wealth of verification within the pages of the Bible that show He exists, that He wants to communicate with us, and that the Bible is His message system. Readers will look at the evidence and find answers to questions such as: Is the Bible inspired by God? To what degree? Is it accurate? What impact will that have on my day-to-day life?

Science—Was the Bible Ahead of Its Time?
Many people today—including Christians—view science and the Bible as contradicting one another. Is that really the case? How do today's scientific discoveries line up with the Bible? A remarkable study affirming that the Bible was ahead of its time on many science-related issues.

What Is the Proof for the Resurrection?
This concise booklet reviews the documentation of biblical prophecies, delves into non-Christian historical writings that confirm Jesus' death, and reveals 12 key reasons for believing in Jesus' physical resurrection.

What Is the Trinity?
Non-Christian sources have long said that Christians believe in three Gods. Is this true? How do we understand the relationship of the Father, Son, and Holy Spirit to each other? Since the Bible doesn't contain the word "Trinity," where did the idea come from? This concise survey spells out what God's Word says about the Trinity and the practical results this truth has in our lives.

What Really Happened Christmas Morning?
Is the Christmas story just another fairy tale? Or is it possible to affirm historically that Christ's birth really happened? This inspiring resource looks at both secular and biblical accounts to uncover the truth about Jesus' birth and the events surrounding it.

What Really Happens When You Die?
When we die, do we go straight to heaven? Is hell a real place, or a figment of human imagination? The Bible reveals a lot about life after death, and how our choices today determine our future destination.

Why Are Scientists Turning to God?
Using the latest scientific discoveries and personal testimonies from modern scientists, the author reveals how God is changing the minds of those who study the creation most closely. Readers will explore this startling progression: What did scientists believe in the past? What three events made mankind feel God was unnecessary? What is bringing scientists back to God?

Why Does God Allow Suffering?
Human suffering—no other issue leads us to question God and His existence more deeply and more often. Can God stop the suffering going on in this world? If He can, why doesn't He? Can He truly be a loving God if He allows suffering to continue? Carefully building on the evidence provided by God's Word, this concise and compassionate resource helps us know God better and understand the role that suffering has in human existence.